The Illusion of Permanence

THE
ILLUSION
OF PERMANENCE

British Imperialism in India

BY FRANCIS G. HUTCHINS

Princeton University Press
Princeton, New Jersey
1967

Printed in the United States of America
by Princeton University Press, Princeton, New Jersey

TO MY PARENTS

Preface

> If a democratic republic subdues a nation in order
> to govern them as subjects, it exposes its own liberty.
> —MONTESQUIEU

THE GOVERNMENT of one country by another inevitably leaves its mark on both ruler and ruled. A relationship is established between two countries by national imperialism which exists at many levels simultaneously. Economic and military arrangements reflect the realities of dominance and dependence. They also modify and are modified by the levels of technology and form of social organization current in each nation. Intellectual preoccupations and popular attitudes of rulers and subjects are similary interconnected, modifying one another while reflecting the particular vantage point which political position and cultural background afford. Developments of all sorts in one country affect developments in the other, making necessary some understanding of both for an understanding of either. This is especially true of Great Britain and India, for their relationship was both lengthy and complex. It has, unfortunately, long been customary to treat English and Indian history as completely distinct topics, though this divorce has never been justified.[1] Since the earliest days of British contact with India the interrelationship between domestic developments in Britian and India has been strong and significant. The nature of society in England influenced the personal character of Englishmen and conditioned the way Englishmen who came to India viewed the country to which they came. Similarly, the evolving course of events in India conditioned the British perspective on a host of subjects. Indian crises leaped to the forefront of attention—the Hastings trial, the Mutiny of 1857—but even in quiescent periods the fact of British power in India encouraged policies and lines of speculation which would have been incomprehensible without it.

---

[1] As Eric Stokes has pointed out in the introduction to his study of the *English Utilitarians and India*, Oxford University Press, 1959.

Until the end of the eighteenth century, India was a prize for European marauders and traders; Indian society at this time was decayed and British society lax. From the time of the Hastings trial, however, in the wake of England's own moral revival, India became an object of interest, as well, to improving, reforming Englishmen. Missionaries began making their way into India, first necessarily by stealth but later with the approval of the East India Company. Englishmen never ceased to trade, but some Englishmen began to concern themselves with other things. "The interests of India" became a subject of serious discussion and ambition. In the era culminating in the reformist Viceroyalty of Lord Bentinck, 1828 to 1835, an energetic effort at the reform and reconstruction of Indian society was attempted. Customs seriously repugnant to the Western imagination—*Sati*, *Thuggee*, female infanticide—were outlawed and the hopes of the reformers far outstripped such purely negative measures. Men such as Thomas Macaulay and C. E. Trevelyan, carrying the missionary impulse into every area of society, looked forward to a complete transformation of Indian life on an English model. There was literally no limit to their aspirations for India; within a generation or so, it was hoped, India's "respectable classes" would be Christian, English-speaking, free of idolatry, and actively engaged in the government of their country. The priorities might be different, depending on whether one partook more of the Evangelical or the Utilitarian perspective. One might prefer to emphasize that the conversion of Indians to Christianity was the key, or conversely, that laws and good government were the primary essential, but the two reform movements nonetheless had a great deal in common. Evangelicals and Utilitarians alike were committed to radical reforms and shared radical expectations of their success. There were even those prepared to predict that India might surpass England as a model of propriety and liberalism. In the opinion of Bishop Heber, the faults of Indians

seem to arise from the hateful superstitions to which they

are subject, and the unfavourable state of society in which they are placed. But if it should please God to make any considerable portion of them Christian, they would I can well believe put the best of European Christians to shame.[2]

If missionaries looked forward to the prospect of Indians setting Europe an example of Christian conduct, social reformers were no less sanguine. "There was an opportunity in India," wrote James Mill, "to which the history of the world presents not a parallel."[3] Mill was excited by the prospect of dictating outright Indian social arrangements and forming Indian society on the basis of Utilitarian principles of social equality and private ownership of property through the making of land settlements directly with the tiller of the soil. England, in short, had an opportunity of making India a haven for individual initiative and free enterprise which the reverence for inherited absurdities had prevented England herself from becoming. The Indian *tabula rasa* seemed the most promising of all bases for the establishment of society on a proper system; for in the eyes of the reformers India seemed very much like a blank page. They found it difficult to concede the vitality or relevance of institutions as alien as those then existing in India. The reformers of the 1820s and 1830s did not possess an accurate impression of the problems confronting them in India, or of the merits of the traditional society they hoped to transform, but it could not be said that they lacked ambition. India excited Bentham and Bishop Heber and James and John Stuart Mill. Reformers and missionaries instinctively turned to India. India required conversion; she needed laws. India appealed to the imagination of the most radical elements in English life. Reformist impulses of a

[2] Letter to Charles Wynn, March 1, 1825, in Reginald Heber, *Narrative of a Journey through the Upper Provinces of India*, London, 1829, III, 333.

[3] Mill, *History of British India*, 1820 edn., London, v, 416. Mill here refers to an opportunity lost, in Cornwallis's decision to make the land settlement in Bengal on an aristocratic rather than a democratic basis. Mill lived to see the opportunity grasped in the settlement of other regions of the country according to Utilitarian principles.

radical and evangelical generation spilled over into India and many people hoped to see in India the fruition of schemes frustrated by the conservatism of English life.[4]

Reformist enthusiasm began to ebb, however, in the years following the departure of Bentinck and Macaulay from India. Bentinck's successor, Lord Auckland, appointed by the graceful Lord Melbourne, found India "boring."[5] The Legal Codes devised by the Law Commissioners under Macaulay's direction lay neglected in the files. The era of the 1840s and 1850s in India lacked a clear ideological cast. The old impulses had waned, while new ambitions and rationalizations had not been clearly formulated. India had meanwhile become involved with vested interests, a place of residence and profitable employment for a class of Englishmen reluctant to see themselves supplanted by Indians. The liberal commitment to India's emancipation was no longer felt, though it was difficult to discard it openly. The Mutiny of 1857 crystallized this situation. Feelings which had been vaguely formed, arguments which had been put forward jestingly, suddenly flamed up with a violence and completeness which is difficult to credit. The new temper of British India did not spring fullblown from the ashes of the Mutiny, but the Mutiny provided the justification for believing what people had already begun to believe some years before. The Mutiny did not change the attitudes of thousands of Englishmen overnight. The attitudes had already changed and only required this opportunity to find a confident expression.

In the latter half of the century thinking about India bore a distinctly different face. While before the Mutiny reformers had

[4] The era of Evangelical and Utilitarian reform in India has been more thoroughly studied than any other period in British Indian history. Excellent accounts of this period are contained in Ainslie Embree, *Charles Grant and British Rule in India*, New York: Columbia University Press, 1962; in Eric Stokes, *English Utilitarians and India*, London: Oxford University Press, 1959; and in Thomas Metcalf, *Aftermath of Revolt, 1857-1870*, Princeton: Princeton University Press, 1964.

[5] Philip Woodruff, *The Men Who Ruled India*, New York: Schocken, 1964, I, 277.

looked to India for the realization of radical hopes frustrated at home, in this period it was the autocrat who sought in India a field to fulfill ambitions stymied in England. India attracted the person who was disturbed by the growing democratization of English life—not the man who hoped to make India more democratic than England was herself willing to become. Once the target of reformers, India had now become the hope of reactionaries. The man who now came to India was likely to be a man excited by the desire to rule rather than reform, concerned with British might, not Indian hopes; a man to whom the permanent subjection of India to the British yoke was not a repugnant thought.

The ideas out of which this commitment to a permanent rule finally evolved had been tossed about from the earliest days of British penetration. "Empire" as a theme had been common for several centuries. The connotations of such a term as Empire in the second half of the nineteenth century, however, were new. Partially it was a result of England's changed position in India; in the midst of the wars of the first half of the century talk of Empire could scarcely be more than optimistic rhetoric, while the secure and relatively peaceful military control of the half-century following the Mutiny gave the idea much more substance. More crucial than this, however, were changes in attitudes of the British in India reflecting changes in the intellectual climate of Europe. Changing conditions in England, and in England's relations to her European rivals, as well as changes in India, contributed to a new frame of mind which had as its governing idea the justness of the permanent subjection of India to British rule.

The following pages trace the origins and development of that idea and describe the way in which it dominated British policy in the later years of the century. The evolving course of events during the nineteenth century is examined in the light of the state of affairs current at the end of the century. What is stressed is the significance of specific events and ideas for the later period. The organization of the work, moreover, is topical, and the different components of the ideology of permanence are treated separately, though roughly in the order of their emergence. In several instances, notably with regard to James and John Stuart Mill, Charles Grant, and James Fitzjames Stephen, the ideas of major, but not in every respect typical representatives of particular schools of thought have been explored at some length to suggest the possibilities for elaboration on the dominant themes of the period. All manner of materials—from official reports to lighthearted novels and diaries—have been drawn upon in the delineation of this ideology, which has involved making connections and putting pieces together which were never synthesized in the beliefs of any single person, or set down in full in a government document. The argument presented here is thus an interpretation, a new ordering of impressions which were not so arranged during the period described. While never visible as a whole in any single place and difficult to trace to the influence of individual persons or events, the ideology of permanence clearly exerted a strong pressure on British life and thought. A permanent *raj* seemed a practical possibility and to be confirmed by racial and political and religious theories as both sound and high-principled. In retrospect, the extent of the British dedication to this illusion of permanence seems to have been both regrettable and dangerous. The Empire, seemingly so stable, was in reality growing ever more fragile; the principles by which the Empire was governed, seemingly so self-evident, were often based on partial impressions and suggested by accidental occurrences. The certainty of a permanent Empire in these years, however, seemed to increase in proportion to its fragility, and to serve for many people as a defense and retreat from reason long after the course of events had proved its impossibility.

British attitudes toward India were of course never a monolithic orthodoxy. The British throughout their connection with India engaged in a dialogue amongst themselves, and if certain approaches and attitudes were dominant at different times they were constantly under attack by those who preferred other approaches and attitudes. When experience and inclination dictated the need for a change of policy there were always formulated alternatives from which to choose. All the diverse attitudes toward Indian problems which gained dominance at different periods in later years were visible in some preliminary form in the controversies of the eighteenth century. The reformers of the early years of the nineteenth century had to fight against a tide of antagonism; and the dominant late nineteenth century mood was subject to the challenge mutely represented by the experience of the earlier period, as well as to the criticism of contemporary malcontents. It is true, however, that the latter years of the century saw an attenuation in the vigor of the debate and that the attitudes of the British in India came closer then to approximating a uniform orthodoxy than at other periods. In the early years of the century criticism was freely indulged in by senior officials; later, criticism came largely from the peripheries of power. The criticism itself was likely to be less basic and searing, and it was easy within a context of dominant conservatism to gain a reputation for radicalism by proposing quite modest changes. The liberal English officials of late nineteenth century India seem singularly pallid replicas of their predecessors, for they did not occupy exalted positions and moreover quarreled only glancingly with the premises dominant in their age. The primary focus of the debate between alternative policies had shifted out of the official community in India. The opposition was now represented not by a school of prominent official opinion but by radicals from England and increasingly by Indian nationalists.

The study of British imperial ideology continues to be relevant to contemporary issues because of the role it played in the Indian nationalist struggle. It is important to understand what it was that Indians reacted against, the peculiar nature of the contact Indians had with the West, in order to appreciate the nature of the reaction. Some Indians accepted the British view of themselves and of Indians, and the British approach toward public policy; others did not. But the ideology of India's rulers could not be ignored by Indians because the rulers set the terms of the debate.

A further area of concern to which an analysis of British imperialism may contribute involves the comparative study of the intellectual and psychological aspects of group and racial confrontations, the evolution of prejudice and stereotypes, and the mentality of dominant classes. British imperialism in India, unique in many respects, nonetheless developed a pattern of relationships and attitudes for which analogies can be found in other societies. In Africa, in the American South and elsewhere, social situations and intellectual viewpoints emerged which invite comparison with those of nineteenth century British India.[6]

It is a pleasure to be able to record a longstanding intellectual debt to Professors Lloyd and Susanne Rudolph, who first introduced me to the field of Indian studies and who have continued to be a source of stimulation and encouragement. Susanne Rudolph was the first director of my doctoral dissertation which formed the basis of the present work and guided me past many pitfalls. I am also grateful for the assistance of Professor Merle Fainsod who subsequently assumed the direction of the dissertation. Others to whom I am grateful for advice and assistance include Professors Rupert Emerson, Bernard S. Cohn, Thomas Metcalf, Judith Shklar, Carolyn Elliott, and Robert Hardgrave.

Financial assistance for the research and writing of my dissertation was provided by the American Institute of Indian Studies,

[6] A number of highly interesting studies have been made of such related topics, which have provided valuable insights for the present work; in particular, Stanley Elkins, *Slavery*, New York: Universal Library, 1963; Philip Mason, *Prospero's Magic; some thoughts on class and race*, London: Oxford University Press, 1962; and O. Mannoni, *Prospero and Caliban, The Psychology of Colonization*, Powesland, trans., New York: Praeger, 1956.

Poona, and by the Committee on Southern Asian Studies, University of Chicago, enabling me to spend a year in India for research, followed by a year at Chicago, where, as a Carnegie Intern, I was able to complete the writing of the dissertation.

FRANCIS G. HUTCHINS

Cambridge, Massachusetts
November 1966

Contents

The Illusion of Permanence

CHAPTER I

Evangelicism, Utilitarianism, and the Origin of the Idea of a Just Rule

> The system will not last fifty years. The moment
> these brave and able natives know how to combine,
> they will rush on us simultaneously and the game
> is up. —SIR CHARLES NAPIER, "CONQUEROR OF SINDH"

IT IS ONE of the many ironies of the British connection with
India that those who first argued for the justness of England's
retention of an Indian empire were opposed to its acquisition.
India was conquered for England by merchant adventurers
such as Robert Clive and Warren Hastings, and gentlemen war-
riors such as Lord Wellesley and Sir Charles Napier, who
thought of England's position in India in terms of profit and
national advantage. The conviction that these conquests could
also serve higher purposes found its origin in the writings of reformers, Benthamite and Evangelical, men such as James Mill
and Charles Grant who considered England's march toward
supremacy in India the product of acts of criminal aggression.

India's conquerors were men molded in an England untouched
by religious or political reform, in an aristocratic society unex-
cited by questions of morality. They conquered India but they
did not despise it. They knew from personal experience that
traditional Indian society and political institutions were viable,
and in many respects admirable, and did not pretend that their
military conquests had produced anything more than the ascendancy of a particular dynasty. They fought and won their
battles by acting consciously in an Indian context and according
to the contemporary rules of the game. As Sir Charles Metcalfe
remarked to Mountstuart Elphinstone, "I think all stirring
times detestable, on one account, which is that pure virtue is

useless in them."[1] Metcalfe and others nonetheless responded to
the call of "stirring times" with the methods they felt were
suited to them, and soon found India prostrate at their feet.

It was precisely this use of what they considered Oriental cunning and violence which so incensed the reformers. James Mill's
six-volume *History of British India* contained a searing indict-
ment of the crimes which he acknowledged had done much to
bring England to her present eminence in India. Mill, for instance, in describing John Malcolm's mission to Persia in 1799,
quoted Malcolm's statement that "The embassy was in a style
of splendour corresponding to the character of the monarch, and
the manners of the nation, to whom it was sent; and to the
wealth and power of that state from whom it proceeded," and
then added his own commentary: "A language this," said Mill,
"which may be commonly interpreted, lavishly, or, which is the
same thing, criminally expensive." But Mill found more to
blame in Malcolm's conduct than mere Oriental ostentation;
the agreement reached between Malcolm and the King of Persia authorized the King to "disgrace and slay" any Frenchman
entering his territory, which drew from Mill this further comment: "Though the atrocious part of this order was, no doubt,
the pure offspring of Persian ferocity; yet a Briton may justly
feel shame, that the ruling men of his nation, a few years ago
(such was the moral corruption of the time!) could contemplate
with pleasure so barbarous and inhuman a mandate. . . ."[2] The
same tone of voice characterized the Evangelical response. Of
the Treaty of Bassein, Charles Grant said in 1804, "We are
chargeable with all the guilt of it, the bloodshed, miseries and
devastations which it has occasioned."[3] The "crimes" of India's
conquerors were continuously condemned by a line of critics
prompted by many diverse motives, stretching from Edmund

[1] Edward Thompson, *The Life of Charles, Lord Metcalfe*, London: Faber
and Faber, 1937, p. 59.

[2] Mill, *History of British India*, 1820 edn., VI, 161-62.

[3] Charles Grant to George Udny, 1 June 1804, cited in Embree, *Charles
Grant*, p. 214.

Burke to Richard Cobden, a tradition with which Evangelicals and Utilitarians were prominently associated.

And yet it was from this tradition of reproof as represented by the Evangelicals and Utilitarians, rather than from the tradition of conquest, that the conviction that England should remain in India permanently was finally to evolve. There were of course critics—Cobden was one[4]—who were totally opposed to the Indian connection, who argued that if India had been sinfully acquired it could only be retained by compounding the sin of acquisition. The more dominant note, however, was that sounded by the reformers, in the argument that England's retention of India was more of an atonement for original sin than an indication that she persisted in that state. The same Charles Grant who expressed chagrin at England's unprovoked assault on India's sovereign rulers also recorded his conviction that England's rule of India should demonstrate "whether conquest" (of which he so often expressed disapproval)—"shall

> have been made in our hands the means, not merely of displaying a government unequalled in India for administrative justice, kindness, and moderation, not merely of encreasing the security of the subjects and prosperity of the country, but of advancing social happiness, of meliorating the moral state of men, and of extending a superior light.[5]

Grant's motive in urging reform was to discover: "upon what general principles may we best hope to make our connection with that country permanent, and, as far as we can, indissoluble?"[6] Mill similarly avoided justifying conquest, while stressing the possibility of compensating "the people of India, for the

[4] Cf., e.g., Richard Cobden, *How Wars are Got up in India*, London: William and Frederick G. Cash, 1853.

[5] Charles Grant, "Observations on the State of Society among the Asiatic Subjects of Great Britain, particularly with respect to Morals; and on the Means of improving it." *Parliamentary Papers* (H. C.), "Report from the Select Committee of the House of Commons on the Affairs of the East India Company," 16 August 1832, Appendix, p. 123.

[6] *Ibid.*, p. 111.

miseries of that misgovernment which they had so long en-
dured,"[7] by "giving to the government of India the benefit of
men capable of applying the best ideas of their age to the ar-
rangement of its important affairs."[8]

To the Evangelical and Utilitarian reformers India seemed in
urgent need of reform. Both Mill's and Grant's estimation of
Indian society represented a radical departure from that which
had been held by both Burke and Hastings. Divided over what
policies England should pursue in India Hastings and Burke
were united nonetheless in an admiring assessment of traditional Indian society; further divided over which were the more
admirable characteristics of this society—Hastings emphasizing
what was permitted to the ruler, Burke countering with an emphasis on the traditional restraints on power—both men agreed
that India should be governed in accordance with its traditional
pattern rather than by imported European techniques. The new,
reforming generation replaced this impression of India as a
rich and highly developed civilization with one which depicted
India as existing in the grossest sort of degradation. The motives
which had led many Europeans to form a more appreciative
opinion of Indian society were ruthlessly exposed. Charles
Grant dismissed with a single gesture the *philosophes* of the
French Enlightenment, polemicists such as Burke, Orientalist
scholars such as Sir William Jones, and nabobs such as Hastings:

> Some modern philosophers . . . whose aim has been to sub-
> vert, together with revealed religion, all ideas of the moral
> government of the Deity, and of men's responsibility to Him,
> have exalted the natives of the East, and of other pagan re-
> gions, into models of goodness and innocence. Other writers,
> with far better views, indignant at the alleged delinquencies
> of Europeans in Hindostan, have described the natives of that
> country as a harmless, kind, peaceable, and suffering race.
> Others, again, speak rather from an admiration inspired by

[7] Mill, *History of British India*, vi, 416.
[8] *Ibid.*, p. 402.

the supposed past taste of the Hindoos, mixed with pity for their present situation, than from experience of their actual qualities and dispositions. And there may be others still, who have not had much personal experience of the evils resulting from the state of society among the Hindoos, but being pleased with their obsequiousness and easily acquiescing in the licentiousness prevalent among them, have been willing to treat their character and proceedings with indulgence.[9]

In devising their opinions of the current state of Indian society and developing proposals for its reform, Evangelicals and Utilitarians acted with a degree of unity which belied the apparent contradictions in their basic beliefs. It was not surprising, however, that the two movements found so little difficulty in cooperating. Though drawing their inspiration from opposed conceptual extremes, Christian piety on the one hand, and secular hedonism on the other, Evangelicals and Utilitarians actually shared much more than a common antipathy to traditional Indian society. As Halevy remarked,

It would be a mistake to establish an irreconcilable opposition between the Utilitarian ethic and the Christian on the ground that the former is founded on pleasure, the latter on sacrifice. For Utilitarian morality cannot be described without qualification as hedonism. It was based simultaneously on two principles. One of these, it is true, was the identification of the good with pleasure; but the other, of equal importance with the former, was the duty incumbent upon man, in virtue of the natural conditions to which his life is subject, to sacrifice present pleasure to the hope of the future, and purchase happiness at the cost of labour and suffering. . . . Benthamism, as its principles were popularized about 1815 by James Mill the Scotsman, was the French philosophy of the eighteenth century adapted to the needs of a nation moulded by a dogmatic and austere religion.[10]

[9] Grant, "Observations," p. 32.
[10] Elie Halevy, *England in 1815*, London, 1949, pp. 586-87. Cf. Melvin

James Mill's view of Indian society combined Enlightenment radicalism with almost equal portions of Evangelical piety. Like the *philosophes*, Mill disparaged the tendency exemplified by Edmund Burke to find legitimation and a presumption of virtue in the mere perpetuation of institutions for a long period of time. "Faults this nation may have," Burke had exclaimed, in reference to India, "but God forbid we should pass judgment upon people who framed their laws and institutions prior to our insect origin of yesterday. . . ."[11] In the radical Enlightenment tradition Mill scorned any such reverence for established custom. He differed from the *philosophes*, however, in making vigorous attacks on Hindu immorality in the name of a superior European virtue.

One of the characteristic activities of the eighteenth century Enlightenment had been the intellectual discovery of the non-European, non-Christian world. Though travelers' reports had been available long before that, it was only in the eighteenth century that they became of more than passing interest to intellectuals, for reasons at the very heart of Enlightenment concerns. Intent simultaneously on the destruction of the exclusive claims of Christianity, and on the assertion of the equality and basic rationality of the entire human race, the *philosophes* perceived that accounts of non-Christian societies directly suited their purposes. The idealized figure of the wise Oriental statesman and philosopher and that of the simple but virtuous savage were employed to ridicule European claims to uniqueness and sufficiency. Non-Christian "superstitions" fared no better than the Christian variety; but neither did they fare worse. Similarly, Oriental despotism was not held up to admiration, but neither was it held up to contempt by comparison with the European state of affairs. There was, rather, an inclination to identify Oriental despotism with the form of government then existing

---

Richter, *The Politics of Conscience, T. H. Green and His Age*, Cambridge, Mass.: Harvard University Press, 1964, pp. 309-10.

[11] Burke, *Works*, London, 1877, VII, 46.

under Christian auspices in Europe, and to link in a common destiny the oppressed peoples of both Europe and the Orient. When the *philosophes* attacked non-European societies they did so as an indirect method of criticizing their own societies.

This was not the case with James Mill, who did not shrink from illustrating Indian inadequacies by pointing to a superior state of affairs in Europe. Dissatisfied as he was with the current condition of England, he was nonetheless prepared to argue emphatically for its superiority over that of India. In doing so he adopted a tone of moralistic righteousness totally alien to the *philosophes*.

Mill's account of Hindu society, for which he relied on missionary accounts to an extent which drew protests from his editor,[12] presumed a standard of proper conduct which would have been completely acceptable to the most rigorous Evangelical. Mill's estimation of what was moral stressed the sanctity of women and the home. He thus found nothing to admire in the Hindu ideal of asceticism which he characterized as "an absolute renunciation of all moral duties, and moral affections. 'Exemption from attachments, and affection for children, wife, and home . . .'"[13] was an aspiration which Mill could only consider a reflection of moral corruption.

Evangelicalism and Utilitarianism ran parallel to one another in a number of important respects. Both sects were highly moralistic in their standards of human conduct, both were products of the rising middle classes in business and the professions. Both doctrines had within them the seeds of egalitarian individualism, and were dedicated to insuring greater scope for the energies of the industrious individual. Both sects, moreover, considered that the principles of probity and hard work which

[12] H. H. Wilson, who edited the later edition of Mill's *History*, said of his sources: "As missionaries . . . they see the errors and vices of a heathen people through a medium by which they are exaggerated beyond their natural dimensions, and assume an enormity which would not be assigned to the very same defects in Christians." *History*, 1840 edn., I, 523.

[13] *Ibid.*, pp. 364-65.

they espoused were of universal applicability. Both were essentially secular; Utilitarianism was avowedly so, Evangelicalism was a most undogmatic and untheoretical religious movement which made work in this world the touchstone of religion. A preoccupation with the quality of life in society was of the very essence of the Evangelical creed. Charles Grant's proposal for introducing Christianity into India, for instance, spoke of the mission movement as a social rather than theological crusade. Grant recommended the introduction of Christianity because it was useful, not simply because it was true:

> It is not . . . the introduction of a new set of ceremonies, nor even a new creed, that is the ultimate object here. Those who conceive religion to be conversant merely about forms and speculative notions, may well think that the world need not be much troubled concerning it. No, the ultimate object is moral improvement. The preeminent excellence of the morality which the Gospel teaches, and the superior efficacy of this divine system, taken in all its parts, in meliorating the condition of human society, cannot be denied by those who are unwilling to admit its higher claims; and on this ground only, the dissemination of it must be beneficial to mankind.[14]

Utilitarians and Evangelicals sought the same goal by different routes: Utilitarians hoped to improve morals by reforming society; Evangelicals hoped to improve society by reforming morals.

The two movements shared optimistic hopes for the rapid transformation of Indian society. The currently debased state of the society was believed to be emblematic of its immaturity rather than its degeneracy. The conditions existing in India, James Mill argued, were similar to those found everywhere among "rude nations" whether they be Red Indian or primitive Anglo–Saxon. Hindu conceptions of the Divinity reminded Mill of those possessed by "the rude tribes of America, wander-

[14] Grant, "Observations," p. 99.

ing naked in the woods."[15] Caste in India reminded Mill of early Britain: "The Druids among the ancient Britons, as there was a striking similarity in many of the doctrines which they taught, also possessed many similar privileges and distinctions to those of the Brahmens."[16] Parallels could be found for Indian manners: "Dr. Forster . . . remarks a great similarity, in many respects, between the manners of the Hindus and those of the Otaheitans."[17] Religious conceptions, social arrangements, and manners, all had their counterparts in other rude societies. Even gross indelicacy embodied in written codes was not unusual at a very early stage of society, as Dr. Henry's citations, modestly veiled in Latin, about the customs of the early Anglo–Saxons, so clearly showed.[18]

Mill thus denied both the uniqueness and grandeur of Hindu civilization, but he did so in order to insist that India was in the mainstream of human development and that India presented no obstacles to social advance which had not been met and overcome elsewhere. When Mill spoke of "our race"[19] he was not referring to the English race but to the human race. Nor did Mill believe India's retardation for so long a period at an early stage of man's normal career reflected in any way discreditably upon Indian capacities. Borrowing from Malthus, Mill argued that "The rapidity with which nations advance through these several states of society chiefly depends on the circumstances which promote population."[20]

It was in this connection that Mill found the opportunity presented the British in India almost intoxicating. England had acquired supreme control over a country which had been prevented by a succession of historical accidents from achieving the advance which might otherwise have been expected of it. England, moreover, possessed in Benthamism the most refined

[15] Mill, *History of British India*, 1840 edn., I, 342.
[16] *Ibid.*, p. 188n.   [17] *Ibid.*, p. 465n.
[18] *Ibid.*, p. 463n.   [19] *Ibid.*, p. 330.
[20] *Ibid.*, p. 176. For a full discussion of society's several stages, cf. *ibid.*, pp. 172ff.

principles of government ever conceived. Mill expected from India, as from a rich field long fallow, a bountiful harvest of social advance from a modest application of Benthamite legal and social reform.

Evangelicals anticipated similar results from religious reform. Charles Grant agreed with Mill that

> We cannot presume from the past state of any people, with respect to improvement in arts, that they would under different circumstances, for ever continue the same. The history of many nations who have advanced from rudeness to refinement, contradicts such an hypothesis: according to which, the Britons ought still to be going naked, to be feeding on acorns, and sacrificing human victims in the Druidical groves.[21]

In terms of practical effect, as well, the two movements supplemented one another in ways not always appreciated or intended by their adherents. The impact of the egalitarian notions of Utilitarianism on Indian society is well known.[22] But the Evangelicals, despite highly conservative views on social policy, also facilitated the leveling process. Evangelicalism, it is true, drew much of its motive force from antagonism to the French Revolution, and sought to prevent a similar outbreak in England through a religious crusade designed to make the lower classes pious and respectful. That the Evangelicals should have contributed to a radical social revolution in India is thus somewhat ironic, but it is also typical. Conservative intentions and radical effects were both integral parts of Evangelicalism, and both were implicit in Charles Grant's program for India.

Grant wrote his tract advocating missionary work in India in 1792, at the height of English hysteria concerning the events in France. It was not a propitious time for advocating radical new departures, and Grant took great pains to convince his readers that the introduction of Christianity into India would not have

[21] "Observations," p. 87.

[22] This is most fully described in Eric Stokes, *English Utilitarians and India.*

dangerous consequences. He argued in fact that Christianity of the English sort was the best defense against revolution, that it was religious systems fraught with superstition, such as French Catholicism and Indian Hinduism which made men politically restive. Grant hoped English Protestantism might keep Indians passive, just as it induced contentment in the English lower orders. Pointing to France, Grant wrote: "The present circumstances of Europe seem emphatically to point out, that nothing but such principles can be depended upon, for keeping our subjects in obedience and subordination."[23] Grant endorsed Bishop Horne's view of the attitudes inculcated by Christianity:

> in superiors, it would be equity and moderation, courtesy and affability, benignity and condescension; in inferiors, sincerity and fidelity, respect and diligence. In princes, justice, gentleness, and solicitude for the welfare of the subjects; in subjects, loyalty, submission, obedience, quietness, peace, patience, and cheerfulness. . . .[24]

Confronting directly the argument that the introduction of Christianity into India might lead eventually to a demand for self-government, Grant dismissed the prospect as founded on a misconception of the nature of Christianity:

> The grand danger with which the objection alarms us is, that the communication of the Gospel and of European light may probably be introductive of a popular form of government and the assertion of independence. The establishment of Christianity in a country does not necessarily bring after it a free political constitution. The early Christians made no attempts to change forms of government; the spirit of the Gospel does not encourage even any disposition which might lead to such attempts. . . . Christianity seeks moral good, and general happiness. It does not, in the pursuit of these objects, erect a peculiar political system; it views politics through the safe

23 "Observations," p. 116.   24 *Ibid.*, p. 99.

medium of morals, and subjects them to the laws of universal
rectitude.[25]

Political conservatism was thus the very foundation of Grant's
plea for Christian missions; social radicalism was equally implicit in his assessment of Indian society which bracketed Indians of all degrees of social eminence in a single category of
depravity. Grant was prepared to undermine ruthlessly the aristocratic structure of Indian society because his contempt for the
impurity of the traditional Indian nobility left him unwilling
to concede that they performed any useful social function whatsoever. To the older, more casual English conquerors of India,
who often kept Indian mistresses, and mixed on terms of rough
equality with the Indian rulers they were conspiring against—
"My old Friend and Antagonist" Metcalfe called Ranjit Singh[26]
—the Indian nobility, for all its violence and cruelty, nonetheless seemed to possess the qualities of a viable ruling class. The
nobility might be erratic and immoral, but they were also lavish
with presents and fond of spectacle, capable of impressing their
subjects. The Evangelical, applying a standard of righteous conduct developed in the setting with which he was familiar in
England, refused to admit such considerations into account and
lent the weight of virtue to the eradication of social privilege.

The leveling influence of moral considerations in British Indian policy had already become evident by the time of Lord
Cornwallis, who became Governor-General for the first time in
1786. Cornwallis, in introducing the Permanent Settlement, had
made an effort to create a class of landlords on the pattern of the
English aristocracy. But it was also Cornwallis, who served in a
sense as a pivot between the old Whig liberalism and the new
Evangelical and Utilitarian liberalism, who was responsible for
the eradication of Indians from important posts in British administration. "I think it must be universally admitted," Cornwallis wrote to the Court of Directors, "that without a large and
well-regulated body of Europeans, our hold of these valuable

[25] *Ibid.*, p. 105.   [26] Thompson, *Metcalfe*, p. 281.

dominions must be very insecure."[27] The Europeanization of the services was based essentially on moral considerations, on the view that uprightness and honesty were more important to the success of British Indian government than the association with that government of Indians. In personal life, Cornwallis strived to follow the standard he had set for the public services, by similarly dissociating himself from the taint inherent in association with the natives of India. Charles Grant noted with approval that "Lord Cornwallis, soon after his arrival in Bengal, refused to be present at an entertainment of this sort [one involving "indecent dancing"] to which he was invited by the Nabob."[28] Grant used as an illustration of the general untrustworthiness of the natives the fact that Cornwallis, universally admired for his integrity, had "reposed no confidence in any of them."

> Though civil and attentive to the natives, *he has reposed no confidence in any of them, nor has he had a single individual, either Hindoo or Mahomedan, about his person, above the rank of a menial servant, contrary to the general usage of men occupying such stations as he filled.*[29]

The initial impact of moral considerations on British Indian administration was the elimination of Indians from positions of trust and responsibility by an administration also concerned to protect the social position of the Indian aristocracy. In subsequent years, moral considerations were to deprive Indians of power and wealth as well, as the Indian nobility came under direct attack in the application of radical land settlement policies[30] and the progressive elimination of princely houses through the Doctrine of Lapse. From the time of Cornwallis until the Mutiny of 1857, the position of the Indian privileged classes was progressively undermined on the basis not only of

[27] Edward Thompson and G. T. Garratt, *Rise and Fulfillment of British Rule in India*, Allahabad: Central Book Depot, 1958, p. 174.

[28] "Observations," p. 31n.   [29] *Ibid.*, p. 36. Italics in original.

[30] For a discussion of land settlement, cf. Stokes, *English Utilitarians and India.*

Utilitarian radicalism but of moral considerations as well. The Utilitarian argument would have had much less weight if it had not been able to utilize Evangelical contempt for the personal character and conduct of the classes it opposed on political and economic grounds. Grant considered "The assertion . . . that the higher natives of India are people of the purest morality and strictest virtue . . . altogether new and in palpable opposition to testimony and experience."[31] Grant, who was so violently opposed to political radicalism, by failing to distinguish between the relative depravity of high and low in India, helped contribute the weapon of moral condemnation to those intent on eradicating Indian classes they held to be unproductive.

The reformers' program offered hope for India's regeneration, and considerable success was attained in the implementation of this program. Evangelicals and Utilitarians, however, also laid the groundwork for the justification for Britain's permanent control of India in ways which were equally complementary.

Both movements were considerably more successful in their negative task of discrediting Indian society and the opinions of those who defended it than in perpetuating zeal for reform. Later generations were inclined to view Indian society contemptuously without enthusiasm for its future prospects. Mill's editor, H. H. Wilson, was concerned about the possible deleterious effects of Mill's description of the Hindus, which he felt was "calculated to destroy all sympathy between the rulers and the ruled. . . . There is a reason to fear that these consequences are not imaginary, and that a harsh and illiberal spirit has of late years prevailed in the conduct and councils of the rising service in India, which owes its origin to impressions imbibed in early life from the History of Mr. Mill."[32] Mill's successors ignored his radical commitment to human equality, emphasizing instead a conception of Indian inferiority to which Mill's own at-

---

[31] Grant, "Observations," p. 119n.
[32] Mill, *History of British India*, 1840 edn., I, vii.

tacks on the current state of Indian society had unintentionally contributed.

A more direct contribution of Benthamism to the imperial ideology was its stress on the role in government of the specialist. To Mill it was no objection that Indian reform was to be introduced by alien experts. In the Utilitarian view, the role of the Legislator, the great spirit who gave laws to a society, was crucial to social advance. Bentham obviously had cast himself in this role for the modern age, but it was further assumed that this was the normal method in which progress was achieved. "In every society," wrote Mill, "there are superior spirits, capable of seizing the best ideas of their times, and, if they are not opposed by circumstances, of accelerating the progress of the community to which they belong."[33] Even the caste system seemed probably to have been introduced in such a fashion by a great Legislator, who, suiting his social innovation to the credulous condition of the populace, had clothed it with the sanctity of a supernatural origin.[34]

If laws were best devised by specialists so also were they best administered by specialists. There was a tendency within Benthamism to consider the essence of politics to be regulation rather than participation, a tendency which strongly appealed to the alien bureaucrats charged with the government of India. Throughout their rule the British were considerably more successful in legislating reform than in eliciting the cooperation and participation of their Indian subjects. It was possible for Mill's successors to maintain that they were governing India for Indians and to feel that there was no incongruity in the fact that this government was not *by* Indians. Mill encouraged the notion that government was properly the business of specialists and thus provided an ideological framework which was employed in defense not only of the need for Indian reform but also of the need for the continuing presence in India of British administrative specialists.

[33] *Ibid.*, p. 178.   [34] *Ibid.*, pp. 181-82.

There were perhaps even more persuasive arguments for permanence in the Evangelical program of moral reform. Many missionaries shared Mill's conviction of the unity and similarity of the human race and bent their efforts to bring India as rapidly as possible up to the British standard. Many felt, it is true, that embracing Christianity would quickly bring India to the forefront of civilization. But there was another side to the movement for moral reform which ultimately proved more important than its optimistic, egalitarian aspect: the mood of charitable condescension.

Charles Grant, though convinced that Christianity would assist Indians to "rise in the scale of civilization,"[35] still held serious reservations about India's future prospects. Grant was certain Christianity would be good for Indians—because it would do anybody good—but he was less convinced that Christianity would make Indians and Englishmen exactly alike. His view of Christianity led him to the conviction that its message was not the same for all and that while it made Englishmen good rulers, it could also make Indians good subjects. Furthermore, however committed an Evangelical reformer might be to potential human equality and to brotherhood realized within the Christian faith, he was also necessarily committed to the belief that there was something special not only about his faith but about himself as a believer. He could not act as the evangelist who brought good tidings and expected only a simple conversion and affirmation of faith. The Evangelical could not accept as a brother and an equal any depraved and ignorant person who paraded himself under the Christian label. While this might have been conceivable for Non-conformist missionaries who were themselves not far removed from a lowly position in their own society, the Evangelicals were respectable members of the Established Church and members of a class which was rapidly taking over the leadership of their own country. They were members of that substantial middle class that had come

[35] "Observations," p. 83.

into positions of wealth and power in business and the professions. They owed their eminence not to inherited wealth and titles but to their own efforts, to the application of energy and intelligence. They did not simply possess a faith; they possessed in addition: habits of mind—frugality, seriousness, dedication to strenuous labor, contempt for pleasure-seeking, lavishness, and elegance—which were more central to their faith than creeds or dogmas or any number of Articles. The Evangelical was consequently more inclined to work for the underprivileged, whether heathen Indians or English workingmen, than acknowledge their equality as human beings and potential believers. The pious works of Evangelicals were often tinged with condescension; the Evangelicals engaged in more thorough concern with demonstrating their own righteousness than hope for the actual enlightenment and elevation of those who served as the object of their endeavors. If an Evangelical reformer did retain the Enlightenment view that all men were equal, he did so usually with the proviso that much would be required before that potential equality became a reality. If mankind not only were converted to Christianity but further adopted habits of mind and action similar to his own, then only could mankind be entitled to a full measure of respect. The argument for the permanent subjection of India to British rule thus also found support in Evangelicalism, in the conviction of the justness of helping the underprivileged, joined to a skepticism about the ability of the underprivileged ever to help themselves. The two reform movements, so zealous for India's rapid transformation, when modified and drained of optimism formed the initial basis for the justification of Britain's presumed right to govern India indefinitely.

CHAPTER II

The Right Sort of Conduct: India's Attraction for Victorian Englishmen

"You know I never liked India, but one always takes a sort of stoical pleasure in doing a very unpleasant duty. You may imagine what zest stable duty may acquire by being regarded as a chronic martyrdom!"[1]

THE ERA of greatest enthusiasm for social reform came to an end almost simultaneously in India and in England in the mid-1830s. The Reform Bill of 1832 capped and completed an era of excitement about social and legal issues in England but foreshadowed a lull in reform efforts rather than the beginning of renewed activity. Macaulay's "Minute on Education in India" in 1835 similarly signaled a major triumph for reform in the decision to support education in the English language, but in India as well reform enthusiasm seemed to have spent much of its strength in conquering its political rivals, leaving little enthusiasm for the more important work of following up its formal triumph. The beginning of Victoria's long reign thus inaugurated a new era, though one whose significance and distinctive characteristics were slow to emerge. The earlier reform movement had largely spent itself; what was to follow was not immediately clear.

Indian reform, it should be emphasized, was "popular" even at its height; Lord Bentinck was not popular with the majority of Englishmen in India, who continued to be more interested in their own emoluments than Indian welfare. The end of the era of greatest reform activity was thus not marked by an energetic crusade in opposition to reform, but simply by the disappearance

[1] William Delafield Arnold, *Oakfield, or Fellowship in the East*, Boston, 1855, p. 440.

of the necessary determination of a committed minority to push reforms at anything exceeding the most glacial pace.

A significant factor in this change of mood among the serious-minded was a widespread crisis in religious belief. The Victorian period, so commonly associated with the ascendancy in society of Christian values, was not in actuality an Age of Faith. It could perhaps be more properly described as an Age of Loss of Faith, for it was not an age in which faith was absent or thought irrelevant; it was an age dominated by an obsessive preoccupation with the crumbling of faith. This period, in which the faith that had inspired Evangelical reformers for a generation was suddenly subjected to such painful scrutiny, approximately coincided with Victoria's reign, beginning in the 1830s and stretching to the end of the century. The growth of doubt about the traditional tenets of Christianity did not provoke a tendency to disregard religion or morality; it produced, on the contrary, a vast proliferation of surrogate faiths which it was hoped would fill the role conventionally played by Christianity as the support of personal morality and social obligation. These faiths ranged from the concreteness of Marxism to the vagueness of Carlyle's Everlasting Yea, from the Spartan agnosticism of Leslie Stephen to the ponderously complex idolatry of Comte. In the words of Melvin Richter,

> The *Ersatz* theologies, the all-inclusive philosophies of life so dear to the nineteenth-century . . . all in their separate ways attempted to enlist religious impulsions in the service of worldly causes . . . to construct secular moralities which would fulfill the same function for modern society as had traditional religions in the past.[2]

The Victorian age, while not an Age of Faith, was thus a time of great moral seriousness in which an almost infinite number of systems and schemes evolved through attempts to find underpinnings for ethical obligations. Among the systems

[2] *Politics of Conscience*, Cambridge, Mass.: Harvard University Press, 1964, pp. 33-34.

of this description which contributed to the ideology of permanence were nationalism, racism, the worship of material progress and force, and the cult of good conduct. The cult of conduct was never quite developed into a "system" or totally divorced from its original identification with Evangelical Christianity. For the majority of Englishmen it meant little more than a vague sense that hard work and sportsmanlike play helped form character. And yet it deserves treatment as a secular religion distinct from Christianity, because for many it became the only thing remaining when doubt had eaten away at the bases of faith and was adhered to with a vehemence proportional to the anguish felt at the loss of that faith. As faith waned Duty became in itself a religion. Good conduct, which had been considered by the Evangelicals to be natural for those with a vital faith, had now become mandatory; once thought the result of belief, good conduct had been transformed into the very substance of faith itself. Even Thomas Macaulay, reared in the bosom of Clapham and confident of India's rapid conversion to Christianity, had difficulty with Christian doctrine. Following his death a quotation from Conyers Middleton was found among his papers, which read,

> But if to live strictly and think freely; to practise what is moral and to believe what is rational, be consistent with the sincere profession of Christianity, then I shall acquit myself like one of its truest professors.

To this quotation, Macaulay had appended the words, "Haec est absoluta et perfecta philosophi vita."[3] Leslie Stephen used plain English: "I now believe in nothing, to put it shortly, but I do not the less believe in morality. . . . I mean to live and die like a gentleman if possible."[4]

Such a point of view made morality more, rather than less, important as faith waned, and turned into an obsession the necessity for insuring that individuals would be constantly sur-

[3] Noel Annan, *Leslie Stephen*, London, 1951, p. 121.
[4] *Ibid.*, p. 198.

rounded by props to good conduct. The individual was now so much more vulnerable, so it seemed, to temptations to dissipation that it was absolutely essential to throw up an impenetrable no man's land between the struggling individual and the very thought or tiniest example of bad conduct. Every street, every conversation, every book thus came to be viewed as potentially an instructor in good or bad conduct, with potential disaster to propriety threatened on every hand. Literature, with its powerful formative effect, was naturally subjected to scrutiny, and an army of censors followed in Bowdler's footsteps. An attempt was even made to do for Indian scriptures what Bowdler had done for Shakespeare, when "an association was formed, including Christians, Mohammedans, and Hindoos, for the purpose of expurgating the native literature to a sufficient amount to supply schools with decent books."[5] In a religion of conduct,

[5] Harriet Martineau, *Suggestions towards the Future Government of India*, London: Smith, Elder, 1858, p. 108. And yet literature, even when most innocent and affecting, was open to serious objection. Henry Lawrence presented his sister with a passage from the *Natural History of Enthusiasm* which made this point. As described by his biographers, "The last day that he was at home, he put into his sister Letitia's hand the following favorite passage that he had written out and marked, 'With Henry's love.' " It gives a good look into his mind:—

The Religion of the heart may be supplanted by a religion of the imagination, just in the same way that the social affections are often dislodged or corrupted by factitious sensibilities. Everyone knows that an artificial excitement of all the kind and tender emotions of our nature, may take place through the medium of the imagination. Hence the power of poetry and drama. But every one must also know that these feelings, however vivid, and seemingly pure and salutary they may be, and however nearly they may resemble the genuine workings of the soul, are so far from producing the same softening effect upon the character, that they tend rather to indurate the heart. Whenever excitements of any kind are regarded distinctly as a source of luxurious pleasure, then, instead of expanding the bosom with beneficent energy, instead of dispelling the sinister purposes of selfishness, instead of shedding the softness and warmth of generous love through the moral system, they become a *freezing center of solitary and unsocial indulgence*,

however, the most important scriptures were lives of the saints, biographies of good men who were models of good conduct. Biography, thus conceived of as a medium for religious instruction, was conformed to standards other than those of psychoanalysis, or even candor. A biographer's responsibility was thought to compel him to suppress facts about his subject which were not edifying, for his task was to instruct and not dissect.[6] Sir John Kaye, for instance, in his biography of Sir Charles Metcalfe, presented him as an example of the way in which one man could serve his country in India, and suppressed all reference to Metcalfe's Indian wife and three sons—one of whom attained considerable eminence and a place in the *Dictionary of National Biography.*[7]

Just as in biography exhortation and edification were considered more important than cleverness in expression or analysis, so in personal life goodness was valued more highly than subtlety, and sincerity than intelligence. One was vulnerable to the lures presented by the oversophistication of one's own mind, no less than to external temptations, and the Victorians felt simplicity and openness of mind were the surest defense against wrongdoing. They considered the development of "character"

---

and at length displace every emotion that deserves to be called virtuous. No cloak of selfishness is, in fact, more impenetrable than that which usually envelopes a pampered imagination. The reality of woe is the very circumstance that paralyses sympathy; and the eyes that can pour forth their floods of commiseration for the sorrows of the Romance or the Drama, grudge a tear to the substantial wretchedness of the unhappy. Much more often than not, this kind of luxurious sensitiveness to fiction is conjoined with a callousness, that enables the subject of it to pass the affecting occasions of domestic life in immovable apathy; the heart has become, like that of Leviathan, "firm as a stone, yea hard as a piece of nether millstone."

Sir Herbert Edwardes and Herman Merivale, *Life of Sir Henry Lawrence,* New York: Macmillan, 1873, pp. 64-65.

[6] For the views of Leslie Stephen, editor of the *Dictionary of National Biography,* on this subject, cf. Annan, *Leslie Stephen,* pp. 222ff.

[7] Thompson, *Metcalfe,* pp. x-xi.

the highest goal, and character was not associated primarily with intelligence or learning, but with the ability to deal with other people. A defense of the importance of character might take the form in India, for instance, of an emphasis on the value of knowledge of men in contrast to a knowledge merely of books. Brigadier-General John Jacob—"Jacob of Jacobabad"— felt formal language study was actually a hindrance to communication with "the mass of natives."

> It should be remembered that while the one young man has been studying books the other has been studying men. The former will be able to read a native book, or to converse with his Moonshee in elegant phraseology, but will be probably quite incapable of understanding the expressions of a peasant. . . . The latter would be quite unable to read a word of the book; but having been associated with the people, would talk with them readily.[8]

The Victorian Englishman at home similarly questioned the value of polite refinements in prosecuting the serious business of life, and sought instead for guides to steadiness and sturdiness of character.

Example in literature and life became the great teacher. Well-regulated conduct was presumed to have an edifying effect on those around one; immoral conduct was considered not only intrinsically bad but bad also for the effect it would have on others. Englishmen further assumed that if the instruction afforded by the display of good character was not lost on their own youthful daughters, it would be equally impressive to their Indian subjects. India, which may have heightened the propensity to immorality of eighteenth century Englishmen, in the nineteenth provided only a further spur to probity. The exposure to Indians of an illustration of British conduct became for the Victorians what missionary endeavor had been for the preceding generation. The transformation of India, which had

[8] Lewis Pelly, ed., *The Views and Opinions of Brigadier-General John Jacob, C.B.*, London: Smith Elder, 1858, p. 12.

once been hoped for from Christian teaching, was now considered to rest on the instruction of Christian example. India, in fact, was held, in Jacob's opinion, by the moral force of British example:

> We hold India, then, by being in reality, as in reputation, a superior race to the Asiatic; and if this natural superiority did not exist, we should not, and could not, retain the country for one week. If, then, we really are a morally superior race, governed by higher motives, and possessing higher attributes than the Asiatics, the more the natives of India are able to understand us, and the more we improve their capacity for so understanding, the firmer will become our power. Away, then, with the assumption of equality; and let us accept our true position of a dominant race. So placed, let us establish our rule by setting them a high example, by making them feel the value of truth and honesty, and by raising their moral and intellectual powers.[9]

In an article in the *Parents Review*, a Rugby graduate stated that in his opinion the Indian Mutiny of 1857 had resulted from a failure by the English in India to act more fully on such principles. He noted that at Rugby he had been taught by the Headmaster, Dr. Arnold, to consider "fighting with the town boys, with those 'of lower social position' contemptible; instead one should help them by acting towards them as 'Christians and gentlemen.' "[10] If Englishmen had conducted themselves toward Indians in such a fashion, acting with a courtesy and restraint designed to inspire respect in those who were less privileged, it was argued, the Mutiny might have been averted. For as this article implied, the natural corollary of the assertion that India was held by the force of good example was that it might be lost by the force of bad example. This situation in which the

---

[9] *Ibid.*, p. 2.

[10] Cf. Edward C. Mack, *Public Schools and British Opinion, 1780-1860*, New York, 1939, p. 257. The reference is to an article in *Parents Review*, December 1895, p. 759.

Englishman assumed he was always "on the stage," always affecting for good or ill those around him by his manner of life, had the effect of making him extremely preoccupied with the prospect that Indians might get a bad impression. As Jacob put it,

> Whatever tends to make European gentlemen "cheap"—to lessen their evident value—to hold up their vices rather than their virtues to the view of the natives—to show them to the natives only in inferior positions, where their powers are not called forth, and where they have little influence for good— must tend to destroy in no slight degree the hold we have on the people. Whatever, on the contrary, raises the European character in the eyes of the natives of India, and in reality, must greatly add to our security and power.[11]

Jacob was concerned about ill-paid Englishmen in inferior jobs who might be venal and corrupt. Others were concerned about the impression made by innocent frivolity:

> To what are called "amusements" in the bigger world of society, Henry Lawrence was no doubt indifferent even as a boy. Coming home one night from a ball to which he had gone with Alexander, George, and Letitia, he said to his sister, "What a wretched unprofitable evening! Not a Christian to speak to. All the women decked out with flowers on their heads, and their bodies half naked." Simple, earnest, and modest, he shrank even then from frivolity and display; and in later years, in India, he never could see English ladies dancing in the presence of native servants or guests, without being thoroughly wretched.[12]

It will be recalled that in *A Passage to India* the English community at the club made themselves desperately uncomfortable to avoid giving a bad impression: "Windows were barred, lest

[11] Pelly, *John Jacob*, p. 3.
[12] Edwardes and Merivale, *Henry Lawrence*, pp. 19-20.

the servants should see their mem-sahibs acting, and the heat was consequently immense."[13]

The Englishmen of Forster's novel were of course a later and lesser breed, whose concern was only negative—that Indians not hold them in contempt—and who had lost all interest in the prospect that "good example" might transform India. The standard of educational conduct upheld by Jacob and Henry Lawrence had a certain nobility about it, though also an element of pathetic self-delusion. It was imagined that always "turning one's best profile" would "have an effect" on Indians and that stern austerity of manner was more impressive than warmth, friendship and sympathy. The "ungrateful children" of the Victorians—Samuel Butler, Lytton Strachey, Virginia Woolf—understood the presumption, and rejected it angrily. Indians were simply mystified. Unacquainted with the context in which stoic stiffness had become associated with superiority of character, they could only observe the British display with puzzlement rather than profit. Ranjit Singh told the visiting Frenchman Victor Jacquemont that he had at first suspected he might be an Englishman, but that a brief conversation had removed his doubts:

> Sur ma nationalité, cependant, il paraît rassuré. Quand je le quittai, après ma première audience, il s'écria que je n'étais certainement pas Anglais. Un Anglais, dit-il, n'aurait pas changé vingt fois de position; il n'aurait point fait de gestes en parlant; il n'eût point parlé sur cette variété de tons, haut et bas; il n'aurait pas ri dans l'occasion, etc.[14]

The Victorian cult of conduct possessed value only for its adherents. The greater strictness and ceremony with which it was observed in regions most alien and uncomprehending, though justified by its presumed effect on the "natives," was in reality

[13] E. M. Forster, *A Passage to India*, New York: Harcourt, Brace, 1924, p. 24.
[14] Victor Jacquemont, *Correspondance*, Paris: Garnier Freres, 1846, 1, 357.

only the necessary reenforcement required by the cult in regions hostile to its claims.

Instead of responding with pleasure or interest to what was unfamiliar serious-minded Englishmen now reacted against it, and clung firmly to their own standards of conduct, thus producing an actual accentuation of English morality. "It has generally been found," noted G. O. Trevelyan,

> that a manly valiant race, which has imposed its yoke upon an effeminate, and unwarlike people, in course of time, degenerates and becomes slothful and luxurious. . . . Thus Marc Antony . . . and his followers became half Egyptians under the influence of the lovely Begum of Alexandria. . . . With the English in the East precisely the opposite result has taken place. The earliest settlers were indolent, dissipated, grasping, almost Orientals in their way of life, and almost heathens in the matter of religion. But each generation of their successors is more simple, more hardy, more Christian than the last.[15]

Frivolity and the pursuit of pleasure were considered destructive of character; pain and discomfort, on the other hand, were felt to be preeminently useful in character-building. Consequently, India came to be valued not for its pleasures, or promise, but precisely because it was possible to be desperately unhappy there. If one went to India it was likely to be described in terms of a sacrifice of comfort, rather than in terms of the prospects for Indian improvement. As Lady S. remarked to Wilfred Blunt, Indian officials "all hated India so much that they ought to be handsomely treated for being obliged to live there."[16] Unhappiness was considered, not something to be overcome, like Bunyan's Slough of Despond, but a necessary condition of moral life. Discomfort and unhappiness were courted in the hope that in so doing one might discover one's duty. If one were unhappy,

[15] G. O. Trevelyan, *The Competition Wallah*, London, 1866, p. 202.

[16] Wilfred Scawen Blunt, *India Under Ripon, A Private Diary*, London: T. Fisher Unwin, 1909, p. 218.

suffering from self-imposed burdens and hardships, it seemed less likely that one might be acting immorally.

This view of life, and the relevance India had to it, are portrayed in Charlotte Brontë's novel, *Jane Eyre* (published in 1847), in the character of St. John Rivers. Rivers, from the time Jane Eyre first meets him, displays signs of the noble yet troubled soul which leads him eventually to become a missionary in India. Returning from performing a difficult errand of mercy, St. John appeared "Starved and tired . . . but he had performed an act of duty; made an exertion; felt his own strength to do and deny, and was on better terms with himself."[17] St. John felt resentful of the beauties of nature and the softness of domestic life because they seemed diversions from the more toilsome way. "He crushed the snowy heads of the closed flowers with his foot";[18] to him the surrounding hills were no more than a stifling prison.

"This parlour is not his sphere," I reflected: "the Himalayan ridge, or Caffre bush, even the plague-cursed Guinea Coast swamp, would suit him better. Well may he eschew the calm of domestic life; it is not his element: there his faculties stagnate—they cannot develop or appear to advantage. It is in scenes of strife and danger—where courage is proved, and energy exercised, and fortitude tasked—that he would have the advantage of him on this hearth."[19]

It is in this connection that India appeals to St. John Rivers. He desires a place to lay "his genius out to wither, and his strength to waste, under a tropical sun."[20] For, says Rivers, "I hold that the more arid and unreclaimed the soil where the Christian labourer's task of tillage is appointed him—the scan-

[17] Charlotte Brontë, *Jane Eyre*, New York: Modern Library edn., 1933, p. 422.

[18] *Ibid.*, p. 388.

[19] *Ibid.*, p. 421. Responsiveness to nature had become for many in itself a form of religion. It was necessary for Rivers to deny this form of communion to himself in order to pursue what he considered a higher morality.

[20] *Ibid.*, p. 398.

tier the meed his toil brings—the higher the honour."[21] Rivers does indeed go to India, and while Jane Eyre's narrative does not follow him there, at the end of the book a summary impression of his work there is given:

As to St. John Rivers, he left England: he went to India. . . . A more resolute, indefatigable pioneer never wrought amidst rocks and dangers. Firm, faithful, and devoted; full of energy, and zeal, and truth, he labours for his race: he clears their painful way to improvement: he hews down like a giant the prejudices of creed and caste that encumber it. He may be stern; he may be exacting, he may be ambitious yet; but his is the sternness of the warrior Greatheart, who guards his pilgrim convoy from the onslaught of Apollyon. His is the exaction of the apostle, who speaks but for Christ, when he says—"Whosoever will come after me let him deny himself, and take up his cross and follow me." His is the ambition of the high master-spirit, which aims to fill a place in the first rank of those who are redeemed from the earth—who stand without fault before the throne of God: who share the last mighty victories of the Lamb; who are called, and chosen, and faithful.

St. John is unmarried: he will never marry now.[22]

While Miss Brontë does not indicate in what manner the Indians at whom he hewed responded to Rivers, it is possible to draw some impression from his effect on the more emotional spirit of Jane Eyre herself. Jane Eyre refused his offer of marriage despite her own interest in the Indian mission field and her great admiration for Rivers, for fear that as his wife she

[21] *Ibid.*, p. 378.

[22] *Ibid.*, p. 493. Cf. the description by Major James Abbott of Honoria Lawrence finding "delight in the solitary tent on the sun-parched plain" and wandering "through the cheerless jungles and scarcely less dreary tracts of cultivated land . . . she might, perhaps have been tempted to bless the very wretchedness of those very circumstances which so enlarged her power to administer to [Henry Lawrence's] happiness." Edwardes and Merivale, *Henry Lawrence*, p. 452.

would be "forced to keep the fire of my nature continually low" and witness her individuality "trampled down" by his "measured warrior-march."[23] "He is a good and a great man; but he forgets, pitilessly, the feelings and claims of little people, in pursuing his own large views. It is better, therefore, for the insignificant to keep out of his way; lest, in his progress, he should trample them down."[24] Jane Eyre rejected this tyranny for herself, but warmly rejoiced to see it exercised in India where she felt its sternness would be beneficial.

A less highly colored impression of the impact of the new, troubled religious mood on the relations between Englishmen and Indians is contained in another novel of the same period, by the brother of Matthew Arnold: William Delafield Arnold's *Oakfield, or Fellowship in the East.* The Arnold family is closely associated with the Victorian crisis of faith. Thomas Arnold, the father of Matthew and William Delafield Arnold, was a prominent Broad Churchman, renowned as the Headmaster of Rugby. Matthew Arnold poignantly lamented the faith he had lost in a series of poems, the best known of which are probably his "Stanzas on the Grand Chartreuse," and "Dover Beach." Possibly even more famous in her own time was Mrs. Humphry Ward, daughter of Thomas Arnold's third son and hence the niece of Matthew and William Delafield Arnold. Mrs. Ward, in her novel, *Robert Elsmere,* which is estimated to have sold approximately a million copies,[25] made the questioning of faith a popular sensation. The hero of her book is a young clergyman who abandons his orders after a crisis of faith, and who ultimately finds solace in constructive work under the guidance of the surrogate faith provided by T. H. Green's philosophy.[26] William Delafield Arnold's story completes the chronicle, carrying the family's sensitivity about conventional faith to India. William Arnold was that unique Victorian prod-

---

[23] *Jane Eyre,* p. 437.   [24] *Ibid.,* p. 446.

[25] Richter, *Politics of Conscience,* p. 379n44. The figure includes translations.

[26] Cf. *ibid., passim.*

uct: a man raised with such a fearsome need for internal honesty that he cannot disguise to himself the loss of faith; and with such a terrible need for faith that he cannot reconcile himself to its loss. With this loss of faith, he did not lose his stern sense of self-imposed duty; he had only lost his joy in the doing of his duty and his ability to communicate his joy to others.

Oakfield, the hero of the novel *Oakfield*—patently Arnold himself—because of difficulties with the thirty-nine articles which forestall him from entering the services of the Church, and because of a streak in his character reminiscent of St. John Rivers which compels him to leave his comfortable home in the Lake Country for the very reason that he finds it unbearably pleasant, abandons a promising university career after completing his A.B. at Christ Church, and secures an appointment as an officer in the East India Company's Indian (non-European) Army. Being, however, of pious inclinations, Oakfield finds Indian regimental life unbearably unpleasant. Since levity is commonly employed in references to young ladies in the officers' mess, Oakfield withdraws to eat alone in his own quarters.

Under any other circumstances such a person as Oakfield might never have been formally enrolled as an army officer. If the Indian Army had been closer than 10,000 miles Oakfield could have ascertained in advance what sort of service he was entering. As it was, he could entertain any illusions he chose concerning the nobility and self-denial of men engaged in such a great work as the civilization of India. Or if commissions had not been the spoils of patronage, and Oakfield had been subjected to any form of military selection or training before his posting to India, it is hard to imagine his ever actually entering such a career. As it was, Oakfield arrived in India innocent and commissioned, a testament that a system of patronage can produce misfits of every description.[27]

[27] Many such "misfits" were arriving in India as the new, more serious generation tried to accommodate themselves to the old-style army. At Dum Dum, when Henry Lawrence arrived there as a young officer, there was "a small band of sincere men voluntarily foregoing many amusements

By refusing to put up with bullying and bad talk, Oakfield
finds himself in a number of fracases. By refusing to duel with
an insolent brute who abuses him, he incurs the displeasure of
his commanding officer and has to stand a court martial to refute the charge of cowardice; even the fine and honorable men
in the Company's service find his code of ethics puzzling. Oakfield repudiates the feudal concepts of honor, he scorns "the
world's report." Ultimately, in the finest Rugby style, he vindi-
cates himself by extraordinary heroism in battle against the
Sikhs and is rewarded with a civil appointment as Assistant
Commissioner at Lahore. In a year or so, however, his health
destroyed by the Indian climate, Oakfield returns to his beloved
Lake Country to die. (W. D. Arnold, following his years in the
army, was appointed Director of Public Instruction in the Punjab, but was forced to return home on sick leave, dying at the
early age of 31 on the journey home, having failed to reach the
Lake Country.)

The bulk of *Oakfield*, into which this leaven of incident is
introduced, consists of elaborate accounts of Oakfield's relations
with a handful of close and sympathetic friends in India. Several of these he converts to his own painful view of life. Several
others he admires because of their devoted, public-spirited dedication to their official duties. Long letters exchanged between
Oakfield and his friends are reproduced; long conversations are
recorded pursuing philosophical questions about the meaning of
life, death, and service. The answers hit upon are deeply intro-

---

and indulgences from conscientious motives, and in spite of the ridicule
of those around them" centering around a residence with the name of
Fairy Hall; Henry Lawrence soon joined this band. Till the end of his
life, Lawrence's religious convictions were unsettled; he confided to a
friend later in life that he "hardly knew what he believed, what he dis-
believed." He in consequence adhered to the cult of conduct, "locking up
the sacred fire in his heart, but exhibiting its effects in self-conquest, increased affection for his fellow-creatures, and more earnest application to
his professional duties and studies." Edwardes and Merivale, *Henry Lawrence*, pp. 451, 523.

spective. Oakfield and his friends are honest and pious. They are also egocentric. They prefer to nurse tender consciences rather than attack the world as joyous evangelists. They live in the world of their own private meditations.

"Well, but what do you mean by examining? Examine what?"

"Examine what there is in any line of life which seems to open itself, that may assist or retard the great object of life."

"Which is—"

"One's own spiritual life."[28]

None of the members of the small circle of Oakfield's fellowship in the East likes India. All of them plan to escape it when they are financially able. India they consider only a painfully educational experience in hardship and deprivation. Oakfield alone might have stayed in India indefinitely if his health had not driven him back to England and an early death. Not because he liked India, however; only because he insisted on punishing himself, only because he was intent on reminding himself that all life was essentially grim and trying.[29] While still in England Oakfield muses, "Sometimes I fancy that I am more driven by a superstitious, unfaithful dread of the happiness of my present life than by any distinct call to go abroad."[30] And far from encouraging others to enter Indian service, Oakfield makes a great effort to persuade his brother not to come to India. Oakfield's brother Herby's announced intention to enter Indian service sets in motion one of the major crises of the book. Herby is only dissuaded when Wykham, himself an Indian officer, makes a special trip to Herby's public school to impress on him that now that he, Wykham, has come into £1,000 a year he in-

[28] Arnold, *Oakfield*, p. 304.

[29] Cf. Henry Lawrence's comment: "The only thing R—d and I could agree upon tonight, that the perfect emptiness of the pleasures of this life was the best proof of a hereafter." Edwardes and Merivale, *Henry Lawrence*, p. 77.

[30] W. D. Arnold, *Oakfield*, p. 15.

tends never to return to the hostile arid land of India. The announcement that Herby has been "saved" from India's clutches
is greeted with sincere rejoicing by all, and Oakfield expresses
his gratitude to Wykham in a letter which reads,

> Let me thank you, my dear Fred, most heartily, for your
> very kind and wise treatment of poor Herby. Indeed it would
> be a sad disappointment to me if he were to come out here;
> one of a family is enough for this place of torment: speaking
> seriously, you know how often we have agreed, that, for one
> man whose character is refined and strengthened by the fiery
> furnace of Indian temptation, there are ten who are carried
> away....[31]

It will be noticed that Oakfield here emphasizes what India
does *to* people, rather than what people can do *for* India. India
is not simply the setting of the novel; it is, in a literal and theological sense, Hell on Earth. It is the testing ground for the spiritual energies of Oakfield and his friends. It is not a challenge
to the optimistic reformer; it is a menace to the physical and
spiritual well-being of good men. The puzzling question the
novel suggests is not whether England will be able to remake
India; it is whether England will be able to survive India. India
is viewed as a pit sucking to their destruction hopeful Englishmen who approach it whether with desire for gain or for reform. Wykham told Oakfield's brother, "I tell you, Herby, you
would hate India; everybody does. The best men, such as your
own brother, who work hard and, as it is said, get on, hate it;
idle, good for nothing dogs, like myself, hate it. Perhaps the
worse like it best....[32]

---

[31] *Ibid.*, pp. 389-90.

[32] *Ibid.*, p. 370. Cf.: " 'I am out here to work, mind, to hold this wretched
country by force. . . . We're not pleasant in India, and we don't intend
to be pleasant. We've something more important to do.' . . . He spoke
sincerely. . . . He expected no gratitude. . . . It was his duty. . . .
How Ronny revelled in the drawbacks of his situation!" Forster, *Passage
to India*, pp. 50-51.

Viewing India as they did through the spectacles of introspection and duty, Oakfield and his friends found it difficult to focus on Indian problems very directly or clearly. Wykham urges, for instance, as one of the reasons why Oakfield's younger brother should not come to India, that there will be little opportunity for military distinction in India for a long time to come since now that the Sikhs are subdued there is no reason to suspect there will be any military activity within the foreseeable future. "The knowing ones say there is to be no more fighting for I don't know how many years. . . ."[33] (*Oakfield* was published in 1855.)

There is of course nothing unusual in this failure to anticipate the Mutiny of 1857, but it is typical. The only imaginable military challenge was one from beyond the borders of the realm. Oakfield and his friends indicate no genuine interest in Britain's own Indian subjects; they are a passive and irrelevant quantity. Oakfield is willing to point out that most people think their own servants better than the general run of Indians; he suggests that perhaps the Indian's propensity to lie is not so infinite as common report would have it, but he feels no affection for Indians. He demonstrates no comprehension that Indians are individuals at all.

> "It is grievous to live among men, and feel the idea of fraternity thwarted by facts; and yet the idea must not be abandoned as false or hopeless. We must not resign ourselves without a struggle to calling them brutes."
>
> "I think we may call them what they are."
>
> "Yes, but be sure of what they are first; you know yourself that there are many good points in the natives."[34]

India never takes on any kindlier features for Oakfield than those of the arid plain and huddled mass. Problems of Indian government are English problems; the object of British efforts appears as a passive quantity. Oakfield feels the tone of British

[33] W. D. Arnold, *Oakfield*, p. 332.   [34] *Ibid.*, p. 332.

Government is too commercial. He is eager for an improved
spirit of self-denial and sacrifice among officials.

Such is Oakfield's program of "Indian reform." He cannot
bring himself to hope for a transformation of India itself. He
shrinks from the idea of England's abandoning India, but only
because it would be an act of moral irresponsibility, not because
anything is to be gained or given by perpetuating the connection. India is Britain's painful cross—the hellish price she has
to pay for having such celestial regions as her own Lake Country. Oakfield's death is almost Christ-like; he has suffered more
than all because he has had to serve in India, and by his great
suffering he has blest his beloved family and allowed them to
stay in the Lake Country; he has saved them by giving his own
life.

Christianity had become for Oakfield what distinguished
Englishmen from Indians, not what would bring them together. Christianity itself had been transmuted from a faith into
a code of ethical self-discipline, which made it easier for Christians to reprove than to convert those who differed from them.
Indians had become characters in a Christian morality play, the
villains in a religious drama in which Englishmen played the
central role.

This preoccupation can be clearly seen in the campaign
against the continuing patronage by the British government of
traditional Indian religious festivals and institutions. One result
of this campaign was the termination in 1838 after many de-
lays of the Government's association through regulation and
taxation with the Temple of Juggernaut. But there were many
additional grievances. Sir Peregrine Maitland, for instance, resigned his position as Commander-in-Chief at Madras to protest the government's association with such rites as the Cocoanut
Festival at Surat. On this occasion, the Governor-General, Lord
Auckland, not very much distraught by the matter, composed
an elegant Minute which argued that

The salutes at Surat are a compliment paid to the return of

the season, when the coast, by the change of the monsoon, is again open to the merchant, and industry and profit are diffused among the commercial, seafaring classes. I would be extremely loath to discontinue any one proper demonstration. We must all, I feel assured, lament that occasions of the kind are so rare, on which it can be shown that the sympathies and feelings of the Government are in unison with those of the people. The day of these observances at Surat seems to be a popular holiday, on which joy is natural and reasonable; and if something of superstition be added to it, this will disappear as intelligence and civilization advance, whilst the holiday and its festivities will, as must be desired, survive. Something of paganism may be traced in our English feasts of May-day and harvest home; something Druidical in the rites of Halloween; more that is catholic in the village mummeries of Christmas; and with such observances, which ought to be upheld while they are gay, and innocent, and popular, will doubtless, much that is now distasteful in India be ranked, as instruction is spread, and classes are mingled, and differences are softened. To time, and the gradual growth of knowledge, I would trust much, and would deprecate in these matters all overstrained fastidiousness of feeling, and a sternness of action which must tend to create alarm, to alienate the people from the government.[35]

Auckland's Minute brought a stinging reply from Sir Peregrine Maitland:

That repugnance to attend such festivals is not the "overstrained fastidiousness of feeling" which the noble Lord supposes, even on the comparatively innocent occasion quoted by him, and that there is something more than a mere tinge of superstition and paganism in them, is plain from the following prayer which is recited at the festival to which he has al-

[35] Minute of April 1, 1837, in *Parliamentary Papers* (H.C.), Returns, 12 Feb. 1858, "East India (Sir Peregrine Maitland)," p. 6.

luded.[36] "Oh, Tapis, Goddess! daughter of the sun, wife of the
sea, pardon all our sins! As the waves follow each other, so
let happiness follow us; in our labour and trade bless us; send
us a flood of money, and preserve us in the possession of
wealth and children." Can it be wondered at that Christians
should revolt at being made parties, even in appearance, to a
solemn invocation of heathen deities; and can it be imagined
that a man who has one serious thought can consider such a
ceremony "as gay, and innocent, and popular" as harvest-
home or May-day feast; and with the example of Egypt, and
Greece, and Rome before him, does the noble Lord himself
really think the "something of superstition" which is to be
traced in them will disappear as intelligence and civilization
advance, while the Government direct, and countenance, and
honour, and assist the people in upholding them?[37]

Maitland felt the bad example offered by British patronage of
such festivals could only serve to reenforce superstition. But
what particularly upset him was not that millions of souls still
remained in the grip of idolatry but rather that Christians
should be expected, even in appearance, to condone it. The ambition of serious-minded men was simply that British government should be conducted in a "Christian manner," and the
hope of seeing India become a Christian nation had virtually
disappeared. Englishmen conceived that to govern India was
their duty and were only further convinced of this by how little they enjoyed doing it and how little they were appreciated
for doing it.

The cult of conduct taught people to find gratification in a
consciousness of the rightness of their own actions rather than
in mere popularity.[38] Though righteous conduct could be in-

[36] Footnote in original: "Translation of the prayer used on Cocoanut
Day at Surat."

[37] *Ibid.*, letter of 1 Feb. 1838.

[38] "His own self-approval was his only aim," Major Abbott said of
Henry Lawrence. Edwardes and Merivale, *Henry Lawrence*, p. 450.

structive it was not to be expected that all would be equally capable of appreciating and profiting from it. Oakfield, for instance, refused to accept the challenge of a bully to engage in a duel, knowing well that this act would be interpreted as cowardice. Sir Peregrine Maitland was not impressed by Aukland's argument that Cocoanut Day should be continued simply because it was "popular." The applause of the vulgar, whether English or Indian, it was known, was rarely the fruit of righteousness. If the virtuous did not actually relish being disliked, an explanation for such a state of affairs was ready to hand; one could not always expect applause from those it was one's painful duty to reprove. England's task was the thankless one of doing for people what she knew had to be done, knowing that the people who were the object of her endeavors would only greet them with resentment. The gulf between Englishmen and Indians seemed to make this inescapable. Oakfield found it "grievous to live among men, and feel the idea of fraternity thwarted by facts"; and yet, regrettable as it might be, the facts seemed plain. "The unprepared mind," observed Harriet Martineau, "whether Hindoo or Mussulman, developed under Asiatic conditions, cannot be in sympathy, more or less, intellectually or morally, with the Christianised European mind."[39] It was Kipling who gave this point of view its classic expression, in his well-known lines:

> Take up the White Man's Burden—
> Send forth the best ye breed—
> Go bind your sons in exile
> To serve your captives' need;
> To wait in heavy harness
> On fluttered folk and wild—
> Your new-caught, sullen peoples,
> Half devil and half child.
>
> . . . .

[39] Martineau, *British Rule in India*, London: Smith, Elder, 1857, p. 289.

> Take up the White Man's Burden
> And reap his old reward:
> The blame of those ye better,
> The hate of those ye guard—
> The cry of hosts ye humour
> (Ah, slowly!) toward the light:—
> "Why brought ye us from bondage,
> Our loved Egyptian night."

In demonstrating as well as building his character the high-principled Englishman strived to expand his capacity for strenuous exertion, in work and play. Activity became virtually an end in itself, for it was the Devil who made work for idle hands. Walking forty miles a day, writing forty volumes of virtuous verse, it scarcely mattered what one did so long as it kept one from wasting time in mere reflection or idle refinements. "To recommend contemplation in preference to action," observed Leslie Stephen, "is like preferring sleeping to waking."[40]

For an Englishman eager to live according to such an ethic, India was ideally suited, for India had always been a place of work. Even when Englishmen went to India simply to make a fortune as quickly as possible they had gone with the idea of working hard, if only so that they might return to England in a short time with means to live at leisure. The cult of conduct contributed the added attraction of self-approbation to the traditional concern with monetary gain, which had for so long enticed Englishmen to India, and produced the Englishman of the middle years of the century who worked as hard on salary as his predecessors had in pursuit of fortune. This extraordinary busy-ness of British Indian life had long impressed observers. Victor Jacquemont commented on it in 1829:

> On n'y vient pas pour vivre, pour jouir de la vie; on y vient, et cela est vrai dans toutes les positions sociales, pour gagner de quoi en jouir ailleurs. Il n'y a pas à Calcutta un seul *man of leisure.*[41]

[40] Annan, *Leslie Stephen*, p. 240.   [41] *Correspondance*, I, 78.

What had amazed the Frenchman Jacquemont delighted Fitzjames Stephen when he arrived to become Law Member of the Viceroy's Council in 1869. Stephen wrote,

> The immense amount of labour done here strikes me more than anything else. The people work like horses, year in and year out, without rest or intermission, and they get hardened and toughened into a sort of defiant, eager temper which is very impressive. . . . I am continually reminded of the old saying that it is a society in which there are no old people and no young people. It certainly is the most masculine middle-aged busy society that ever I saw, and, as you may imagine, I don't like to fall behind the rest in that particular.[42]

English diversions from work—they could scarcely be called relaxations—were equally strenuous, and equally masculine. There was nothing frivolous about such English pastimes as riding and pig-sticking. Active exercise of this sort was felt to have as important an effect on character as work itself. It produced "manliness," by which was implied the ability to lead others as well as to control oneself. Sir Charles Metcalfe, for instance, posed a problem for his Victorian biographer, Kaye, not only because of his Indian family but also because of his apathy toward athletics. Kaye wrote of the youthful Metcalfe, "I would rather think of a fine open-spirited boy, boating, swimming, playing, even getting into mischief at school, and in the holidays spending half his time on the back of a pony." Such, however, was unfortunately not the case. And yet, concluded Kaye gallantly, "If he had been captain of the boats, and beaten Harrow and Winchester off his own bat, he could not have grown into a manlier character."[43] Exceptions of course required acknowledgement, but about the normal route to manliness, Kaye left his reader in no doubt.

Such a preference for manly diversions involved an equal con-

[42] Leslie Stephen, *The Life of Sir James Fitzjames Stephen*, New York: Putnam's 1895, pp. 244-45.

[43] Thompson, *Metcalfe*, p. 11.

tempt for intellectual and aesthetic pursuits. John Beames describes the plight of one of his colleagues in the Civil Service who "imprudently brought a piano to the Panjab with him. Such refinement was unpardonable. . . . I'll smash his piano for him,' John Lawrence was reported to have said, when he first heard of such a degradation as a Panjab officer having a piano."[44] "Their ignorance of the Arts was notable," commented Forster of the Englishmen in *A Passage to India*, "and they lost no opportunity of proclaiming it to one another; it was the Public School attitude; flourishing more vigorously than it can yet hope to do in England."[45]

The growing emphasis on games at the public schools in the Victorian period mirrored the change in society at large, from concern with piety to concern with conduct. Rugby, as reformed by Thomas Arnold, had united an interest in sports with a strong intellectual training and a heavy religious emphasis. Later headmasters developed the emphasis on sports to the extent of virtually disregarding the other aspects of Arnold's concern, as ability at games was encouraged in the hope that it would be the prop to virtue which Christian faith had provided to earlier generations.[46] This cult of games is today generally associated with the Victorian public schools, where it was made an integral part of education, but the cult could trace its origin well back beyond the introduction of Thomas Arnold's reforms at Rugby and the consequent transformation of the majority of the public schools. Vigorous sports as such had been traditional in the English countryside, and characteristic of Englishmen in India from the earliest times. Sport, like other aspects of the cult of conduct, was not created *de novo* to form a support for character, but rather was simply adapted from an inconsequential part of life, a casual recreation, into an activity fraught with

[44] John Beames, *Memoirs of a Bengal Civilian*, London: Chatto and Windus, 1961, p. 103.
[45] *Passage to India*, p. 40.
[46] Cf. Mack, *Public Schools*, p. 351.

moral purpose when faith began to lose its persuasiveness as a molding force.

The adaptation of sport to moral ends was a measure of the change occurring in the class affiliations of earnest people. The traditionally stern, hardworking Non-conformists were now enjoying the rewards of several generations of application, and were more inclined to identify themselves with the Establishment. The aristocratic classes were simultaneously becoming more moral and orderly in their conduct. The result was the transformation of formerly trivial and exclusively aristocratic pastimes into serious pursuits of a much more broadly defined upper class.

The idea of the value of sport as a training in leadership may well have had its origin among the British in India, and in very practical considerations in no way connected with the loss of Christian faith. In India, where warfare "closely resembled fox-hunting," it was not at all unreasonable to conclude that pig-sticking and tiger-shooting, the Indian variants of the English fox hunt, were the best possible practical training for the conquest of continents. Edward Thompson described General Lake, hero of the Maratha campaigns, as "the best type of English traditional general, active and affable and bluff, the fox-hunter on parade. 'It mattered not at what time of the morning the army commenced its march, there was Lord Lake in full uniform, buttoned to the chin, powdered and peruqued.' He rose at two a.m. to dress, the result of good ways acquired in Lincolnshire, where the bucks, Lord Yarborough told Malcolm, were at immense pains to ride out properly attired, so as to leave 'a genteel corpse' if they broke their necks. War to Lake was merely fox-hunting on a grand scale and its tactics were exactly similar. You found your quarry, then you rode hard at him with all the pack you had. This was generalship, as he had always understood it."[47]

A taste for sporting exercise and the outdoor life was almost

[47] Thompson, *The Making of the Indian Princes*, London: Oxford University Press, 1943, p. 72.

as essential for the civilian administrator in times of peace as for
the military commander. The civilian was expected to cover his
district constantly on horseback, and frequently to live under
canvas for months at a time while settling land revenue or simply touring in the cold weather through remote areas within his
district. Under such circumstances sporting exercise, whether it
be a daily ride, or a protracted hunting expedition involving
scores of people and a train of provisions, might very naturally
be considered the best possible training for leadership and command. Similarly, the difficulty Englishmen found in adjusting
to the Indian climate made exercise seem from an early period
a necessary safeguard against physical no less than moral de-
generation. The dangers of lassitude and lethargy resulting
from the heat convinced Englishmen that the only defense was
an almost frantic defiance. The boisterous dancing parties and
fierce exertions of late eighteenth and early nineteenth century
English society in India may not have been the healthiest answer to the Indian climate, but it anticipated the response Victorian Englishmen subsequently made to the dangers of a de-
bilitating moral climate. Jacquemont found the English in the
Calcutta of 1829 "galloping endlessly, like automats."

> Puis, quand le soir amène quelque fraîcheur, on monte à
> cheval, et jeune et vieux galopent pendant une heure, comme
> des automates, sans but; ils rentrent en nage chez eux, et pour
> se préparer une nuit facile et légère, se mettent à table où ils
> restent deux heures, et d'où ils ne se retirent que pour aller au
> lit. Il y a un très-grand fonds de bêtise dans cette exhibition de
> *manliness* que les Anglais se croient obligés de faire.[48]

To the English in India such vigorous exertion was the secret
of health, and it was recommended for numerous ailments, including that of excessive thinking. "Ride on horseback," wrote
Charles Metcalfe's mother, herself a veteran of many years in

[48] *Correspondance*, I, 84-85.

India, to her unathletic son. "When intense thinking is joined
with the want of exercise, the consequences must be bad."[49]

The Victorian public schools accepted the presumption that
games were incomparably the best training in leadership, as well
as the presumption that their responsibility as schools was to
direct boyish aspirations to public service as the highest calling
in life. Anthony Powell reminisced of his school days at Eton:
"Teaching was efficient and it was assumed, or so it seemed to
me, that every boy would at one time or another be in some
such position as viceroy of India, and must be brought up with
this end in view."[50] The boys at the second-rate public school in
Kipling's novel, *Stalky & Co.*, had a song which ran,

> It's a way we have in the Army,
> It's a way we have in the Navy,
> It's a way we have at the Public Schools,
> Which nobody can deny![51]

Many men went directly from school into the services; those
who proceeded on to University might find there much the
same spirit as was maintained at school. Jowett's Bailliol in particular was instilled with the spirit of public service. By the close
of the century it could count among its graduates one-sixth of
the Indian Civil Service and three successive viceroys.[52]

When the product of such a brand of education entered the
ranks of British Indian officialdom, he was likely to discover
that his training had been an excellent preparation for what he
had to cope with. One of Dr. Arnold's prize students at Rugby,
for instance, whom Arnold asked "to put down disorder in a

[49] Thompson, *Metcalfe*, p. 34. John Beames ascribed the death of one
of his colleagues in the Civil Service to similar causes: "The result of this
excessive overwork on the health of a stout, full-blooded man who required
a great deal of exercise to keep him well, was fatal." Beames, *Memoirs*,
p. 218.

[50] Anthony Powell, "The Wat'ry Glade," in Graham Greene, ed., *The
Old School*, London, 1934, p. 152.

[51] Kipling, *Stalky & Co.*, New York, 1909, p. 226.

[52] Richter, *Politics of Conscience*, p. 52.

boarding-house"[53] became the renowned Hodson of "Hodson's Horse" who won fame by helping to "put down" the Mutiny of 1857. Fitzjames Stephen drew an extended analogy between the Indian Civil Service and a public school, which was summarized as follows by his brother, Leslie Stephen:

> The little body of Englishmen who have to rule a country comparable in size and population to the whole of Europe, without Russia, seem to him to combine the attributes of a parish vestry and an imperial government. The whole civil service of India, he observes, has fewer members than there are boys at one or two of our public schools. Imagine the Eton and Harrow boys grown up to middle age; suppose them to be scattered over France, Spain, Italy, Germany, and England; governing the whole population, and yet knowing all about each other with the old schoolboy intimacy. They will combine an interest in the largest problems of government with an interest in disputes as petty as those about the rules of Eton and Harrow football.[54]

The analogy was anything but coincidental. In many ways Indian official society was just that: public school boys grown to middle age still retaining the basic attitudes they had acquired at school. India appealed to the person who had responded to the atmosphere of a public school; and the public schools consciously attempted to imbue their students with an aspiration to service of the Empire. And if not all Indian officials were products of the very best schools, or even of any public school, all at any rate honored the public school ideal.

An important aspect of this ideal was contempt for early marriage. Celibacy permitted a man to perpetuate the society of his all-male public school and to engage with his schoolmates in the rewarding, manly pursuits of warfare and administration in remote and hostile regions, to which his education had urged him to aspire. The dangers of premature matrimony were among

[53] Mack, *Public Schools*, p. 273.
[54] Leslie Stephen, *James Fitzjames Stephen*, p. 242.

the lessons learned by the boys in the public school in Kipling's, *Stalky & Co.*

> "Doesn't our Beetle hold with matrimony?"
>
> "No, Padre; don't make fun of me. I've met chaps in the holidays who've got married housemasters. It's perfectly awful! They have babies and teething and measles and all that sort of thing right bung *in* the school; and the masters' wives give tea-parties—tea-parties, Padre!—and ask the chaps to breakfast."[55]

Unlike the Hindu who held that a man should marry early and then in later life adopt celibacy and austerity, the Victorian man was prepared to contemplate marriage only when fully established in society, and even then only on terms which left him relatively free to continue to pursue his own life undisturbed. In India it was common for a man to be separated from his wife and children for months or years at a time, as they sought more salubrious regions or returned to England for education while he remained at his post. Women were honored in their absence as superior beings, as the Vestal Virgins of the religion of conduct. Colonel Sleeman observed that "in our 'struggles through life' in India we have all, more or less, an eye to the approbation of those circles which our kind sisters represent—who may, therefore, be considered in the exalted light of a valuable species of *unpaid magistracy* to the government of India."[56] Women were elevated to a pedestal—where they were expected to stay. The ideal wife reverenced her husband and did not presume to meddle in his affairs; she did not follow him to his places of work and relaxation which continued to be safely masculine. The purity of women was championed by men horrified at the thought of their having anything to do with real life, with *their* life. Belief in feminine purity was the opposite of belief in feminine equality. Purity connoted weakness, a spirituality which

[55] *Stalky & Co.*, p. 161.
[56] Lt. Col. W. H. Sleeman, *Rambles and Recollections of an Indian Official*, London, 1844, p. iv.

was too fragile to face the grim realities of life head on. English women, in this respect like Bengali men, were not considered suited to public affairs because public affairs were the proper domain of masculine men. If one assumed that violent exercise was the best training for political leadership, it was simple enough to conclude that politics was a realm suited only for men physically, and hence morally, strong.

It is instructive to contrast this mid-Victorian attitude with that expressed at the beginning of the century by James Mill in his *History of British India*. Mill's assumption had been that the domination of public life by men possessing merely physical force was characteristic of the rude, early stages of man's development. In Mill's view,

> As society refines upon its enjoyments, and advances into that state of civilization, in which various corporeal qualities become equal or superior in value to corporal strength, and in which the qualities of the mind are ranked above the qualities of the body, the condition of the weaker sex is gradually improved, till they associate on equal terms with the men, and occupy the place of voluntary and useful coadjutors.[57]

On this issue Mill's son, John Stuart Mill, sided with his father, though in advocating female emancipation he was going decidedly against the Victorian grain. That enthusiastic champion of masculinity, Fitzjames Stephen, writing from Calcutta, announced that regardless of "what Mill and other old maids in breeches may choose to say, *you* know my will that obedience is the very essence of married life, and that it is not a servile but an honourable and blessed thing."[58]

The product of a Victorian public school was likely to be well disposed toward the masculine society of British India. He would also be likely to place a high premium on the value of strong leadership. The playing fields of Eton led to the frontier, not to the conference table. A man confident of his capacity for

[57] Mill, *History of British India*, 1840 edn., 1, 447.
[58] "Letter to Minnie," dated Calcutta, 19 December 1869, *Stephen Papers*.

leadership, trained to believe that this was a man's highest calling, was likely to be interested in demonstrating his ability to
lead and uninterested in being supplanted by clever but unathletic native subordinates. The British were taught to find satisfaction in the "feeling that one is working and ruling and making oneself useful in God's world,"[59] and much that still sur-
vives in India serves as a tribute to the practical results of such
an attitude. Aggressive leadership is not always, however, the
most efficient method of getting things done. The very effectiveness of "masterful activity" in a setting in which one's subordinates are receptive and cooperative may blind one to its potential
for disaster in a setting in which they are hostile and recalci-
trant. Nor is a training in leadership an adequate substitute for
specialized knowledge in the making of decisions in areas
which require technical competence. The concept of "leadership" for which Englishmen were trained proved ultimately to
be both limited and constricting, for it actually incapacitated
them for dealing with unanticipated challenges, challenges
which were inconceivable according to all they had been taught
to believe. Even warfare fell prey to the trained specialist. "We
are beginning to see the price exacted, though late," wrote Edward Thompson in 1943 "by the tale of easy victories and by the
kind of cantonment and station life which they encouraged,
during decades when European countries were building up se-
verely professional armies."[60] The Victorian confidence in the
gentleman amateur who was "not very bright, but good at
games" affected nearly all aspects of English professional life,
and seriously hampered England's adjustment to the requirements of the modern world for trained intellect.[61] The playing
fields of Eton were not an adequate preparation for all the challenges English leadership was to encounter in the twentieth century; neither Gandhi nor the German General Staff were much

[59] Beames, *Memoirs*, p. 223.   [60] Thompson, *Princes*, p. 63.
[61] For a full discussion of this point, cf. Rupert Wilkinson, *Gentlemanly
Power, British Leadership and the Public School Tradition*, London: Oxford University Press, 1964.

impressed by a man who was "not very bright, but good at games."

Nor was the effectiveness of sport as great as was assumed in producing even that sort of character the Victorians strove consciously to cultivate. Games were assumed to have a direct effect on morals. "Ugly lusts for power and revenge melted away and even the lust for women assumed—so it was said—reasonable proportions after a day in pursuit of pig."[62] Frustrations no doubt might be relieved at a pig's expense; lusts for power and revenge, however, were more probably mollified, if at all, by the companionship and teamwork associated with sport, the experience of working together in good-humored fellowship, rather than by the pursuit of pig per se. Exercise taken in isolation would appear to have no probable temporizing influence on such feelings. So far as the subduing of sexual passion was concerned, pig-sticking had not had this effect earlier in the century, and the assumption that it did was clearly the result of the common Victorian habit of associating what was difficult to do with what was desirable to attain.

While events of the twentieth century have served to demonstrate the limitations of the Victorian cult of conduct, its practical effectiveness in many spheres in the nineteenth century was notable; nowhere did it seem better vindicated than in India. India was a haven for the masculine man, where the virtues inculcated in the public schools seemed indispensable. India was a place of work, where one did not expect to enjoy oneself, or earn affection for one's labors from any but those who admired the flexing of a strong arm. The British Indian official, held in reverence by a devoted and often absent wife, and surrounded by Indians dependent on his capacity for work and leadership, could truly feel that his dedication to the cult of conduct had served him well.

[62] Woodruff, *Men Who Ruled India,* ii, 180.

CHAPTER III

Concepts of Indian Character

Of the people, so far as their natural character is concerned, I have been led to form, on the whole, a very favourable opinion. They have, unhappily, many of the vices arising from slavery, from an unsettled state of society, and immoral and erroneous systems of religion. But they are men of high and gallant courage, courteous, intelligent, and most eager after knowledge and improvement with a remarkable aptitude for the abstract sciences, geometry, astronomy, &c., and for the imitative arts, painting and sculpture. They are sober, industrious, dutiful to their parents, and affectionate to their children, of tempers almost uniformly gentle and patient, and more easily affected by kindness and attention to their wants and feelings than almost any men whom I have met with.

—BISHOP HEBER, 1825[1]

The natives, as far as I have seen, have nothing attractive in their character; indeed, as Gil Blas said, when he was with the actors, "I am tired of living among the seven deadly sins."

—HONORIA LAWRENCE, 1837[2]

THE Victorian Englishman in India, by his situation as well as temperament, was singularly ill-suited to gain a favorable impression of Indian character. "No one can estimate very highly the moral and intellectual qualities of people among whom he resides for the single purpose of turning them to pecuniary account," G. O. Trevelyan remarked, referring to the business community, but the statement could be applied with almost

[1] Heber, *Narrative*, III, 333.
[2] Letter to Mrs. Cameron, dated 28 December 1837, in Edwardes and Merivale, *Henry Lawrence*, p. 104.

equal force to the official classes.[3] The official classes were similarly motivated in coming to India by considerations of status and monetary reward, available only at India's expense. An Englishman, moreover, whatever his purpose or position in India, found himself automatically endowed with privileges which made unstrained relations with Indians virtually impossible. His contact was primarily with menials and subordinates, and many a young official formed his first impressions of Indians while presiding over a criminal court. As Miss Martineau observed, "We are apt to take our notions of the natives from the inferior specimens which press upon our observation, either from their numbers or their servility."[4] In addition, the Victorian temperament posed nothing but difficulties. Closely regulating his own thought and actions by a rigid code of conduct, the Englishman, far from finding refreshment in the diversity of human conduct, attached exclusive virtue to his own pattern of behavior, and found in Indian behavior a comprehensive rejection of every standard he had learned to value. The polarization of the Victorian and the traditional Indian character, as it appeared to Englishmen, was so extreme, that it is not surprising that Honoria Lawrence had the sensation she was living among the seven deadly sins.

The Victorian age was preeminently one of self-conscious progress in which man was thought capable of turning nature to his own purposes; India seemed fatalistic, hopelessly wedded to constricting custom and indifferent to human life and the material world. The Victorians emphasized the ideal of dominant masculinity, admiring a man who was physically strong, fond of vigorous sports, and capable of vast amounts of work. In contrast: "The physical organization of the Bengalee is feeble even to effeminacy. He lives in a constant vapor bath. His pursuits are sedentary, his limbs delicate, his movements languid."[5] The Victorian was taught to value simplicity, honesty, and plain

---

[3] *Competition Wallah*, p. 261.   [4] *Suggestions*, p. 99.
[5] Thomas B. Macaulay, "Warren Hastings," in *Essays and Poems*, Boston, n.d., II, 566-67.

dealing. In contrast, "What the horns are to the buffalo, what the paw is to the tiger, what the sting is to the bee, what beauty, according to the old Greek song, is to woman, deceit is to the Bengalee."⁶ "Besides, your native positively likes to fee Jacks-in-office. During the progress of a Governor through his province, all the rajahs and zemindars who come to pay their respects to the great man are never content unless they pay their rupees to his servants. They would not enjoy their interview thoroughly if they got it gratis."⁷ The Victorians were sober, undemonstrative, unaesthetic, convinced that art should be morally improving and censorious of that which was not; Indians were depicted as sensuous, extravagant, and delighted by immorality in art. To the Victorian family and country were sacred; "The Bengalee . . . would see his country overrun, his house laid in ashes, his children murdered or dishonoured, without having the spirit to strike one blow."⁸ The Victorian was frugal and unostentatious in externals, and though in India he lived on a scale which was lavish by English standards, he was still usually intent on saving a large portion of his income for remittance home. In contrast,

I will mention a very common trait in the Native character, which is, that although at the head of a large body of well-mounted and armed men [Nawab Golaum Kadir] is now living close to the cantonments, in a small and tattered tent (at which a half-batta sub-altern would turn his nose up); and his followers, I fancy, live under the canopy of heaven; but so it is: with Blacky, everything is for display, and many a dashing fellow carries his fortune in his horse and accoutrements, and should he have more than enough for that, he hires such a chap as himself to ride behind him, and perhaps

⁶ *Ibid.*, p. 567. These quotations are from Macaulay's description of Nuncomar.
⁷ G. O. Trevelyan, *Competition Wallah*, p. 233.
⁸ Macaulay, "Warren Hastings," p. 567.

does not spend half-a-dozen rupees a month on everything else.[9]

The Victorians, who placed Accumulation very close to Godliness,[10] considered the Indian fascination with gaudy apparel, lavish weddings, and entertainments highly unfortunate, if not sinful. And finally, on the score of sexual morality, the Victorians held rigidly to notions of chastity and self-restraint, and pictured their womenfolk as models of innocence and purity. Indian religion struck them as no less than a systematic encouragement of lust; the Indian conception of women, and the position of women in Indian society seemed the epitome of barbarity.

Such a catalog of disparate qualities, seemingly united only by their common defiance of values which the Victorians held dear, might seem difficult to ascribe to any single individual; on the contrary, it was only necessary to demonstrate that any given individual was indeed a "native" to have proved that he possessed them all. To take an example from a region and a religion different from those of Nuncomar, the Bengali Hindu of Macaulay's celebrated caricature, consider the description of a Kashmiri Muslim, "Sheik Imammoodeen, the Governor of Cashmere," which appeared in the *Calcutta Review* of July 1847:

> The Sheik is, perhaps, the best mannered and best dressed man in the Punjaub. . . . [H]is figure is exquisite. . . . His smile and bow are those of a perfect courtier. . . . Beneath this smooth surface of accomplishment and courtesy lies an ill-sorted and incongruous disposition: ambition, pride, cruelty, and intrigue, strangely mixed up with indolence, effeminacy, voluptuousness and timidity. . . . Deeply engaged in the intrigues and revolutions of Lahore, he was never to be found at

[9] Henry Lawrence, in a journal written for his sister, October 1830. Edwardes and Merivale, *Henry Lawrence*, p. 68.

[10] Miss Martineau, noting the prevalence of poverty in India, commented that the people "cannot live—much less accumulate." *Suggestions*, p. 82.

the crisis of any of them; and so completely are all his aspirations negatived by indecision, that he spent six months of his Cashmere government in wavering between three schemes for his own personal aggrandisement [before choosing] the most senseless of the three. . . .[11]

The emergence of the Victorian conception of Indian character, which ultimately became so conventionalized that it was assumed to apply to any given native, resulted from a blend of observation and preconception. As Harold Isaacs has noted, stereotypes are never entirely false.[12] Stereotypes would be easy enough to explode if they were patently untrue. Stereotypes, however, are formed, not out of the air, but by the selection and emphasis of observations of reality which seem to conform best with one's preconceived notions. The Victorian image of Indians was thus not entirely false in detail, but as a generalized picture it was highly colored by the artificiality of the relations Englishmen had with Indians, by the values which they brought with them to India, and by what they wanted to see in Indians.

To some extent, impressions were shaped by either willful or unintentional misunderstandings. Both Englishmen and Indians inevitably viewed one another in ways conditioned by their own culture, and consequently often dismissed as mere perversity actions which were entirely rational in the context of values which were not understood. By traditional Indian standards, Englishmen could seem extremely immoral. As the Abbé Dubois commented,

How, indeed, could a Brahmin, or any other Hindu have any real feelings of friendship or esteem for Europeans so long as the latter continue to eat the flesh of the sacred cow, which a Hindu considers a much more heinous offense than eating human flesh, so long as he sees them with Pariahs as

[11] Edwardes and Merivale, *Henry Lawrence*, p. 396.
[12] Cf. his discussion of American stereotypes of Asia, in *Images of Asia, American Views of China and India*, New York: Capricorn, 1962, pp. 379ff.

domestic servants, and so long as he knows that they have immoral relations with women of that despised caste?[13]

In contrast, most of the Indian customs which shocked Englishmen (including even such violent customs as widow-burning) possessed a certain reasonableness in the broader context of Indian social and religious values. The Indian custom of giving presents was part of a system of conventional politeness, though the only word the British could find in their own experience to describe such a system was corruption. And what was described as "deceit" and "dishonesty" could very often be mere courtesy; it was more polite, according to Indian notions, to agree to do something even if you did not intend to do it, in order to avoid giving offense. Among people who understood the convention, misunderstandings were not liable to arise. Many illustrations of Indian "double-dealing" seem often to have been simply the product of such a misunderstanding of Indian language or etiquette.[14]

Even when Englishmen and Indians were actually following comparable patterns of behavior misunderstandings arose because of the differing ways in which the same inclination was indulged in the two societies. What, for instance, constituted extravagance? Henry Lawrence considered Nawab Golaum Kadir extravagant because he supported a number of retainers, which he may well have done as much out of charity as for display. But the "extravagant Indian" was also portrayed as eating the simplest food and not caring where he slept. To the Englishmen, the comforts of a settled home and imported English cuisine did not seem luxuries, even though Nawab Golaum Kadir obviously considered them such. And what constituted sensuousness and indolence?

[13] J. A. Abbé Dubois, *Hindu Manners, Customs and Ceremonies*, trans. Beauchamp, London: University Press, 1959, p. 305.
[14] An intriguing study of this process of mutual misunderstanding based on diverging preconceptions has been written, which discusses the relations between French colonialists and the inhabitants of Madagascar. See Mannoni, *Prospero and Caliban*.

"By Jove, sir," exclaims the major, who has by this time got to the walnut stage of argument, to which he has arrived by gradations of sherry, port, ale, and Madeira—"By Jove!" he exclaims, thickly and fiercely, with every vein in his forehead swollen like whipcord, "those niggers are such a confounded sensual lazy set, cramming themselves with ghee and sweetmeats, and smoking their cursed chillumjees all day and night, that you might as well think to train pigs. Ho, you! *punkah chordo*, or I'll knock—Suppose we go up and have a cigar!"[15]

The truth of the matter was that Indians could match the British in moral disapproval of acts which violated their traditional notions of propriety, and the British were just as capable of indulgence as the Indians they excoriated. The normal human tendency to see the mote in the other person's eye and ignore the beam in one's own was here exaggerated by the fact that the mote and beam were of different substance. Englishmen saw more immorality in Indian actions than was there because they did not understand those actions, and failed to perceive the comparability of many of their own vices because they assumed a somewhat different form.

Added to these considerations was the tendency to ascribe to those whom one dislikes or is eager to disparage failings which are feared and disliked in oneself.[16] This undoubtedly contributed to the Victorian predilection for ascribing to Indians precisely those traits which Victorians were taught to consider most reprehensible in their own lives. If one were ashamed, for instance, of one's own sexuality, it was a psychological relief to contrast one's own still relatively superior state with the presumably unlimited sexuality of those one disliked.

The importance of predilections and preconceptions in form-

---

[15] Russell, *My Diary in India, in the Year 1858-1859*, London: Routledge, Warne and Routledge, I, 50-51.

[16] Philip Mason describes the tendency to project "all he dislikes in himself on to the people of another class or another race," in *Prospero's Magic*, pp. 57ff.

ing British impressions of Indian character can be seen by contrasting the Victorian attitude with that which had been common only a few years before. In the eighteenth century, Englishmen had come from a country less narrowly constrained; and, moreover, had come to India as "mere boys," where they were shaped as much by Indian as by English influences. Such men were less likely to recoil from an appreciation of India's diversity, if only because their remembrance of England was less strong. In particular, if they lived not exclusively at Calcutta, but in addition in areas remote from other Englishmen and English women—travelling in sovereign Indian states and associating with Indians not dependent on British will, they found much to inspire enthusiasm. Travelling among the Sikhs in 1808, Captain Matthew had found it "impossible to fancy myself in a foreign country,"[17] so hospitably was he received. David Ochterlony, who though born in Boston, Massachusetts, spent most of his life in northern India, and who according to legend had thirteen wives who took the air each evening riding on thirteen elephants, ended his life in India, "the only country in the world where he can feel himself at home."[18] The warm appreciation of the Indian character expressed by Bishop Heber was not uncharacteristic of the feelings of many people in the period before Victoria's reign. To the Victorians such appreciation seemed not only incomprehensible but immoral.

Much more important than the simple fact that the Victorians found the Indian character distasteful, were the causes to which were attributed Indian failings. The reformers of the early years of the century had also disparaged Indian character, but in doing so had ascribed its depravity to remediable causes. The most important alteration in the Victorian approach was thus not in its main impressions of what Indians were like but in its attempt to conceive those failings as inherent and incurable. Whereas the reformers had traced the origins of Indian depravity to religious and social causes, to the Victorians it seemed

---

[17] Thompson, *Princes*, p. 159.   [18] *Ibid.*, p. 184.

a result of the more intractable considerations of climate and race. As Henry Beveridge wrote in 1876,

> Carlyle says that the most important thing about a man is his religion. . . . It seems to me that it would be truer to say that the most important thing about an individual man is the character of his parents, and about a people, the race to which it belongs. Certainly, I do not think, in looking at the Bakarganj people, that the most important thing about the majority of them is whether they are Hindus or Mahome-dans. They were Bengalis before they were Hindus or Mahomedans.[19]

The Victorians treated with great concern the effect the Indian climate might have on their own constitutions. It was presented as an objection to the prospects of European settlement that children reared in India would not have the same stamina as those reared in a brisker climate and that "the European constitution cannot survive the third generation."[20] Thus preoccupied with the effect of climate on themselves and their children, the Victorians naturally held that it was even more crucial in molding Indian character, which had been subject to tropical influences much longer. Alleged Indian languor, sensitivity, fatalism, constitutional feebleness, preference for despotic institutions, and sexuality, were all depicted at various times as necessary results of India's "constant vapor bath."

Such speculation could claim a respectable antiquity, its history running all the way from Hippocrates to Montesquieu. Hippocrates apparently considered a tropical climate an important though only contributory cause of "indolence," striking a balance between climatic and political considerations.[21] Montes-

[19] Henry Beveridge, *The District of Bakarganj; Its History and Statistics*, (1876), pp. 211-12, quoted by Lord Beveridge in *India Called Them*, London, 1947, p. 6.

[20] *Parliamentary Papers*, (H. C.), "Select Committee on Colonization and Settlement (India)," 1857-1858, Vol. VII, Fourth Report, question #9767.

[21] Cf. Mill, *History of British India*, 1840 edn., I, 481n.

quieu held that climate did indeed determine character in many respects. "Cold air constringes the extremities of the external fibres of the body," he observed, while "warm air relaxes and lengthens the extremes of the fibres; of course it diminishes their force and elasticity. People are therefore more vigorous in cold climates."[22] Montesquieu felt that climate did have an effect on character, but avoided passing judgment on the relative merits of the character formed in different climates: "In cold climates they have very little sensibility for pleasure; in temperate countries, they have more; in warm countries their sensibility is exquisite...."[23]

Montesquieu's theory of climatic determination was furthermore in no sense destructive of the notion of basic human equality; Englishmen, he felt, would have been no different from Indians if they had grown up in India. Nor did Montesquieu consider it a justification for inaction. If climate determined human inclinations, this in Montesquieu's eyes was no reason why inclination should be considered invincible to correction by suitable regulation. Though the tropics might require legislation which would be superfluous in colder regions, there seemed no reason why, if such legislation were devised, the civilization of the tropics might not acquire the virtues of those existing farther north.

The English reformers of the early years of the nineteenth century were less responsive to the attractions of the character Montesquieu had believed to be induced by warmth and also highly skeptical that climate was its cause. The reformers either belittled climatic theories as of minor significance, or dismissed them as totally false. They were no more inclined to attribute Indian depravity to the heat than they were to ascribe their own virtues to "constringed cutis," "compressed papillae," and "paralysis of the miliary glands."[24] Charles Grant believed that "in

[22] Montesquieu, *The Spirit of the Laws*, trans. Nugent, New York: Hafner, 1962, p. 221.

[23] *Ibid.*, p. 223.   [24] *Ibid.*, p. 222.

developing the causes of the Hindoo character, too much seems sometimes to have been imputed to the climate."[25]

> If the character of the Hindoos proceeded only from a physical origin, there might be some foundation for thinking it unalterable; but nothing is more plain, than that it is formed chiefly by moral causes, adequate to the effect produced: if those causes therefore, can be removed, their effect will cease, and new principles and motives will produce new conduct and a different character.[26]

Grant felt that Indian physical weakness was in large measure attributable to diet. "The inhabitants of foreign descent, who continue the use of animal food, especially the Armenians, a sober people, are more robust than the Hindoos."[27] For the many other presumed effects of the climate—indolence, fatalism, sensuousness, sexuality, etc.—Grant found more than adequate explanation in the Hindu systems of law and religion. It seemed scarcely surprising to him that Indians were excessively preoccupied with sex when "Representations which abandoned licentiousness durst hardly imagine within the most secret recesses of impurity, are there held up in the face of the sun to all mankind, in durable materials, in places dedicated to religion."[28] Grant suggested that a similar encouragement of promiscuity in England through the placing of lewd sculptures prominently on public buildings might well have a similar effect on English morals.

The Abbé Dubois described graphically the nonclimatic influences molding Indian attitudes toward sex:

> The instincts which are excited at an early age by the nudity in which they remain till they are seven or eight years old, the licentious conversation and obscene verses that their parents delight in teaching them as soon as they begin to talk, the disgusting expressions which they learn and use to the de-

[25] Grant, "Observations," p. 42.　　[26] *Ibid.*, p. 87.
[27] *Ibid.*, p. 42.　　[28] *Ibid.*, pp. 69-70.

light of those who hear them, and who applaud such expressions as witticisms; these are the foundations on which the young children's education is laid, and such are the earliest impressions which they receive.

Of course it is unnecessary to say that, as they get older, incontinence and all its attendant vices increase at the same time. It really seems as if most of the religious and civil institutions of India were only invented for the purpose of awakening and exciting passions towards which they have already such a strong natural tendency. The shameless stories about their deities . . . the public and private buildings which are to be met with everywhere bearing on their walls some disgusting obscenity . . . all these things seem to be calculated to excite the lewd imagination of the inhabitants of this tropical country.[29]

James Mill, after consulting his sources, came to an even more emphatic rejection of climate as a formative influence. He, like Grant, considered the "lightness and feebleness" of the Indian physique a result of diet.[30] But while Grant stressed the fatalism of Indian religion as the primary cause of indolence, to Mill it seemed the result of the insecurity of property:

> The love of repose reigns in India. . . . "It is more happy to be seated than to walk; it is more happy to sleep than to be awake; but the happiest of all is death." Such is one of the favourite sayings, most frequently in the mouths of this listless tribe, and most descriptive of their habitual propensities. Phlegmatic indolence pervades the nation. Few pains, to the mind of the Hindu, are equal to that of bodily exertion; the pleasure must be intense which he prefers to that of its total cessation.

Here Mill rightly sensed a challenge to the Benthamite theory of pleasure and pain which was predicated on the assumption

[29] Dubois, *Hindu Manners*, p. 308.
[30] *History of British India*, 1840 edn., i, 478.

that all men shared with the industrious Englishman a preference for the pleasures obtainable only by hard work. Replying to the challenge, Mill continued,

> This listless apathy and corporeal weakness of the natives of Hindustan, have been ascribed to the climate under which they live. But other nations, subject to the influence of as warm a sun, are neither indolent nor weak; the Malays, for example, the Arabians, the Chinese. The savage is listless and indolent under every clime. In general, this disposition must arise from the absence of the motives to work; because the pain of moderate labor is so very gentle, that even feeble pleasures suffice to overcome it; and the pleasures which spring from the fruits of labor are so many and great, that the prospect of them, where allowed to operate, can seldom fail to produce the exertions which they require . . . there is but one cause, to which, among the Hindus, the absence of the motives for labour can be ascribed; their subjection to a wretched government, under which the fruits of labour were never secure.[31]

In Mill's eyes, Indian sexuality was also a reflection of the pattern normal in all "rude" societies. "In the barbarian," he wrote, "the passion of sex is a brutal impulse, which infuses no tenderness."[32] Mill similarly attributed Indian "effeminacy" not to delicacy and reluctance to take exercise, but to the primitive state of Indian society. He noted that

> Much attention has been attracted to the gentleness of the manners, in this people. They possess a feminine softness both in their persons and in their address. . . . Mildness of address is not always separated even from the rudest conditions of human life, as the Otaheitans, and some other of the South-Sea islanders, abundantly testify. "The savages of North America are affectionate in their carriage, and in their conversations pay a mutual attention and regard, says Charlevoix, more

[31] *Ibid.*, pp. 480-81.   [32] *Ibid.*, pp. 445-46.

tender and more engaging, than what we profess in the cere-
monial of polished societies."[33]

Mill and Grant went to such pains to discredit climatic in-
terpretations because they realized how effective a means they
were of discouraging the motive to reform. Montesquieu, it was
true, had felt regulation could curb propensities instilled by climate. But the reformers desired much more than merely the
introduction of regulations to check natural tendencies; they as-
pired to see the tendencies themselves transformed. What Montesquieu had felt was simply a result of a cold climate—love of
work, stern self-discipline, etc.—Grant and Mill believed were
norms of conduct based on universally valid principles and ac-
cessible to peoples in all climes. Grant considered industrious-
ness the product of a love of virtue; Mill conceived of it as resulting from the love of postponed pleasures. Neither considered this impulse, so similar though diversely described and
justified on divergent grounds, to be the monopoly of any single
race or climate.

The Victorian revival of climatic theories coincided with the
waning of reform enthusiasm. The Victorians were inclined to
agree with Montesquieu that the Indian temperament was the
product of special Indian conditions, just as their own temperament was the product of the "climate," both physical and
moral, of England. But they were also inclined to agree with the
reformers that the peculiar English temperament possessed pre-
eminent moral validity, a view Montesquieu would have considered ludicrously narrow. In the hands of the Victorians climatic theories thus became a justification for the English presence
in India because of England's presumably exclusive ability to
provide India with rulers of a vigorous frame, which was constantly refreshed by visits home and to the hills. Climate, which
for Montesquieu had been the ground for universal law acknowledging basic human equality, had become a justification for
imperialism.

[33] *Ibid.*, p. 465.

Climatic theories, furthermore, in the nineteenth century had begun to fade, with almost imperceptible shadings, into theories of racial distinctness. The scientific study of race emerged only after extremely haphazard and tentative gropings in the course of the century, and in the early stages of speculation about racial characteristics, climate played an important role. Before Darwin, racial distinctness was usually considered the result either of separate Divine creations or of the effect of climate working over a period of time.[34] In regard to India, climatic explanations were more commonly employed because of the absence of the obvious differences which distinguished Mongolians and Negroes from Europeans. In the case of Indians, it seemed more logical to imagine the effect of a tropical sun slowly darkening the color of the skin and eyes and hair, for other physical differences were minor. And yet, even though such a climatic explanation for racial distinctness was in a sense liberal, in its assumption that Indians and Englishmen had evolved from the same stock, it was nonetheless capable of illiberal elaboration. One might insist that over the ages climate had wrought a change in Indian racial character which made it totally distinct from that of the English. Montesquieu, adhering to a radical doctrine of human equality, had imagined that Englishmen would be just exactly like Indians if they grew up in India; one generation was enough. The Victorians, on the other hand, conceived that the effect of climate over untold generations had transformed Indians into an almost totally different race, and that a gap existed between the races which could not be produced—or eradicated—in any small number of generations. When contrasted to the differences existing between Englishmen and Indians the similarity of facial features seemed inconsequential to the editors of an encyclopedic anthology of Indian informa-

[34] For a discussion of pre-Darwinian study of race, cf. William Stanton, *The Leopard's Spots: Scientific Attitudes toward Race in America, 1815-1859*, Chicago: University of Chicago Press, 1960; and Philip D. Curtin, *The Image of Africa, British Ideas and Action, 1780-1850*, Madison, Wis.: University of Wisconsin Press, 1964.

tion presented to the British public in 1858—the year following
the Indian Mutiny and a year before the publication of *Origin
of the Species*. They wrote:

> In point of race the Hindoos have been regarded by nat-
> uralists as belonging to what they call the Caucasian, and even
> to the same family of that race as the white man of Europe!
> But this is a fantastical notion, for which there is hardly even
> so much as the shadow of a foundation. The only three points
> in which any analogy has been discovered between the
> Hindoo and the European are the oval form of the face, the
> shape of the head, and traces of a certain community of lan-
> guage. In every other respect the points of contrast are incom-
> parably more decisive than those of resemblance. The Euro-
> pean is white, the Hindoo black. . . . The European is taller
> than the Hindoo, more robust, and more persevering. Even
> in the rudest stages of civilization, the European has exhibited
> a firmness, perseverance and enterprise, which strikingly con-
> trast with the feeble, slow, and irresolute character of the
> Hindoo. In the performance of ordinary labor, in those em-
> ployments where there are means for drawing a just compari-
> son, the labor of *one* Englishman is equal to that of *three*
> ordinary Indians.[85]

[85] *India: Geographical, Statistical, and Historical*, Compiled from the
London *Times* Correspondence, McCullock and Others, London: George
Watts, 1858, pp. 81-82. In 1923 the United States Supreme Court declared
that an Indian's skin color was sufficient to designate him of a distinct
race in "common understanding."

The claimant in the case, a Punjabi Sikh who had entered the country
in 1913 and served with American forces in the First World War,
claimed to be "a descendant of the Aryans of India, belonging to the
Caucasian race (and, therefore) white within the meaning of our
naturalization laws." In a decision handed down on February 19, 1923
the United States Supreme Court disallowed this claim. Justice Suther-
land, who wrote the majority opinion, found that a Hindu was not,
after all, a "white person" in terms of the common understanding: "The
words of the statute are to be interpreted in accordance with the under-

"Racial" theories such as this were no more than the conventional impression of Indian character appended to such evident physical differences as that of skin color, which appeared to give them the quality of scientific objectivity. In 1792 Charles Grant had insisted that there existed in India "the universality of great depravity . . . a general moral hue, between which and the European moral complexion there is a difference analogous to the difference of the natural colour of the two races."[86] Grant made this comment in a work designed to show that Indian depravity was not due to inherent causes but to ones entirely subject to remedy. The furthest thing from his mind was the suggestion that Indians were morally blackened *because* they were dark in color, but it was precisely this view which gained currency in subsequent years. Climatic explanations of Indian depravity were amplified by racial notions which conceived that, whether the result of climate or not, Indians constituted a distinct and inferior race.

Thus, extreme sexuality, which Montesquieu had attributed to the climate, and to which, he presumed, anyone would be subject if he lived in the tropics, was now identified not simply with the heat but also with the "darker races." Englishmen were not prepared to concede that Indian residence increased their own sexual appetites, or those of their womenfolk, and thus found it necessary to attribute Indian inclinations to something more than the climate. Miss Martineau felt the majority of the "supposed constitutional vices of our Indian natives" were actually the result of training and circumstances. The only exception to this rule she specified was "lust" which she felt compelled to ad-

---

standing of the common man, from whose vocabulary they were taken." It was not a matter of racial superiority or inferiority, he went on, but of acknowledging a racial difference which, in the case of the Hindu, "is of such a character and extent that the great body of our people instinctively recognize it and reject the thought of assimilation." Isaacs, *Images of Asia*, p. 284.
[86] "Observations," p. 33.

mit "may probably be implicated with a basis of race, though mainly due to training."[37]

"Training" had seemed a more than adequate explanation to the reformers. The Evangelicals had argued that Indian religion was the cause of Indian depravity; to later generations, Indian religion seemed a reflection of Indian depravity, not its cause. The "dark" and "tropical" Indians were assumed to possess, in common with Negroes in Africa and America, sexual impulses unknown to Europeans. Such impressions, moreover, were not permitted to remain the disinterested observation of outsiders, for the Victorians chose to conceive Indian sexuality as a direct physical threat to themselves. It was a "well-known fact" to the British community in India that "darker races were physically attracted by the fairer, but not vice versa."[38] This would not have been so easy to confirm in the early portion of the nineteenth century, when sexual relations between Englishmen and Indian women were common. In fact, the bulk of testimony seemed to be on the opposite side. "The deep bronze tint is more naturally agreeable to the human eye than the fair skins of Europe," wrote Bishop Heber, "since we are not displeased with it even in the first instance, while it is well known that to them a fair complexion gives the idea of ill-health."[39] What was "well-known" in 1829 was just the reverse of what was "well-known" fifty years later, and it is clear that it was amongst the English rather than amongst Indians that this reversal had taken place Indians had not suddenly reversed their ideas about the attrac-

[37] Martineau, *Suggestions*, p. 96.

[38] "Here Mr. McBryde paused. He wanted to keep the proceedings as clean as possible, but Oriental Pathology, his favourite theme, lay around him, and he could not resist it. Taking off his spectacles, as was his habit before enunciating a general truth, he looked into them sadly, and remarked that the darker races are physically attracted by the fairer, but not *vice versa*—not a matter for bitterness this, not a matter for abuse, but just a fact which any scientific observer will confirm." Forster, *Passage to India*, pp. 218-19.

[39] Heber, *Narrative*, 1, 4. Philip Mason discusses the Victorian notion of tropical sexuality, in *Prospero's Magic*.

tions of English complexions, or suddenly developed sexual passions previously unnoticed. The change was the result of the influence of revulsion and fear, shame and insecurity, of the attempt to justify dislike and defensiveness by the perception of an imagined threat; in other words, of changes in British attitudes for which Indians could scarcely be held responsible.

A similar evolution in British thinking was taking place in regard to those Indian characteristics which had been considered by the reformers to be the result of India's long-standing political disorder; Indian servility, quarrelsomeness, obsequiousness and dishonesty—the absence, in short, of the open, honorable, and manly conduct which Victorians valued so highly. "A predisposition to cunning and childish subtlety exercised upon words" was "one of the greatest weaknesses of the natives."[40] Chaotic, indiscriminate, mendacious self-seeking was everywhere rampant, splitting even families apart:

> Discord, hatred, abuse, slanders, injuries, complaints and litigations, all the effects of selfishness unrestrained by principle, prevail to a surprising degree. Seldom is there a household without its internal divisions and lasting enmities, most commonly, too, on the score of interest. The women partake of this spirit of discord. Held in slavish subjection by the men, they rise in furious passions against each other, which vent themselves in such loud, virulent, and indecent railings as are hardly to be heard in any other part of the world.[41]

The reformers commonly ascribed such conduct to the unsettled conditions of Indian life and India's subjection throughout many years to erratic and rapacious despots. The Abbé Dubois, for instance, wrote,

> I think that we may take as their greatest vices the untrustworthiness, deceit and double-dealing which I have so often had occasion to mention, and which are common to all Hin-

---

[40] Fitzjames Stephen, *Memorandum on the Administration of Justice*, no title page or page number, copy in National Archives, New Delhi.

[41] Grant, "Observations," pp. 28-29.

dus. It is quite impossible to fathom their minds and discover what they really mean; more impossible, indeed, than with any other race. He would indeed be a fool who relied on their promises, protestations, or oaths, if it were to their interest to break them. All the same, I do not think that these vices are innate in them. It must be remembered that they have always been until quite recently under the yoke of masters who had recourse to all sorts of artifices to oppress and despoil them. The timid Hindu could think of no better expedient with which to defend himself than to meet ruse with ruse, dissimulation with dissimulation, and fraud with fraud. The prolonged use of weapons for which excuse may be found in their rulers, ended by becoming a habit which it is now impossible for them to get rid of.[42]

And yet it could be argued that Indians were deceitful, not because they had been so long oppressed, but rather because they were suited for no other condition. Macaulay, for instance, noted that "During many ages [the Bengali] had been trampled upon by men of bolder and more hardy breeds. Courage, independence, veracity, are qualities to which his constitution and his situation are equally unfavourable."[43] Macaulay felt Bengali "deceitfulness" was "constitutional" and that the fact the Bengali had been trampled on for so long was not simply an unfortunate accident but rather no more than he could expect. The Victorians, with their emphasis on physical strength and martial prowess, were not inclined to consider a propensity to be conquered only a minor flaw. If Indians were often conquered, it was because they were weak, not because they were unfortunate, and weakness to the Victorians was the hallmark of an inferior race.

The Victorians pictured the decadence and disarray of Indian society as a reflection of Indian racial character rather than the primary deterrent to its true expression. The decline of enthusi-

---

[42] Dubois, *Hindu Manners*, pp. 306-307.
[43] Macaulay, "Warren Hastings," in *Essays and Poems*, pp. 566-67.

asm for remaking Indian society and replacing Indian religion led to a more general acceptance of the notion that Indian society and religion were only what Indians deserved. If it were assumed that the condition of Indian society was not the result of a chain of unfortunate historical accidents but, instead, an expression of the peculiar genius of the Indian people, it followed that attempts at total social or religious reform were futile. Conceiving of Indian society in this fashion became a sufficient explanation for leaving it as it was. Indians were thought incapable of appreciating or adopting successfully superior British habits and institutions.

Undoubtedly the subtlest and most influential procedure for suggesting an inherent Indian racial inferiority was that which implied, with seeming generosity, that Indians were children requiring protection. The young Winston Churchill spoke fondly of Indians as "primitive but agreeable races."[44] To John Beames, his Sikh language instructor seemed "Like most Panjabis of those days . . . a kindly, simply-hearted old child."[45] Such was now the attitude which many Englishmen held toward the representatives of a civilization which had attained sophistication at a time "when the ancestors of English dukes still paddled about in wicker canoes, when wild in woods the noble marquis ran."[46]

It had been common from the time of James Mill to identify developed civilization exclusively with the European variety, and to designate Indian culture—its antiquity notwithstanding —as characteristic of an early stage of human development. Indians were lumped together with other non-European peoples, all of whom were pronounced primitive because of their lack of European culture. A further consideration was that within India Englishmen had begun to turn their attention to peoples who fitted more closely the stereotype of childlike primitivism, to the

[44] Winston Churchill, *My Early Life, A Roving Commission*, New York: Scribners, p. 104.
[45] Beames, *Memoirs*, pp. 100-101.
[46] G. O. Trevelyan, *Competition Wallah*, p. 217.

peasant cultivators and tribal groups whom the British could patronize and encourage as supporters against the emerging urban middle classes.

The likening of Indians to children might not have been politically oppressive if the stress of the analogy had been—as in Mill—on the prospects for Indian maturation. C. E. Trevelyan spoke confidently in 1838 of the time when Indians would "grow to man's estate."[47] By those no longer enthusiastic to witness Indians entering into "man's estate" such phrases might be retained but implicitly extended over an indefinite span of time. It was also possible to abandon the concept of the child's maturing altogether, and to consider the Indian's childlike state a permanent condition.

One way of arguing this contention was to state that Indians showed early promise which was later unfulfilled. J. C. Marshman, in testimony before a Parliamentary committee in 1853, stated that "A native boy at the age of 16 is much sharper and much more advanced than an English boy of the same age; but you will find that the native, after he has left school, very rarely improves himself."[48] G. O. Trevelyan noted James Mill's comment that Indians "display marvellous precocity in appreciating a metaphysical proposition which would hopelessly puzzle an English lad," adding: "This is high praise as coming from the father and preceptor of John Stuart; for it is hard to conceive a metaphysical proposition which could have hopelessly puzzled John Stuart at the most tender age."[49] Sir Ashley Eden argued that child labor legislation was unnecessary in India because "A child of eight in Europe is a helpless baby: in India he is almost a man of the world."[50]

These men were possibly correct in their observations. Stanley

[47] C. E. Trevelyan, *On the Education of the People of India*, London, 1838, p. 187.

[48] *Parliamentary Papers*, (H. C.), 1852-1853, Vol. xxix, question #8722, 21 July 1853.

[49] G. O. Trevelyan, *Competition Wallah*, p. 48.

[50] S. Gopal, *The Viceroyalty of Lord Ripon*, London, 1953, p. 58.

Elkins has examined the comparable contention made about slaves in the American South, and concluded that slaves did possess the qualities of early precocity and subsequent apathy which were attributed to them, but that this was a result, not of their racial character, but of the system of slavery itself, that the childishness of the adult slave was a product of the system in which he found himself, and not a justification for that system.[51]

The theorists of Indian childishness might be answered in the same fashion. In 1838 C. E. Trevelyan observed that

> Native children seem to have their faculties developed sooner, and to be quicker and more self-possessed than English children. . . . When we go beyond this point to the higher and more original powers of the mind, judgment, reflection, and invention, it is not so easy to pronounce an opinion. It has been said, that native youth fall behind at the age at which these faculties begin most to develope themselves in Englishmen. But this is the age when the young Englishman generally commences another and far more valuable education, consisting in the preparation for, and practise of some profession requiring severe application of mind; when he has the higher honors and emoluments opened to his view as the reward of his exertions, and when he begins to profit by his daily intercourse with a cultivated intellectual and moral society. Instead of this, the native youth falls back on the ignorant and depraved mass of his countrymen; and, till lately, so far from being stimulated to further efforts, he was obliged to ask himself for what end he had hitherto laboured. Every avenue to distinction was shut against him; and his acquirements served only to manifest the full extent of his degraded position . . . what may we not expect from these powers of mind, invigorated by the cultivation of true science, and directed towards worthy objects![52]

Trevelyan agreed that Indian ambition and intellectual vigor

[51] Elkins, *Slavery*, Chap. III.
[52] C. E. Trevelyan, *Education of People of India*, p. 111.

flagged with the end of adolescence, when the period of rote learning ended and the time for original thought and professional application was reached. But Trevelyan sought an explanation for this not in a theory of innate racial characteristics but in an examination of the social factors conditioning motivation. The degraded state of Indian society, far from challenging the individual to further exertions beyond schoolwork, increased its demands on the individual as he matured to conform to its constricting traditions. And what Indian society encouraged British government completed by refusing access to participation in the government of the country.

The Indian, possessed of precocious verbal facility, adept at memorization, was thought to falter when something more was required, when intellectual progress resulted only from prolonged self-discipline and original inquiry. Similarly, Indians were depicted as skillful in the execution of projects but deficient in the qualities of leadership. An argument of general application to the problem of self-government, it was most fully developed in relation to the army. British officers never tired of eulogizing the martial qualities of their native troops, or of emphasizing their utter helplessness without the direction of European officers. Lord Roberts, the Commander-in-Chief from 1885 to 1893, reported that an old Indian soldier once addressed these words to him: "*Sahib, ham log larai men bahut tex hain magar jang ka bandabast nahin jante.*" ("Sir, we can fight well, but we do not understand military arrangements.") To these words, Roberts added the following exegesis: "What the old soldier intended to convey to me was his sense of the inability of himself and his comrades to do without the leadership and general management of the British officers."[53] Sir Patrick Grant, writing on July 16, 1858, recorded his opinion that Indian sepoys "have no confidence whatever in the very best native officers, and deprived of their European officers (as I think it will be ad-

[53] Roberts, *Forty-one Years in India*, 1905 edn., I, 183, quoted by Nirad Chaudhuri in "The Martial Races of India," *Modern Review* (Calcutta), July 1930, p. 46.

mitted late events have abundantly made manifest) except behind walls or other protection native troops are a mere armed rabble."[54]

Men such as Roberts and Grant believed that Indians were incapable of assuming leadership, and illustrated their point by reference to the trusting simplicity of the ordinary soldiers in the ranks. But the British officer class was not ordinarily recruited from among ordinary British soldiers. Sir Charles Napier considered the better sort of Indian absolutely on a par with English officers. Arguing in 1853 for better treatment for Indian officers, he wrote, "The fair-faced beardless Ensign, just arrived from England . . . has the makings of a first-rate soldier, so have the Native Indian gentlemen at his age."[55] Napier answered the theorists of the innate childishness of the Indian soldier just as Trevelyan had answered those who talked of the failure of early Indian precocity, attributing the current state of affairs not to Indian inability but to the lack of opportunity.

The majority of Victorian Englishmen, however, assumed that all Indians possessed childlike qualities that were ineradicable, and were, moreover, too devoid of innocence, too dangerous to be considered only children. Kipling's phrase "half devil and half child" was a literal description of the common attitude. Indians were "at once childish and ferocious,"[56] possessed of a "mixture of treachery, childishness, and ferocity that could be bred only in the same jungle with the tiger who crouches, springs, gambols, and devours."[57] Indian childishness was a racial quality which did not promise an advance toward maturity, but rather was permanently linked to the menace and

[54] Letter of Grant's, in "Appendix to Minutes of Evidence taken before the Commissioners appointed to inquire into the Organization of the Indian Army," *Parliamentary Papers*, (H.C.), 1859, "Report of the Commissioners Appointed to inquire into the Organisation of the Indian Army."

[55] Sir Charles Napier, *Defects, Civil and Military, of the Indian Government*, London, 1853, p. 255.

[56] Edwardes and Merivale, *Henry Lawrence*, p. 337.

[57] *Ibid.*, p. 320.

power of grown men—men who could be tamed but never entirely trusted. Sexual aggressiveness, constitutional deceitfulness,
and the incapacity for maturity and leadership were combined
in the conception of Indians as grown children whom the British had the difficult task of chastening and commanding. It
seemed vain to hope that such children would ever develop further or be in a position to dispense with the services provided by
the parent nation.

CHAPTER IV

The Response to the Mutiny of 1857 and the Abolition of the East India Company

> Our learned men said the Company's Raj was to
> come to an end in 1857, being one hundred years
> since their first great battle; but they did not say
> another English rule would succeed it,—far more
> hard, much more harsh. The Companee Bahadoor
> and its officers were much kinder to the people of
> India than the Sirkar is now; and if it were not for
> the old servants of the Company, it would be far
> worse than it is.[1]

It has long been customary to assert that the Mutiny of 1857[2] resulted in a serious worsening of relations between Englishmen and Indians. It is not correct to say, however, that the Mutiny *caused* the change in attitude. The British response to the Mutiny gave a definite shape to Imperial attitudes in the following decades, providing in abundance justification and illustration of the presumed need for a new policy of governance. But the Mutiny only provided the proof; it had not in itself created the new attitudes which it was seen to justify. The particular manner in which Englishmen responded to the Mutiny

---

[1] Sitaram, *From Sepoy to Subadar: Being the Life and Adventures of a Native Officer of the Bengal Army Written and Related by Himself*, Calcutta, 1911, para. 311.

[2] The uprising of 1857 was termed a mutiny by the British because they wished to emphasize its treasonous nature and in addition to convey the impression that it was confined to the Indian troops of the British Army. It is clear, however, from recent scholarly researches that while it began as a military mutiny the uprising quickly assumed the character of a popular rebellion. In using the term "Mutiny" here to refer to this rebellion I do so only for convenience—because it was thus referred to by the people whose views I am discussing—and not because I share their impression of the nature of this revolt. On this subject cf. Metcalf, *Aftermath of Revolt*, Chap. ii; and S. N. Sen, *Eighteen Fifty-seven*, Calcutta, 1957.

was not necessary or inevitable, but a reflection of a prior shift in thinking which had begun long before the Mutiny broke out.

The Mutiny could be used as an argument in support of almost anything. The advocate of virtually any policy could argue to his own complete satisfaction that the Mutiny had resulted from the failure to adopt the particular reform which he had been espousing all along. "As regards the mutiny," wrote General Jacob, "I see no reason to change a thought or a word which I have formerly expressed on the subject of our rule in India . . . as I have been endeavoring to convince the public during the past ten years, the consequences [of not adopting the policies Jacob recommended] could not be other than we now see them."[3] The Mutiny could be portrayed as the result of England's having done too much, or too little, been too harsh or too gentle. Disraeli, for instance, who in 1858 was still hostile to Britain's adventures in overseas administration, spoke with considerable sympathy of the Mutiny as a justifiable Indian protest against British harshness.[4]

The fact that the Mutiny provoked an immediate cry for repression, which was followed once the event was passed by a call for cautious retrenchment, reflected changes in both the social and intellectual conditions of British India. The insecurity of the British community as an alien group in a hostile country naturally contributed to the frenzied, indiscriminate nature of the British response. Perhaps more significant, however, was the fact that the official classes condoned and rationalized this popular frenzy in the context of their own highest principles. Instead of deploring the inhumanity and racist excesses of terror-stricken Englishmen many officials spoke of the need for wreaking a terrifying vengeance as the inexorable requirement of stern justice.

Long before the Mutiny gave occasion for its expression, the tendency encouraged by the cult of conduct to be implacable in rage when crossed had become evident. This was one aspect of a

[3] Pelly, *Jacob*, p. 421.

[4] Metcalf, *Aftermath of Revolt*, p. 73.

stern self-righteous character which sought for absolute imperatives in a particular form of behavior. To contradict such imperatives, to act upon different premises, was viewed not only as
defiance but as a demonstration of depravity. If absolute virtue
were to be associated with one form of behavior, absolute evil
could easily be ascribed to contradictory behavior. Of the young
Henry Lawrence, Major James Abbott wrote that when "anything mean or shabby roused his ire, the curl of his lip and the
look of scorn he could put on, was most bitter and intense."[5]
Jane Eyre discovered when she irritated St. John Rivers by refusing his offer of marriage "what severe punishment, a good,
yet stern, a conscientious, yet implacable man can inflict on one
who has offended him."[6] India in 1857 discovered the same truth.
By revolting against the British, Indians were in effect not only
challenging their control of the country but their religious convictions as well. By demonstrating that they had failed to be
impressed by the display of Christian conduct with which British rule had provided them, Indians revealed quite simply that
they were the incarnation of Satanic evil. Charles Arthur Kelley, M.A., of the Bengal Civil Service, wrote of Nicholson's role
in suppressing the Mutiny in the following terms:

> With brand upraised and white plume flashing far,
> What haughty chieftain holds the front of war?
> Well knows the foe that warrior in the fight
> Stern as the storm and terrible as night;
> Not his to dread the battle's blood-red waves,
> Nor the wild rush of Heaven-detested slaves.[7]

Pinpointing the exact nature of the British response, Sir William Russell spoke of the avengers as the devotees of a religion
which was not the religion of Christian faith and love, calling
them "as cruel as convenanters without their faith, as relentless

[5] Edwardes and Merivale, *Henry Lawrence*, p. 16.

[6] Brontë, *Jane Eyre*, p. 440.

[7] Thompson, *The Other Side of the Medal*, London: Hogarth, 1925,
p. 101.

as inquisitors without their fanaticism."[8] The final stage in the transformation of Christianity, from a potential bond between Englishmen and Indians into an English tribal creed, was reached with the conception that the Christian God was fighting side by side with the English against "Heaven-detested slaves." In the years immediately preceding the Mutiny it had become customary to assert that India had been acquired not by a succession of evil crimes of personally accountable individuals, as the earlier reformers had contended, but rather as part of a Providential design. Sir John Kaye, who became the leading historian of the Mutiny, writing in 1853 discerned in India's acquisition "so many finger-prints of the 'hand of God in History,' which he who would read the annals of the Company aright, should dwell upon with reverence and humility."[9] The position of God in the battle was consequently above discussion:

> A . . . parson . . . said to me "Did you observe the ball and cross on the top of the church?" "Yes." "Well; the sepoys fired at them. The ball is full of bulletholes; the cross is untouched!" My good friend wished to imply that something of a miraculous interposition had diverted the infidel missiles, and I did not desire to shake his faith by observing that the cross was solid, whilst it was evident the ball was hollow.[10]

The reversal in British policy following the Mutiny, from a confident assertion of Western values in the reorganization of every aspect of Indian society to a new inclination to appease and conciliate Indians, also reflected, not a sudden change of heart induced by the "disillusionment" of the Mutiny, but much more importantly the broad changes in British values which had been evolving for some years. British reforming zeal had been flagging for several decades, and it was for this reason that the Mutiny was taken as proof that social reform efforts should be

[8] Russell, *Diary in India*, ii, 259.

[9] *The Administration of the East India Company*, London: Richard Bentley, 1853, p. 660.

[10] Russell, *My Indian Mutiny Diary*, ed. Edwardes, London, 1957, p. 177.

either abandoned or slowed down and extended over a long period of time. It had seemed for a brief period following the Mutiny that the mood of righteousness with which it was suppressed would also revive the determination to transform Indian society. Administrative and legislative reforms, such as the reorganization of the army and the police, and the implementation of Macaulay's long-dormant Legal Codes, were quickly taken up. There was some feeling that the best way to prevent future mutinies was to proceed more rapidly to destroy traditional Indian mores. Reform efforts to improve the rationality of the instruments of British Government made considerable headway at this time of heightened fervor, but the keynote of, British social policy became conciliation. Preoccupation with preserving a state of affairs in India which was advantageous to British interests made the Government more prepared to tolerate what would have earlier been called abuses, if it was felt that they contributed to the security of British rule.[11]

The response to the Mutiny within India, then, both the initial flaring of righteous wrath and the subsequent retreat into a preoccupation with conciliation, though brought to a head by the Mutiny, actually reflected changed conditions which had been slowly taking shape in the preceding decades. For the English at home, however, the Mutiny came as a much greater shock. Within England there were few people who could say confidently, "I told you this would happen," because the majority of Englishmen had remained in total ignorance of Indian affairs until the fateful catastrophe of 1857. The Mutiny did indeed revolutionize thinking about India for the English electorate who held ultimate control of Indian destinies in their hands.

This public had never before taken an interest in Indian events; even the Hastings trial had been primarily of domestic

[11] An examination of this shift to a conservative and conciliatory policy in innumerable areas of British concern is the main theme of Professor Metcalf's *Aftermath of Revolt*, in which this shift is documented in detail. Cf. also Chap. viii below.

interest as a partisan issue and had occurred at a time when politics of any description was of interest to a much more restricted public. The English national excitement over the Indian Mutiny was an important episode in the development of popular interest in England's overseas enterprises, which provided the political basis for the imperial adventures of later years. Several decades later, when a more self-consciously imperial mood began to reemerge, Professor James Seeley coined the famous phrase that England had acquired an Empire "in a fit of absence of mind." This felicitous and flatteringly paradoxical expression did not mean, however, that the Empire had been acquired by accident, but rather, in the more precise phrase of Harriet Martineau, "without the national cognizance."[12] The Empire was acquired through the initiative of a small number of Englishmen who had not the least illusion about what they were doing. The important change to which Seeley's phrase pointed was the sudden growth of popular interest in Britain in the activities of these small bands of Englishmen overseas and an inclination to consider their exploits a reflection of the will and intentions of the nation, and their victories thus a creditable achievement, reflecting honorably upon every Englishman. This appearance of popular imperialism, which was crucially important for British Indian history, owed a considerable debt to the national response to the Mutiny of 1857.

This response echoed and applauded the righteous tone set by Englishmen in India. What knowledge the electorate did possess of the nature of Indian society came almost exclusively from missionary sources whose aim was to depict India in as picturesquely unfavourable a light as possible, in an effort to arouse support for the missionary movement. India had entered the general English consciousness in the first half of the century as an illustration of the extreme limit of the abominable depravity which might flourish beyond the pale of the Christian religion. No more abusive epithet existed in the Christian vocabulary than that which labelled a person "worse even than an Indian."

[12] Martineau, *Suggestions,* p. 4.

("This child, the native of a Christian land, worse than many a little heathen who says its prayers to Brahma and kneels before Juggernaut—this girl is—a liar!")[13] Literary exoticism and the work of appreciative Oriental scholars had little effect on this generally negative impression. For the British public India was firmly established as the quintessence of depravity. Until 1857, however, India had seemed remote, and its depravity little more than theoretical, requiring of England only missions, and presenting to England no direct threat whatsoever.

At a stroke the Mutiny made India both grimly real and relevant. The tales of atrocities committed against English men, women, and children attached British attention to India in a more immediate and personal way than any missionary tract could hope to achieve. Remote and eccentric English adventurers were one thing, innocent women and children, another. Here India seemed to strike at the inner core of the English nation. The English public followed with horrified fascination the unveiling of every minute detail of Indian perversity. The Mutiny had made "every nook and corner of [India] as fearfully interesting to the people at large as the interior of Africa to the Parks of Peebles, and the Polar regions to the Franklins and Kanes."[14] The sudden national transformation made a deep impression on Thomas Macaulay who recorded:

> The cruelties of the sepoys have inflamed the nation to a degree unprecedented within my memory. Peace Societies, and Aborigines Protection Societies, and Societies for the Reformation of Criminals are silenced. There is one terrible cry for revenge. The account of that dreadful military execution at Peshawar—forty men blown at once from the mouths of cannon, their heads, legs, arms flying in all directions—was read with delight by people who three weeks ago were against all capital punishment.[15]

The nation demanded the ruthless suppression of the Mutiny

[13] Brontë, *Jane Eyre*, pp. 65-66.   [14] Martineau, *British Rule*, p. 13.
[15] G. O. Trevelyan, *Macaulay*, II, 366.

and greeted as a fitting climax to a year of turmoil the announcement of the imposition of direct Crown rule. The first significant contribution of public opinion to British–Indian relations
was a ringing endorsement of the justness of India's subordination and an insistence that it be made more firm and effective
through Crown rule. Indian government, which had always
been something of a closed preserve, a vested interest, a field of
service and enrichment for one segment of the population only,
was now adopted as its own by the nation as a whole. India had
been in a sense annexed psychologically because of the popular
interest which now followed India's reconquest. India "belongs
to us,"[16] Miss Martineau stated confidently, speaking the national mind. The abolition of the East India Company and the
establishment of Crown rule were the assurance the nation required that India did indeed now "belong" to the nation, and
not just to a handful of Englishmen. The abolition of the Company sounded the death knell of liberal hopes for India's rapid
transformation and liberation from English control, by providing a firm rock of British popular support on which India's British rulers could construct their theories of permanent control
with confidence that they would not be deserted by the nation at
home upon which their power ultimately depended. In this respect, the greatest defeat suffered by the rebels of 1857 was
caused by the realization of their own objective: the abolition of
the rule of the East India Company. The Company's rule did
indeed come to an end, just as the Indian prophets had foretold
—"but they did not say another English rule would succeed it."

It has long been conventional to regard the Mutiny as the
cause of the changes in attitudes of the British in India, but to
regard the abolition of the East India Company as no more than
an inconsequential administrative revision. The truth of the
matter seems to be just the reverse. The attitudes of the British
in India had already changed; the Mutiny's greatest direct effect
was in arousing popular support in England for British rule of
India, which was expressed in the demand for Crown rule. In

[16] Martineau, *British Rule,* p. 3.

an odd and almost accidental fashion, the abolition of the Company was a rejection of the promise of Indian self-government. The association of liberal principles of government with the rule of the East India Company, and the importance for them of its termination, have been generally overlooked because of the seeming triviality of the change on a formal level. The strenuous defense of the Company made at the time of its abolition by John Stuart Mill and others has been generally held to have been founded on apprehensions which were not borne out by events and consequently of little lasting interest. While it is true that a number of these apprehensions were indeed unfounded, Mill's instinct was nonetheless sound in sensing that the Company's abolition involved an important issue of political principle.

The reforms of 1858 were on the surface little more than a shuffling of titles and faces—and more often titles than faces. Canning, the last Governor-General, was the first Viceroy. Stanley, the last president of the Board of Control, stayed on to become the first Secretary of State for India. Sir Charles Wood, who succeeded him as Secretary of State, was a former President of the Board of Control. The new Council of India, which was established to advise the Secretary of State, looked suspiciously like a combination of the Board of Control and the Court of Directors. The Statute of 1858 provided that seven of the first fifteen members of the Council were to be members of the superseded Court of Directors. Indian government, which had previously been triple, was now only double. While before a Parliamentary Board of Control had supervised the Court of Directors of the Company which in turn had regulated the conduct of the government in India, now the Secretary of State for India and his Council dealt directly with the Governor-General in India. Though the Company's Court of Directors had been abolished, prominent directors such as Ross Mangles and Sir Frederick Currie were appointed to the new Council. Moreover, the cadre of the Company's career servants in India was not affected, and the system of selection by competitive examination inaugurated by the Company was continued under the Crown. The continuity of personnel was undoubtedly more important than the alteration of titles. And yet, some faces did disappear with the change of titles, among them that of John Stuart Mill. Mill held the office of Examiner of India Correspondence, a senior post in the Company's London bureaucracy. (Mill's father, the author of the six-volume *History of British India*, had also been Examiner.) The younger Mill had been in the service of the East India Company for a total of thirty-five years at the time of its abolition. He nonetheless resigned his position after the failure of efforts to avert the abolition of the Company of which he was, in his own words, "the chief manager," and refused to serve in the revised government. Mill's account of this episode in his autobiography, presumably written a decade or more after the event, which speaks of the "folly and mischief of this ill-considered charge,"[17] reveals that the strong feelings he entertained on the subject had not subsided in the interval or been mollified by the course of subsequent events.

The Company however was in jeopardy long before the Mutiny, and probably would have been superseded in the normal course of events even if the Mutiny had not intervened to accelerate the process. In the Charter Act of 1853 the customary twenty-year extension had been refused, and the intention of Parliament to abolish the Company before another twenty years had passed was made abundantly clear. The primary reason for the Company's retention had been apprehension concerning the acquisition of India's valuable patronage by one of the major parties if Parliament were to govern India directly. The establishment of a system of entry to the Civil Service by competitive examination in 1853 seemed at last to have provided an alternative procedure for insulating Indian patronage from party avarice, and proved perfectly effective in this respect in subsequent decades. The apprehension concerning Indian patronage was, however, the dominant note sounded by the Company's defenders in 1858, and the insulation of India from Parliamen-

[17] J. S. Mill, *Autobiography*, London, 1944, pp. 211-12.

tary meddling was described as one of the chief merits of the system of government which they feared was about to be superseded. Abolishing the Company, in the view of such dedicated liberals as John Mill, Charles Trevelyan, and Harriet Martineau, would be simply tossing India into the jaws of the aristocracy, while the preservation of the Company, and the retention of patronage among the middle classes which they feared could only be thereby insured, seemed a blow struck in India's own interest.

The threat of the expropriation of Indian patronage by the aristocracy was vividly depicted by Harriet Martineau, who considered it a

> blessing ascribable to the East Indian Company [that it keeps] open a broad area of public employment for middle-class occupation. The *Times* professes to be weary of the subject of the popular character of the Indian service; and it is easily conceivable that the Minister, also, is weary of the warnings issued to the public within the last few weeks, under the existing danger of this field of patronage being taken possession of, like every other, by the aristocracy. . . . India [is] the only avenue to that service of the State in which every class should be more or less exercised. . . . Under imperial government, called parliamentary, there would be large retrenchments of the outlay for Indian objects on every hint of a question in Parliament; while, on the other hand, it would speedily be made worth while for high-born youths to go out and "represent the aristocracy" in the Indian service.[18]

Mill also stressed the middle class character of the Indian service in testimony before a Parliamentary Committee. "The general course in which the patronage flows," he said, "is among the middle classes."

> 2492. What do you mean by the middle classes? [Mill:] I mean, in the present case, by the middle classes, the classes

[18] Martineau, *Suggestions*, p. 141.

unconnected with politics, or with the two Houses of Parliament.[19]

This defense of middle class employment involved much more than mere concern with a vested interest, for it also reflected assumptions about the character of the middle class and the aristocracy. Miss Martineau considered the middle class inherently pacific and the aristocracy instinctively predatory, and the eminence of the middle class consequently intimately involved with the prospects for international peace and progress. Both Mill and Miss Martineau had little use for the state of current politics, considering it a diversion of the aristocracy. India's interests, it was felt, could be best protected by men of the middle classes professionally occupied with Indian affairs, who had made it their special field of study and expertise.

In 1852, when Mill appeared before a Parliamentary Committee, he was asked,

2918. What do you think would be the consequences of Parliament interfering more frequently and more extensively in the government of India? [Mill:] I think that many bad and few good consequences would result. The public opinion of one country is scarcely any security for the good government of another . . . there are very few cases in which public opinion is called into exercise; and when it is so, it is usually from impulses derived from the interests of Europeans connected with India, rather than from the interests of the people of India itself.

. . . .

whenever . . . interest was excited in Indian questions they would become party questions; and India would be made (which I should regard as a great calamity) a subject for dis-

[19] *Parliamentary Papers* (H. C.), 1852-1853, Vol. xxx, Testimony of 21 June, 1852.

cussion of which the real object would be to effect a change in the administration of the Government of England.[20]

Mill and Miss Martineau misjudged the nature of both Parliamentary politics and the middle class rulers of India. They attempted to make a virtue of the Company's remoteness from politics by presuming that political activity could never serve Indian interests. And yet the very history of the East India Company disproved this. As C. H. Philips has shown,[21] the periods in which the East India Company had the greatest independence were not when it was most isolated from Parliament but when it had the greatest influence within Parliament. Ignoring Parliamentary politics was not a sufficient program for insuring liberal goals. Nor were the nonpolitical specialists who governed India so pacific as Miss Martineau supposed, or so liberal as Mill supposed. Though of middle class origin, their aspirations were to imitate the distasteful habits of the aristocracy; they were by no means pacific. As Sir John Kaye observed, "In India every war is more or less popular. The constitution of Anglo–Indian society renders it almost impossible that it should be otherwise."[22] Warfare was the simplest route to distinction, profit, and incidentally, aristocratic titles. Englishmen went to India, not to exemplify the supposed middle class virtues, but to acquire the supposed aristocratic vices.

The presumably liberal instincts of India's middle class governors were however an essential element in Mill's political philosophy. The idea of a disinterested vested interest, a progressive, self-liquidating expert, formed the crucial link between the Utilitarian and the liberal facets of Mill's thought. The philosophy of Bentham and James Mill had been founded on principles both atomistic and universal. James Mill, while retaining much of this point of view, was also deeply influenced by the

[20] *Parliamentary Papers* (H. C.), 1852-1853, Vol. xxx, Testimony of 22 June, 1852.

[21] In his *The East India Company, 1784-1834*, Manchester: Manchester University Press, 1940, p. 299.

[22] Thompson, *Princes*, p. 30.

current of liberal nationalism of his day, and by a conception of government involving educational participation as well as mere regulation. His discussion of Indian affairs joined the Utilitarian interest in regulation by experts to these goals of his own by the notion of an educational autocracy acting along Benthamite lines—which would be dedicated to preparing India for participation in her own government as an independent nation. The tenuousness of the marriage between these two conceptions can be seen in Mill's own comments about India, which reveal a reluctance to abandon the goal of Indian independence, as well as a reluctance to relinquish expert regulation by Englishmen as a present and indefinitely continuing reality. When asked about the long-range objectives which he hoped to see realized in India, Mill replied,

> 3117. . . . I do not think you could make a native Governor-General, but I think natives might in time be appointed to many of the higher administrative offices.

> 3118. Do you think they might be members of Council? [Mill:] Not, I should think, at present; but in proportion as the natives become trustworthy and qualified for high office, it seems to be not only allowable, but a duty to appoint them to it.

> 3119. Do you think that in those circumstances the dependence of India upon this country could be maintained? [Mill:] I think it might, by judicious management, be made to continue till the time arises when the natives shall be qualified to carry on the same system of Government without our assistance.[23]

In 1858 Mill composed a lengthy *Memorandum of the Improvements in the Administration of India during the Last Thirty Years*, which contained a clear statement of his view of the East India Company's activity as an enlightened autocracy.

[23] *Parliamentary Papers* (H. C.), 1852-1853, Vol. xxx, Testimony of 22 June, 1852.

He described the Company's energetic activity in the construction of dams and roads, the administration of revenue and justice, the promotion of education and health, the pacification of aborigines and the suppression of barbaric practices. The *Memorandum* stressed the unique character of Indian problems and the need for remedies and governmental policies specially adapted to Indian needs. "In a country like India," he argued, for instance, "the direct aid of Government to industry is required, for a variety of purposes which, in more advanced countries are sufficiently, and even better, provided for by private enterprise."[24] The purpose of Indian government was to sponsor reforms, stimulate activity and development, and educate Indians to manage their own affairs. The East India Company had been assigned the delicate task of regenerating the Indian nation, assisting it in reaching the stage at which it could continue to develop by its own efforts. Mill wanted to see India governed by a self-liquidating despotism and considered the East India Company quite a reasonable approximation of that ideal.

The significance of the opposition by such liberals as Mill, C. E. Trevelyan, and Miss Martineau to the Company's abolition has been overlooked because it was couched in the wrong terms. The liberals defended the Company's middle class nature, and their apprehensions seemed to have been misplaced when Indian officials continued to be middle class in origin. But the liberals had been defending not a class interest but a set of principles which they identified with a particular class. They were actually thoroughly justified in considering the abolition of the Company a repudiation of the "middle class" preparedness to place Indian interests above British. A plausible case can be made for the justness of the Company's claim to have represented Indian interests even in opposition to British national interests—because of the idealism of individual Company servants, and because of the Company's limitations. The Company, in

[24] *Memorandum*, London, 1858: published anonymously by the East India Company.

protecting its vested interests from other Englishmen, was also protecting India from unlimited exploitation.

In February of 1858, when its fate was already visible, the Company submitted a Petition written by Mill to Parliament, which stated:

> . . . Your Petitioners cannot contemplate without dismay the doctrine now widely promulgated that India should be administered with an especial view to the benefit of the English who reside there; or that in its administration any advantage should be sought for Her Majesty's subjects of European birth, except that which they will necessarily derive from their superiority of intelligence, and from the increased prosperity of the people, the improvement of the productive resources of the country, and the extension of commercial intercourse. Your Petitioners regard it as the most honourable characteristic of the government of India by England, that it has acknowledged no such distinction as that of a dominant and a subject race; but has held that its first duty was to the people of India. Your Petitioners feel that a great portion of the hostility with which they are assailed, is caused by the belief that they are peculiarly the guardians of this principle and that so long as they have any voice in the administration of India, it cannot easily be infringed. And your Petitioners will not conceal their belief that their exclusion from any part in the Government is likely, at the present time, to be regarded in India as a first successful attack on that principle.[25]

The Company, in defending its exclusive monopoly, claimed that it had employed that monopoly in India's own interest, and implied that dissatisfaction with the Company's rule was stimulated by the unprincipled avarice of Englishmen eager to take unfair advantage of England's ascendancy in India. The Company, in other words, was defending its privileges by references to high-minded principles, suggesting that those who were eager

[25] Hansard, *Parliamentary Debates*, 3rd Series, Vol. 148, Appendix.

to share its privileges were not so high-minded. With all due allowance for the partial hypocrisy of such a stand, and for the fact that the Company did exploit private Englishmen when it was advantageous to do so, it would seem that the Company was justified. By 1857 a sizeable body of English traders and planters had grown up in India and had organized themselves into a vocal pressure group. They felt the Company was unsympathetic to British commercial interests and reluctant to take the side of the English against Indians. The efforts of Macaulay and his successors to institute a measure of equality in the administration of justice had produced a violent reaction in the Calcutta press and a succession of memorials and petitions to Parliament. Private Englishmen in India, far from feeling that the English government in India stood firmly behind them, on the contrary felt unrepresented. They instinctively appealed over the heads of the Company's administrators to opinion in England and to Parliament to bring the Company to reason.

It can scarcely be argued that the Company had been derelict in its duty in acting in such a manner. The "Report of the Committee of Parliament on the Affairs of the East India Company" in 1833 had laid down guidelines for the Company as follows:

> On a large view of the state of Indian Legislation, and of the improvements of which it is susceptible, it is recognized as an indisputable principle, that the interests of the Native subjects are to be consulted in preference to those of Europeans, whenever the two come in competition; and that therefore the Laws ought to be adapted rather to the feelings and habits of the Natives than to those of Europeans.[26]

In the light of such specific instructions, the aggrieved tone of the Company's Petition of 1858 is understandable; it was Parliament which had reversed itself and abandoned the large-minded liberalism which it had in the first instance urged on the Company.

[26] Reprinted in R. Muir, *The Making of British India, 1756-1858*, Manchester, 1915, p. 305.

The argument that the abolition of the Company was in some degree a response to the pressure of white settlers and traders in India is given further support by the fact that at the same time Crown rule was being debated in Parliament a Committee of Parliament was established to examine the question of white settlement in India. On March 16, 1858 Parliament created the Select Committee on Colonization and Settlement (India), designed "to inquire into the Progress and Prospects, and the best Means to be adopted for the Promotion of European Colonization and Settlement in India, especially in the Hill Districts and Healthier Climates of that Country."[27] Petitions from white residents in India detailing their grievances against the Company's government were referred to this Committee and its establishment was clearly designed as a demonstration of official interest in the welfare of private Englishmen resident in India. Almost no one on the Committee or amongst its witnesses questioned the desirability of English settlement. Even the qualifications which were raised were minor in contrast to the bulk of affirmative and optimistic testimony.

The Committee met to receive the testimony of witnesses on twenty-nine separate days from March through July, the period during which the form of Indian government was being decided. (The "Act for the Better Government of India" received Royal assent on August 3, 1858.) This Committee, explicitly devoted to the problem of encouraging English settlement, was informed by one witness that "There is a strong feeling of the general dislike on the part of the governing officers, the civilians as we call them, against the European settlers."[28] When asked to state his own feelings about the value of increased European settlement, however, the witness (an Indigo planter) was quite emphatic.

> 9897. Are you of opinion that greater European superintendence wherever it can be safely adopted in India, should be introduced? [Saunders:] It is the one thing wanted.

[27] *Parliamentary Papers relating to India*, 1857-1858 (H. C.), Vol. VII.
[28] *Ibid.*, J. Saunders testimony 23 July 1858, question #9815.

9898. You coincide with the great majority of the witnesses in that respect? [Saunders:] Yes; there cannot be two opinions upon the subject.

.   .   .   .

10257. (Chairman:) Can you suggest anything which might encourage settlement of Europeans in that part of the country [The Northwest Provinces]? [Saunders:] The general improvement of the courts and the knowledge that everyone connected with the Government wished to encourage the settlement of Europeans.

10258. In fact, the converse of the policy which (according to your previous statement) has been so far a good deal adopted? [Saunders:] Certainly.

Parliament, which had committed itself to the furtherance of European settlement in 1833, and had instructed the Company to implement and encourage this policy, found in 1858 that the Company in practice was still unsympathetic to private English exploitation. One purpose Parliament had in view in superseding the Company clearly was to reassure English settlers in India that their interests had not been forgotten and to provide a more secure and sympathetic framework for English commercial exploitation of Indian resources than had so far developed under Company administration. English settlers, in the words of one Petition to Parliament, felt themselves "entitled to demand as Englishmen,"[29] treatment which stood in frank defiance of the Company's claim to deal with Englishmen and natives impartially. Settlers felt "entitled to demand as Englishmen" that the courts of their adopted country recognize their status as a privileged racial minority.

At the time of the Charter renewal of 1833, Parliament had instructed the Company to open its settled territories to unrestricted exploitation by Englishmen; at the same time, it insisted on a priority for Indian interests. The inherent contradiction in

[29] *Ibid.,* Appendix No. 37, p. 238, Petition from Bengal nonofficials.

the two policies was not apparent at the time. It was only when a community of private Englishmen had actually established themselves and begun to voice their demands for privileged treatment that Parliament was forced to choose between a policy of safeguarding British interests and one dedicated to Indian progress toward self-government. In 1833, philanthropic liberalism had been in the ascendant, and uncontradicted by the protests of a strong vested interest. Twenty-five years later, liberal idealism was waning in English public life, making more appealing the course of least resistance in bowing to the clamors for the protection of British investments in India, even at the expense of India's own interests. Some decades later, W. W. Hunter commented, "The old official dislike to English settlers, which had once formed a political feature of the Company's rule, still lived on as a powerful tradition during some years after the country passed to the Crown," and lamented the "long bill of costs that the Indian Government has had to pay for the word 'interloper,' as applied to non-official Englishmen in India, and for the traditions which that word left behind."[30] As Hunter indicated, nonofficial Englishmen were never popular with the official classes. The Company's abolition, however, had undercut the effort to treat English settlers and Indians on equal terms; under the Crown, officials and settlers increasingly identified their own interests in a common effort to maintain a privileged position. The Company's servants had been employed by an autonomous agency charged with the task of Indian regeneration; the officials of the Crown served British imperial interests, including the protection of the interests of Englishmen residing in India. The official classes lost some of the uniqueness that had set them apart from other Englishmen, but in return were assured that their services were employed in building up an enduring empire, and that their efforts were clearly endorsed by the nation. It was an exchange perfectly acceptable to Indian officials, now themselves more preoccupied with British power

[30] *Life of the Earl of Mayo*, London, 1876, II, 273.

than with Indian prospects. The main significance of the abolition of the Company was this symbolic endorsement of British permanence in India, whose credibility and justifiability had been slowly growing in the preceding decades.

In view of this, the words of the Queen's Proclamation which announced the assumption of Crown rule while promising free entry into her service without reference to race, are sadly ironic. These words have been often quoted by Englishmen in the twentieth century with the implication that Crown rule instituted a new era in the association of Indians with the government of their own country.[31] But there was nothing new in the promise contained in the Queen's Proclamation; precisely the same guarantee was given in the renewal of the Company's Charter approved by Parliament in 1833. The Queen's sentiments were common to the liberal era just ending, but a source of embarrassment in the years to come. On May 17, 1900 the Secretary of State for India, Lord George Hamilton, confided to the Viceroy of India, Lord Curzon, his belief that the inclusion of the words in the Queen's Proclamation referring to "the principle that perfect quality was to exist, so far as all appointments were concerned, between Europeans and Natives" was "one of the greatest mistakes that ever was made."[32]

The East India Company might at any time have been abolished by Parliament. A trading company could afford to be viewed according to an accounting of profit and loss. The imposition of Viceregal government was an investment of British prestige forestalling the possibility of a severance of connection quietly and without fuss. Fitzjames Stephen argued in a letter to the *Times* of January 4, 1878 that the Mutiny had

---

[31] The "keynote" of the post-Mutiny era, wrote F. H. Skrine in 1903, for instance, "was struck by the Queen's Proclamation of 1858 . . . regarded as their Magna Charta by educated Indians." F. H. Skrine, I.C.S., Introduction to W. W. Hunter, *The India of the Queen*, p. xii.

[32] Hamilton to Curzon, 17 May 1900, Hamilton Papers, v., 169. Quoted in Hira Lal Singh, *Problems and Policies of the British in India 1885-1898*, Bombay: Asia, 1963, pp. 72-73.

raised the Imperial Joint Stock Company to its proper place
... [as] a permanent member of the Government of England.

It was once possible to groan over the sins of the East India
Company and to represent their history as something other
than a part of the history of England. This is no longer possible. The Government of India is now, at all events, in form
as well as in substance, a distinct, avowed part of the doings
of the English nation.

In 1891 W. W. Hunter summed up the changes that had tak-
en place between the earlier and later years of the century by
quoting a statement made by Charles Metcalfe in 1820. "Shall
we ever contrive," asked Metcalfe

> to attach the native population to our Government? and can
> this be done by identifying the interests of the upper classes
> with our own? Is it possible in any way to identify their in-
> terests with ours? To all three questions, if put to me, I should
> answer No!"

It was in this despair of ever conciliating India [continued
Hunter] that the ablest of the Company's servants went
through their lives. . . . Can we ever conciliate India? This
was the vital question to which the ablest administrators deliberately answer No, in the India of the Company. It remains
the vital question to which we deliberately answer Yes, in the
India of the Queen. As a matter of fact, the task of conciliation has been accomplished. It is the beneficent legacy which
the past thirty-three years of the Queen's rule in India now
hands down to the incoming century.[33]

"The administrators" of the Company had made a "deliber-
ate" statement that in their opinion England ought not to anticipate remaining in India for long. "The administrators" of the
Crown with equal deliberation felt that there was no compell-
ing reason why India should be free or why they might not remain in India indefinitely.

[33] Hunter, *India of the Queen*, p. 55.

CHAPTER V

British Indian Society:[1] A Middle Class Aristocracy

England in the East is not the England that we
know.   —CHARLES DILKE, 1869[2]

What do they know of England who only England
know?   —KIPLING'S MOTHER, 1889[3]

IT IS DIFFICULT to understand British ideas about India without
an appreciation of the conditions of English life in India.
*Whether one shares Dilke's view—that an Englishmen would
be horrified by what he saw in India of his countrymen—or that
of Kipling's mother—that an Englishman could learn a great
deal of value from what went on in the English settlements in
the East—it is clear that life in the East was distinctive.*

The most obvious fact of social life in nineteenth century India was the distance between the two races, distance in every
sense of the word. The English created for themselves in India
a social world intended to be as much like life in England as
possible. Of course it was not the same, if only because it was
the result of such a conscious attempt at re-creation. It was a
highly artificial society, so tightly knit that it exerted a com-
pelling pressure on all of its members. It was a society dedicated
to keep alive the memory of English life, hence inclined to foster
feelings of self-pity and dissatisfaction with the imperfect rep-
lica—which was all that was possible under Indian conditions.
Englishmen even in the early years had rarely been enthusiastic
about Indian amusements; by the latter half of the century Eng-

[1] The term "British Indian" is used here in preference to the common
term "Anglo-Indian" to avoid possible confusion. During the period of
British rule Englishmen in India referred to themselves as Anglo-Indians.
The term is currently used most commonly to refer to those of mixed
British and Indian parentage.

[2] *Greater Britain*, p. 525.

[3] Kipling, *Something of Myself*, New York: Charles Scribner, 1937, p. 87.

lishmen who had once suffered patiently through the nautch[4] were scarcely even aware that distractions existed beyond the environs of English society. The nautch was supplanted by the amateur theatrical and the pursuit of sport.

This insulated life could be enjoyable. Winston Churchill, for instance, coming to India as an Army officer fresh from Sandhurst, found the way of life of a British officer to his liking, and proceeded to throw himself into it with all his enthusiasm. It was a life which consisted essentially of frontier expeditions, and garrison encampment; and garrison life consisted almost exclusively of polo. By use of political influence (his father had been Secretary of State for India) Churchill managed to get himself assigned to a frontier expedition about which he wrote a popular book which scooped the market from a more staid and methodical account. Back in camp, Churchill and his companions "devoted ourselves to the serious purpose of life. This was expressed in one word—Polo."[5] Every day Churchill played polo for hours on end. "I rarely played less than eight [chukkas] and more often ten or twelve."[6] Then there was whist, drinking at the club, and dining with important officials to whom Churchill had introductions. The striking thing about Churchill's narrative of the way in which his Indian years were spent is his total absorption with the British community. Churchill—and he was typical of hundreds and thousands of others in this respect—spent three years in India without apparently meeting any Indian other than a menial. "Just before dawn, every morning, one was awakened by a dusky figure with a clammy hand adroitly lifting one's chin and applying a

[4] The "nautch" was the entertainment which Indian hosts typically provided for European guests. A nautch was a dance performance which Evangelicals considered indecent, but which eighteenth century Englishmen thought dull, monotonous, and interminable. The dances performed were most often of the North Indian *katak* type, which is characterized by much intricate footwork and a minimum of melodic variety and bodily movement.

[5] Churchill, *My Early Life*, p. 106.

[6] *Ibid.*, p. 108.

gleaming razor to a lathered and defenceless throat."⁷ This was the extent of the contact which the future prime minister had with the inhabitants of the country which he later fought so hard to retain within the empire. Indians for the British who lived in this protected world were little more than human scenery; they had lost all individuality.

Englishmen whose official position forced them into social contact with what John Beames called "big natives" viewed such encounters as an onerous obligation. Beames himself was a distinguished scholar of Indian languages for whom there existed no problem of communication, but even so he considered social contact with Indians a wearisome business. In sketching a typical day, Beames wrote,

> When I got home I had a cup of tea, and then received any native Rajas or other gentlemen. This was a tedious and tiresome business, but before six I had generally got rid of them and drove with my wife. . . . Our drive generally ended at the club in the Fort, where we met nearly everyone in the station, both men and women.⁸

Beames did not even feel it necessary to state explicitly that "everyone" referred only to the English community.

Contained within the simple fact that such a life was possible, remote from Indians in the midst of India, is an indication of the change which had taken place in Britain's imperial position. British India had become a settled fact, and employment in India had become a career to which one would normally devote all his active years. Though Englishmen still remained "birds of passage" the passage had been lengthened to encompass almost the entire span of life. It was consequently both more feasible and more desirable to set up an approximation of English life in India rather than simply live for the moment in the Indian style, postponing until one's return to England the enjoyment of "home things."

⁷ *Ibid.*, p. 107.
⁸ Beames, *Memoirs*, p. 225.

The reconciliation to Indian residence as a permanent condition was facilitated by the discovery of the hill station. The first British residents in India had languished in India's coastal ports, at Surat, Bombay, Madras, and in the swamps of Calcutta amidst the pestiferous vapors of India's least salubrious climate. Although they had always lived apart from the Indian quarter, or "Blacktown," they nonetheless underwent the same discomforts, just as they partook of the same pleasures as did the more important Indian inhabitants. They tried to endure the heat; they tried to enjoy the nautch; but neither effort was a success.

By the 1830s, the hill station had already demonstrated its attractions; the custom of resorting to the hills for the hot months grew steadily with the progress of the century. By the end of the century, entire governments were trekking twice a year to and from the hills; the Viceregal government to its seat in the Himalayas at Simla, the various provincial governments to their own minor replicas. Officials whose duties prevented them from enjoying the pleasure of an office chair at Simla packed off their wives and children to avoid the grilling on the plains. The pattern had been set by the 1830s. The increased use of the hill stations only awaited improvement in communication by rails and telegraph. At the outbreak of the Indian Mutiny, for instance, the Commander-in-Chief was at Simla.

When Macaulay arrived in India in 1834 to take up his duties as Law Member of the Governor-General's Council, he was asked to attend upon Bentinck not at Calcutta but at Ootacamund. From Madras he "travelled the whole four hundred miles . . . on men's shoulders. I had an agreeable journey on the whole."[9]

Macaulay's first taste of India was a trip of four hundred miles "on men's shoulders," at the end of which he found a snug English village where he could enjoy toasting his feet before a roaring fire. Of Ootacamund Lord Lytton wrote in 1877,

For the first time I have seen Ootacamund. *Having* seen

[9] G. O. Trevelyan, *Macaulay*, 1, 327.

it, I affirm it to be a paradise, and declare without hesitation that in every particular it far surpasses all that its most enthusiastic admirers and devoted lovers have said to us about it. The afternoon was rainy and the road muddy, but such beautiful *English* rain, such delicious *English* mud. Imagine Hertfordshire lanes, Devonshire downs, Westmoreland lakes, Scotch trout streams, and Lusitanian views![10]

Hill-station life undoubtedly put administrators in a better mood and enabled them to get through a larger amount of work. Dilke noted:

> The climate of Simla is no mere matter of curiosity; it is a question of serious interest in connection with the retention of our Indian empire. . . . There is clearly much loss of time in sending dispatches for half the year to and from a place like this. . . . On the other hand, the telegraph is replacing the railway day by day, and mountain heights are no bar to wires. This poor little uneven hill village has been styled the "Indian Capua" and nicknamed the "Hill Versailles"; but so far from enervating the ministers or enfeebling the administration, Simla gives vigor to the Government, and a hearty English tone to the State papers issued in the hot months. . . . In 1866, the first year of the removal of the Government as a whole and publication of the Gazette at Simla during the summer, all the arrears of work in all offices were cleared off for the first time since the occupation by us of any part of India.[11]

Simla did indeed give a "hearty English tone" to Indian government; in fact, it produced an Indian government from which India and Indians were infinitely remote. The viceroy lived at Simla in an English Gothic country house perched on an Himalayan summit, 8,000 feet in the air. Hill stations removed much of the irritation of Indian life, reconciling Englishmen to a life of permanent exile, but only by isolating them

[10] Hilton Brown, *The Sahibs,* London, 1948, p. 27.
[11] Dilke, *Greater Britain,* p. 443.

almost entirely from contact with Indian society. During the cool months Englishmen enjoyed a fabricated English life on the plains; during the hot months spiritual isolation was reenforced by physical isolation as well.

The pleasures of hill-station life were equally attractive to nonofficial Englishmen. A new society of hill-dwelling, estate-managing Englishmen had developed. Tea and coffee prospered on the cool but equable slopes of the hill ranges of India and Ceylon, and were supplanting opium and indigo as objects of British investment; the opium trade was dwindling, and indigo had always involved a rather unpleasant struggle with the peasant cultivator on the plains. Growing tea and coffee on the hill ranges was a clean and healthful occupation, offering the enterprising the possibility of establishing a park-like country estate. And because these were estates cleared and planted by Englishmen, labor could be more effectively controlled. Instead of returning as Hastings and so many others had done to purchase a country seat in England, many Englishmen actually created country seats for themselves in India in attractive surroundings, just as they did in comparable regions of east Africa.

One result of the changed conditions of British residence in India was an increase in the number of English women. The importance of their presence has been often commented on, and if anything exaggerated.[12] Victorian Englishwomen are often viewed as the direct cause of changes resulting from a general shift in values and manner of life. The Englishwoman's presence in India exemplified the more settled conditions of British rule. Her own attitudes and the attitudes of Englishmen regarding her reflected the general Victorian mood. Narrow moralism, domesticity, and racial bigotry were, however, not necessary attributes of her sex, as a comparison of Victorian women with the smaller number of Englishwomen who came

[12] Cf., e.g., J. K. Stanford, *Ladies in the Sun, the Memsahibs' India, 1790-1860*, London: Galley, 1962; Percival Spear, *The Nabobs*, London: Oxford University Press, 1963; and Dennis Kincaid, *British Social Life in India, 1608-1937*, London: G. Routledge & Sons, 1938.

to India in the eighteenth century clearly indicates. English-women did not personally cause a narrowing of outlook in English society and a widening of the gap between the two races. It is difficult to envision, for instance, the continuing prevalence in the Victorian period of semi-permanent liaisons between Englishmen and Indian women even without the presence of Englishwomen. It seems more correct to say that British Indian society caused a narrowing of outlook among Englishwomen by refusing them the opportunity of pursuing interests outside its confining limits. Englishwomen in India—like the mistresses of plantations in the American South—were permitted to perform acts of charity, but were presumed to be unsuited by their purity and gentility for a more active role in society.

The presumed gentility of their womenfolk was a part of the British pretense of aristocratic status, which Englishmen in India shared with American plantation owners. Englishmen had always come to India to make money, and the objective of obtaining money had usually been a rise in social status. The first merchant adventurers, the "nabobs," made vast fortunes in a brief span of years and returned to England with the ambition to move in aristocratic circles. The sons of the middle class who accepted positions in India in the nineteenth century were equally attracted by the lure of a large income. But the attraction had now become a large salary rather than the prospect of unlimited fortune, and entailed a career-long commitment to life in India. The salary was not so large as to stir ambitions of saving enough in short order to return to England with the means to live like an aristocrat. Englishmen directed their attention to the rewards of steady service in India rather than to the more elusive ones offered by English society and politics. The ambition of using India as an avenue of advancement in the English social scale was not lost sight of; it was simply transplanted to Indian soil.

Englishmen in India were thus committed, by the unwritten terms of the understanding which had brought them to India, to living in a manner well above the station from which they

had sprung in England. India's function was to turn Englishmen into "instant aristocrats." This passion for gentility was
prevalent even among "the middle and lower classes of Europeans in India, every one of whom considered himself a 'Sahib'
or gentleman."[13] And since the objective was to become *English*
aristocrats, the pattern had of necessity to approximate that of
England as closely as possible. "No Collector's wife will wear
an article of Indian manufacture . . . and all her furniture, even
to her carpets, must be of English make."[14]

The effect of such efforts, so far as actually impressing the
English aristocracy at home was concerned, resembled that of
most efforts of "imitation gentlemen." The nabobs who had returned immensely wealthy from India had been able to buy
their way into society, as well as into Parliament. British Indian
aristocrats had nothing more substantial to support their claims
than pretense. Their aristocratic posture was not transferable;
they could only live like aristocrats in India, they could neither
live like nor pretend to be aristocrats in England itself. The
British living in India took their standards from home, adhering to them with a strenuousness that attempted to compensate
for the refusal at home to admit their pretensions. Fitzjames
Stephen found British Indian officials "a very sensitive and
rather forlorn race . . . who since competition and its results
have not so many connections in England as they used to have"
and who feel "that they are undervalued and snubbed in English society. . . ."[15]

Another result of the changed conditions of British life was
the growth in currency of the use of the term "nigger" to refer
to Indians. Such a refusal to distinguish between varieties of
"black men" indicated the growth of an indiscriminate racism;
it also suggests the extent of segregation which now existed in
British society. The use of such a term could only be possible in
a society from which Indians were excluded, and in which the

---

[13] Beames, *Memoirs*, p. 132.
[14] Blunt, *India Under Ripon*, p. 248.
[15] Stephen to Lytton, 24 November 1876, Stephen Papers.

person using the term was reasonably sure of sharing certain assumptions and shorthand expressions with those he was addressing. Such a word could only have come into common usage in a society which was both closed to and united in antipathy toward the people referred to in this inaccurate as well as impolite fashion. The first use of the word "nigger" in polite viceregal society may well have been on February 6, 1840, on which date Emily Eden, the sister of the Governor-General, Lord Auckland, confided to her journal,

> One sees how new arrivals must amuse old Indians. He [General E.] cannot, of course speak a word of Hindostanee, neither can his aide-de-camp. "My groom is the best of us, but somehow we never can make the bearers understand us. I have a *negro* who speaks English but I could not bring him dak." I suppose he means a native. . . . He can hardly have picked up a woolly black negro who speaks Hindostanee. I wish I knew.[16]

It is doubtful that "General E." used the form of the word which Miss Eden saw fit to transcribe into her journal. Perhaps this manner of referring to Indians was totally new to her, but this also seems doubtful. It would appear that she is here pretending to a confusion which is in reality a polite reprimand.

Racial bigotry, with its accompanying looseness of invective, was clearly growing in the years Miss Eden was in India. While at Simla Miss Eden invited the wives of the members of the unconvenanted service to participate in a charity fair she was interested in. This, she records,

> was rather a shock to the aristocracy of Simla, and they did suggest that some of the wives were very black. That I met

[16] Emily Eden, *Up the Country*, London, 1930, pp. 389-90. "Traveling *dak*" was the fastest mode of transportation before the completion of the railroad. The customary method of mail delivery, the *dak* system was a sort of human Pony Express. Individuals who traveled *dak* were carried in light palanquins by relays of runners. A person's entourage would proceed more slowly—by steamboat, animal-drawn conveyance, or foot.

by the argument that the black would not come off on their works. . . ."[17]

It is noteworthy that such comments were not confined to drifters at the periphery of British Indian society, but were also expressed—and more often as time went on—by the dominant official classes as well. G. O. Trevelyan observed: "That hateful word [nigger] which is now constantly on the tongues of all Anglo–Indians, except civilians and missionaries, made its first appearance in decent society during the years which immediately preceded the Mutiny."[18] "Decent society" was not insulated from such language. This is significant because it indicates that, however great and important the distinctions within British–Indian society might be, the gap existing between all Englishmen and Indians was even greater. British–Indian society had always been a mixed bag, an uneven sorting of the very best and the very worst elements from England. Jacquemont in 1829 had noted that *"Immédiatement au-dessous de la plus haute société, vous trouvez le tuf le plus vulgaire et le plus commun."*[19] The stratum of vulgarity at the bottom of English society in India distressed all observers of Indian affairs. Dilke recounts attending a native drama in Bombay in which "An Englishman was introduced and represented as kicking every native that crossed his path with the exclamation of 'Damned Fool': at every repetition of which the whole house laughed."[20] Shortly after this experience, Dilke encountered a British recruit,

> uproariously drunk, kicking every native against whom he stumbled, and shouting to an officer of another regiment, who did not like to interfere: "I'm a private soldier, I know, but I'm a gentleman." . . . In some fifty thousand natives holiday-making that day, many of them Christians and low-caste men, with no prejudice against drink, a drunken man was not to be seen.

[17] *Ibid.*, p. 159.
[19] *Correspondance*, I, 79.
[18] *Cawnpore*, London, 1910, p. 36.
[20] Dilke, *Greater Britain*, p. 512.

It is impossible to over-estimate the harm done to the English name in India by the conduct of drunken soldiers and "European loafers." The latter class consists chiefly of discharged railway guards and runaway sailors from Calcutta—men, who, trailing across India and living at free-quarters on the trembling natives, become ruffianly beyond description from the effect upon their originally brutal natures of the possession of unusual power.[21]

The paradox of Indian life was that the ordinary extremes of behavior of British domestic life were exaggerated, while the extremes of social distance were infinitely reduced. The viceroy of noble birth, and the disorderly soldier such as the one observed by Dilke, or the one who sparked the "Cow Row" at Lahore by "wounding" several cows in "self defense,"[22] were united by a bond which would not have existed in England. The official Englishman could not dismiss vulgar Englishmen with the contempt the aristocracy would have employed at home, for the simple reason that his own pretension rested on the same grounds as that of the common soldier. His claim to an aristocratic status rested on a basis any Englishman could claim with equal justice. The English nation, in its entirety, was depicted as an aristocracy with respect to India; the whole English nation was "the aristocracy of nature."[23] While the official Englishman might deplore the conduct of the vulgar Englishman he was trapped by the realization that if he sacrificed the vulgar specimens among his countrymen by holding them up to ridicule, he was jeopardizing his own position. Wilfred Blunt describes going to a dinner given by an Indian host and

[21] *Ibid.*, p. 517.

[22] Henry Lawrence reported that it began "owing to the brutal conduct of a European artilleryman towards some cows . . . a herd of cows pressed upon him, and in self-defense (as he says) he cut at them. He might, at any rate, have been contented to use the flat of his sword. Three or four animals were wounded." The event took place in 1846. Edwardes and Merivale, *Henry Lawrence*, p. 391.

[23] *Suggestions*, p. 152.

discovering that the well-intentioned Indian had invited two English couples of vastly differing official status; the Indian host had simply not perceived the important distinctions which would have been so clear to any Englishman. Blunt wondered what would happen. To his amazement, the official and the commoner spoke cordially to one another, and managed to co-exist throughout the evening without visible friction. In this case the Indian was more perceptive than the visiting Englishman. Englishmen in India, high and low, *were* of a class, sharing a common lot and forced to bury the differences which would have separated them in England. The Englishman based his claim to aristocratic rank not on religion, or intelligence, or education, or class—factors which might have admitted qualified Indians to the same rank—but squarely on his membership in a dominant national group. Any member of the English nation could thus claim, with reasonable confidence of success, an aristocratic status in India with its attendant privileges. Sir William Russell observed that

> The Judges of the Courts tell me that they are much troubled by the pseudo-aristocratic prejudices of all classes of Europeans against paying their bills till they are forced into court. Today an officer was summoned by his servant for wages due . . . he wrote to the Judge to say he hoped he would not be required to appear . . . adding—this, mind, to the Judge of the Court!—he would take good care to put it out of the fellow's way to summons him again, as he had "no notion of putting up with such conduct on the part of a *dog of a native!*"[24]

Russell himself observed the following scene:

> I was rather amused at one of [Lord William] Hay's cases this morning. An officer, entered and sat down at table. After compliments, as the natives say—
>
> Briton (Loquitur)—"I say, Lord William, I want to ask

[24] Russell, *Diary in India*, II, 118.

your advice. Can I lick a fellow for serving me with a summons—a writ you know?"

Lord William—"No. If you lick a man you must take the consequences. Do you owe the money?"

Briton—"Why, yes; but the d——d nigger came up and annoyed me, and I want to give him a hiding. It's too bad that gentlemen should be insulted in this way by those confounded impudent rascals about the courts. . . . The whole country's going to the d——l! How can you expect gentlemen to come here to be insulted by those bazaar blackguards and those confounded summons-servers? I'll lick——" etc. . . .[25]

Judges such as Hay might indeed complain at having to put up with such conduct; the crucial consideration is that they *did* put up with it, thereby acknowledging a kinship which was distasteful but unmistakable. The exceptional situation of an island of Englishmen in the midst of an Indian sea forced them together. They were all equally implicated in the conspiracy to win profit and a rise in status from the Indian connection, and all would suffer equally from a common downfall. The result was an extraordinary confraternity of feeling among Englishmen and an extraordinary sensitivity to criticism of any of their number. During the trial before the Calcutta Supreme Court, which convicted the Reverend James Long for libel in publishing a fictitious account of the activities of several English indigo planters, the presiding judge, Sir M. L. Wells, spoke to the jury about the play (*Nil Durpan*) as follows:

It was urged that it only related to some exceptional instance . . . [but] it was impossible to speak of them otherwise than as a filthy insinuation against a society of helpless ladies who, under the mask of a general type, were cruelly stabbed in the dark. If it meant anything, it was not merely a slander against the wives of planters, but also against the Magistrates

[25] *Ibid.,* ii, 95-96.

and the planters. The Jury, the civilians, the soldiers, and merchants in this country alike had their common origin from that middle class whose daughters were here so shamefully maligned. Those ladies came to this country to share a life of toil and hardship with their husbands, far from the friendship and protection of their friends and were entitled to be respected and protected.[26]

Judge Wells was in effect threatening the jury by telling them they could not afford to ignore a slander against one of their own nation because the position of their entire class was imperilled thereby. All Englishmen in India were brought together by a common presumption—and a common threat.

The challenge to British pretensions was imagined to be permanent and ever-present. Sir Patrick Grant, for instance, extended the notion of the similarity between Indians and Negroes by contending that they shared a common dislike for the white man. Grant opposed the suggestion that India might be garrisoned by "hottentots" by saying,

> I am of opinion that there is in the heart of every black man an inherent dislike of the white man, which will always lead him to sympathize with those of his own colour, however they may differ in race, creed or country. . . . I am strongly opposed to the expedient of enlisting the inhabitants of the tropical climates for service in India, for I am convinced that as a general rule the black man will always fraternize with the black man against the white man.[27]

The feeling that all Englishmen were natural allies against the nonwhite races was echoed in this feeling that all black men must inevitably dislike them. All Indians were implicated in

[26] Official transcript of trial proceedings, Calcutta Supreme Court, July 20, 1861, reprinted in Dinabandhu Mitra, *Nil Durpan or the Indigo Planting Mirror*, trans. Dutt, Calcutta: Sri Debi Prasad Mukhopadhyaya, n.d.

[27] "Papers Connected with the Re-organization of the Army in India Supplementary to the Report of the Army Commission," *Parliamentary Papers*, 1859; Memoranda by Grant dated June 16, 1858 and July 16, 1858.

the Mutiny of 1857, inasmuch as the Mutiny was considered typical of what might be expected from all Indians at any time. When Lord Mayo was assassinated by a convicted criminal while visiting a penal colony, the response of Englishmen was intense and indiscriminate. Fitzjames Stephen described the funeral procession:

> One man told me that on his way home, he felt possessed by such fury, against anyone who might be connected with the murder, that he walked with a kind of charge through a group of people, who looked as if they enjoyed "the show" and gave a shove to a big Mohammadan who looked insolent, at which, he said, "the man went down like a bag of feathers." I saw some suspicious-looking fellows grinning and sneering and showing their teeth myself, and I felt as if I could have killed them. No one who has not felt it can imagine how we all feel out here in regard to such matters. When Lord Mayo was stabbed I think every man in the country felt as if he had been more or less stabbed himself. . . . There was a dead silence nearly all the way; the natives standing or squatting in their apathetic way, and the Europeans as grim as death. All that was to be heard was the rattle of the gun-carriage, and the tramping of the horses, and the minute-guns from the fort and ships. . . . Troops and cannon and gun-carriages seem out of place in England . . . but it is a very different matter here, where everything rests upon military force. The guns and the troops are not only the outward and visible marks of power, but they are the power itself to a great extent, and it is very impressive to see them. . . . If one is to have fancies on such a matter, it is pleasant to think that [Lord Mayo] is not to lie here in a country where we can govern and where we can work and make money and lead laborious lives; but for which no Englishman ever did, or ever will, or can feel one tender or genial feeling. The work that is done here is great and wonderful; but the country is hateful.[28]

[28] Leslie Stephen, *Life of Fitzjames Stephen*, pp. 293-95.

The relationship between official and nonofficial Englishmen was intrinsically ambiguous, because the reality of their mutual dependence was belied by the formal obligation of India's career officials to rule disinterestedly on behalf of all Britain's subjects. Officials did favor Englishmen, but were reluctant to appear to do so; nonofficials did secure privileged treatment by various devious means though they were publicly snubbed and formally impotent.

All this was apparent to Charles Dilke, who found the conduct of nonofficial Englishmen highly distressing. His proposal to remedy the situation was to increase the number of white settlers. The prospect of the Vale of Kashmir peopled with English settlers and the hill-ranges covered with English-run plantations pleased Dilke because he was both an English racist and politically a liberal. He enjoyed the vision of the English race flooding over the world, filling every vacant continent and valley, wresting fertile regions from the aborigines; and, because he was a liberal, he looked forward to the liberalizing influence the presence of a large body of white Englishmen might have on the workings of the English despotism in India. Dilke did not approve of race relations as he saw them in India, and yet he urged that

> The union of interests and community of ideas which would rise out of well-ordered [white] settlement would do much to endear our Government to the great body of the natives. As a warning against European settlement as it is, every Englishman should read the drama "Nil Darpan."[29]

Dilke's optimism was founded on the assumption that white settlers in India would have the same interests as the native inhabitants, would feel that their interests were the same, and in agitating against the bureaucratic autocracy in their own interest would also be agitating for the interests of the natives. As it transpired, the increase in white settlement went hand in hand with an increasing insistence on Government protection

[29] Dilke, *Greater Britain*, p. 449.

of white interests against Indians. Settlers did introduce the methods of political agitation—and extralegal coercion—into India, and they did teach Indians how to use them; but they taught Indians their effectiveness in urging their own interests against Indian interests, and what Indians learned they learned by bitter experience from their antagonists.

Private Englishmen were not prepared to align themselves with Indians because they claimed (successfully) to belong to a privileged social class by virtue of their national identity. They were able to maintain their superiority in regard to Indians though they were never conceded full equality with officials. Internally British Indian society was subtly stratified in ways which might justify its description as the world's first classless, bureaucratic society. The parallel between British India and Soviet Russia has obvious limitations, but is not altogether beside the point. Both societies obliterated conventional distinctions of class, but produced an even more rigid ordering within the classless society by making social rank depend exclusively upon official position. Wealth, hereditary standing, artistic or literary ability, and success in electoral politics were all irrelevant. The official class was both closed and technically all-powerful; no alternative routes to eminence and influence existed to confuse and soften the stark outlines of official rank. The officials were arrayed along a scale of precedence reflecting their standing in the monolithic bureaucratic hierarchy. The rest of British Indian society was composed of Englishmen who felt a basic equality as Englishmen with even the most exalted of their countrymen, but were nonetheless compelled to defer to those in bureaucratic positions.

A successful speculator, or a "merchant prince" may force his way into good society in England; he may be presented at court, and flourish at court-balls; but in India he must remain for ever outside the sacred barrier, which keeps the non-official world from the high society of the services.[30]

[30] Russell, *Diary in India*, II, 152.

And yet, even the highest of Indian officials felt their social pretensions disallowed in England. The British in India made claims to social rank ignored at home, but drearily mechanical within India itself. Because one's social claims were only respected within India, there was little temptation to return home. But the British never became Indianized, as had earlier conquerors. Earlier conquerors had not possessed a foreign home from which they continuously drew their standards and which induced them to look upon India only as a place of permanent exile. The British kept themselves apart with all the exclusiveness of an Indian caste, but unlike a true caste they could never be fitted into the larger Indian society. Indians had to acquiesce to their peculiar exclusiveness, and resign themselves to enabling middle class Englishmen to play at being English aristocrats, or ask them to leave. Englishmen gave Indians not only a geographically united nation; English aloofness also helped foster in reaction an awareness of a special Indian identity. No one who has studied Indian nationalism will think social distinctions a small matter. Most Indian nationalists at some stage in their lives sought acceptance in English society; and all could testify to the formative effect on their ideological development of some small act of British exclusiveness.

CHAPTER VI

Technology, Force, Democracy

Whatever happens, we have got
The maxim gun, which they have not.[1]

ENGLISHMEN of the Victorian period found it difficult to share
the Evangelical conviction that Christianity could provide a
bond which would unite all mankind. Victorians had either
lost their own faith in Christianity or turned it into a labyrin-
thine code of conduct which was self-evidently inaccessible to
all humanity. The evangelizing spirit did persist, however—
though less in England than in other parts of Europe—in the
service of various secular faiths which seemed to their devotees
capable of succeeding where Christianity had failed, in providing the basis for human brotherhood. This spirit animated
much of socialist thinking, as well as the creed of liberal, pacifist
nationalism exemplified by Mazzini. If all the world were so-
cialized, or organized in freely self-governing nations, so it was
argued, then human brotherhood would spring up naturally
of its own accord. Artificial barriers would fall. Christian missionaries had considered religious superstition such a flimsy
barrier; now social vested interests and alien governments were
depicted in the same light as surmountable obstacles on the path
toward universal amity.

The development of science and technology stirred similar
hopes in many liberal minds. Here at last, it was felt, a true
common denominator had been found, a faith which could both
unify and exalt mankind. The study of science, joined with the
spiritual improvement resulting from material progress, it was
hoped, would at last bind humanity together. Miss Martineau
spoke lyrically of this prospect:

Let a man of each race on the globe meet all the other dele-

[1] Quoted by Edward Thompson in his *Princes*, p. 63.

gates at any point of convergence: it is probable that each will insist on some theological dogma which will appear impious or absurd to all the rest; and, as for philosophy, the abstract Chinese, the inquisitive Hindoo, the narrow Mussulman, the allegorical German, the figurative Arab, the dogmatic Scotchman, the analytical Frenchman, the misty Anglo-American, the literal Red Indian, the sentimental Russian etc., will speak, each in his own language of ideas, exciting more opposition than sympathy among all the rest. But, introduce science, and what immediate and necessary agreement there is among them all, from the moment they understand the terms, and verify the facts! The practicable qualities of all objects afford an inexhaustible field of study for all manner of men; and the only area in which there is any hope of peace and progress, as long as opposing races remain otherwise unreconciled.[2]

Technology, it was hoped, would enable men at last to understand one another, and guarantee once and for all the peace of the world.[3] But while liberal minds found in science a vindication of liberal hopes and anticipated that it would act as a servant of liberal ends, those of different inclinations perceived alternative meanings in the obviously revolutionary emergence of modern science. The industrial revolution had taken place first in England; was this only an accident, or proof of English national superiority? Science required rigorous study and the application of disciplined procedures; were all equally capable of such activity, or was scientific prowess an exclusively European possession? Advanced technology made Englishmen more powerful than Indians; was this only a historical accident or proof that Englishmen were also better than Indians? Englishmen possessed technology and Indians did not; was scientific knowledge to be broadcast to the world, as the mission-

[2] Martineau, *Suggestions*, p. 104.

[3] Raymond Aron discusses the belief that technology could guarantee peace, in his *War and Industrial Society*, London: Oxford University Press, 1958.

aries had spread the Christian faith, or was it to be monopolized and exploited by Englishmen for their own ends? Obviously, technology spoke no single message to all minds; in India, it was destined to become the servant, not of human brotherhood, but of British imperial dominance. For the dedication to material progress was adapted by Englishmen to the same end to which Christianity had ultimately been adapted, as a proof of the gulf existing between Englishmen and Indians, rather than a possible means of bridging it. Just as Christianity had evolved from a creed available to all into an identification with the peculiarly British kind of character, so science came to seem something which could only be appreciated after an extended period of conditioning. As with other liberal faiths, such as the faith that India would some day be free and self-governing, the belief in the efficacy of technology for Indian improvement, when it survived at all, was assumed to apply only after such a vast number of years that it was effectively nullified as a basis for a progressive policy. Indians would first have to take seriously their present life, dedicate themselves to material improvement and the conquest of nature, abandoning fatalism and other-worldliness before science could speak to them. Just as Christianity was "not a piece of conjuring, which you only have to announce for its magical effects to appear,"[4] so equally did science require, not just its announcement, but a gradual acclimatization. "The only true method is now, for the most part, agreed on: the natives must pass through a great process of secular education—that of life under improved conditions."[5]

For the present, and for perhaps an indefinite future, the development of science could serve only to make Englishmen more acutely aware of the differences existing between themselves and their Indian subjects. Technological improvements had to be made in India for the intellectual as well as material benefit of Indians; but Indians could not be expected either to understand or endorse these improvements. Englishmen were

[4] Arnold, *Oakfield*, p. 125.   [5] Martineau, *British Rule*, p. 289.

forced to take the hard, ungrateful road of doing for their subjects what they knew to be best, without expecting in return either affection or appreciation:

"Look at us here," said Mr. Middleton to Oakfield, "on board this steamer, and there at those multitudes engaged in their harsh-sounding, unpleasing, but animated devotion, and you will see the problem we were speaking of the other day, stated broadly enough. What an inconceivable separation there apparently and actually is between us few English, silently making a servant of the Ganges with our steam-engine and paddle-floats, and those Asiatics, with shouts and screams worshipping the same river...."[6]

The Parliamentary hearings of 1857-58 contain a narrative of the confrontation of the Indian and English sense of priorities.

9974. I was a member of a road committee when the first plans for roads were taken into consideration [testified Mr. Saunders]; the magistrate called a meeting of all the influential natives in the district to consult with him on the subject of making roads. The natives' view in the first instance, was to make a road, say from Agra to a point on the Ganges, which appeared to us English to be of no great advantage, and on inquiring why they should prefer that line, they said that it would be a very pious work; that it would be for the benefit of all pilgrims of Central India who came on a pilgrimage to that special point on the Ganges.

9975. [Mr. Campbell] What point was that?—Soron Ghat. The Magistrate represented to them that that line would be of very little benefit to the commerce of the country. . . . We separated; but the magistrate carried his opinion into force, and commenced a road from Allygurh towards Agra.[7]

The English could never forget that their own view of public policy was one considerably more dedicated to technological

[6] Arnold, *Oakfield*, p. 128.
[7] *Parliamentary Papers*, 1857-1858, Vol. VII.

progress and material development than that of their Indian subjects. Nor were they inclined to consider this difference of merely incidental interest; it seemed, on the contrary, an emphatic demonstration of the more advanced state of English civilization, since progress in the refinement of civilization was now largely gauged by the extent of concern for and the development of industry and technology.

One of the attractions of technology was that it seemed to provide objective criteria of judgment. Miss Martineau's conviction that a scientific fact would instantaneously be agreed upon by men of all religious and national backgrounds has already been noted. It was with a similar feeling that at last the argument had been safely put on the ground of indisputable scientific fact that the claim for the superiority of English civilization was now put forward. The issue of the relative merits of Indian and English civilization might have remained in doubt so long as the argument was confined to a comparison of literary and religious texts or patterns of morality. The student of English literature could argue that Indian literature was inferior on the score of moral worth and historical validity; the missionary could argue that Indian religion and conduct were similarly inferior. And yet, as Miss Martineau pointed out, the judgment was still essentially founded on mere opinion. India, it had to be admitted, did possess a rich and distinctive culture, and complex and sophisticated religions. However much it might be deplored, it was certainly not inconceivable that a person, whether English or Indian, might prefer the Indian tradition. By the measure of technological achievement, conversely, there seemed to be no ground for disagreement or even discussion. As the preference for judging civilizations in such terms grew, so did the feeling that at last the issue of the relative merits of English and Indian cultures could be resolved on an objective, scientific basis. The process of "grading" different cultures was reduced to a conveniently simple and incontrovertible standard. As E. B. Tylor put it in 1871:

Civilization actually existing among mankind in different grades, we are enabled to estimate and compare it by positive examples. The educated world of Europe and America practically settles a standard by simply placing its own nations at one end of the social series and savage tribes at the other, arranging the rest of mankind between these limits according as they correspond more closely to savage or to cultured life. The principal criteria of classification are the absence or presence, high or low development, of the industrial arts . . . the extent of scientific knowledge, the definiteness of moral principles, the condition of religious belief and ceremony, the degree of social and political organization, and so forth. Thus on the definite basis of compared facts, ethnographers are able to set up at least a rough scale of civilization. Few would dispute that the following races are arranged rightly in order of culture:—Australian, Tahitian, Aztec, Chinese, Italian.[8]

So long as the industrial arts remained at the head of the list, and the standard in religion, culture, and politics was set by the industrially advanced nations, there could indeed be few who would dispute Tylor's ranking—or Dilke's likening of Indians, who could not be "credited with . . . the railways and bridges of their English rulers or with the waterworks of Bombay city,"[9] to the nations at the bottom of Tylor's list. The very attempt to rank civilizations on a single scale made the result a foregone conclusion. The possession of technology was now employed to confirm what religious and social reformers had so long assumed.

The emergence of Social Darwinism seemingly simplified the process of ranking even more; it suggested that there need be only one criterion, and that one admirably objective—the cri-

[8] Tylor, *Primitive Culture: researches into the development of mythology, philosophy, religion, art and custom,* London: John Murray, 1871, I, 23-24. Quoted by George Stocking, Jr. in "Matthew Arnold, E. B. Tylor, and the Uses of Invention," *American Anthropologists,* LXV, No. 4, August 1963, 790.

[9] Dilke, *Greater Britain,* p. 519.

terion of strength, of military force. The society which could muster the military strength to defeat another by this simple token was assumed to have demonstrated its superiority as a civilization. Ancient glories, literary treasures, profound religions, or intricate handicrafts had no relevance if they could not contribute to the mounting of a technically advanced, militarily superior armed force. Fitzjames Stephen spoke of England's conquest of India, for instance, as the result of an equitable "competitive examination which lasted for just 100 years, and of which the first paper was set upon the field of Plassey, and the last (for the present) under the walls of Delhi and Lucknow."[10] The reformers, who had urged the construction of a permanent foundation of friendship between India and England on the basis of shared sentiments produced by common institutions, had done so from the conviction that mere military control was of all forms of relationship between peoples, the most fragile. In the later years of the century, Englishmen did not shrink from asserting that British rule was primarily based on force, because such a basis for rule had itself been transformed from a charge which moral men were eager to refute, into an actual sanction of the moral superiority of that rule.

"Religion is not propagated by force," Charles Grant had insisted in 1792. "Compulsion is . . . subversive of the rights of private judgment and conscience, and totally contrary to the spirit and genius of Christianity."[11] Religions, said Fitzjames Stephen in 1873 "are and always must be essentially coercive

[10] *Letter to the Times*, 4 January 1878. Stephen claimed to have learned the importance of force on the playing-fields of Eton—in a passage which revealed that Stephen, like many other confident advocates of force, was himself something of a physical weakling: "I was on the whole very unhappy at Eton and I deserved it; for I was shy, timid, and I must own, cowardly . . . the process taught me for life the lesson that to be weak is to be wretched, that the state of nature is a state of war, and that Vae Victis is the great law of Nature." Annan, *Leslie Stephen*, p. 19.

[11] Grant, "Observations," p. 99.

systems."[12] Religions were spread, in Stephen's view, by "military power, if the early converts are fighting men; it may be power derived from threats as to a future state—and this is the commonest and most distinctive form of religious power of which we have practical experience."[13] Consistently with this view, Stephen advocated that England convert India to English religion by force, though by religion he meant law and order:

> The establishment of a system of law which regulates the most important part of the daily life of a people constitutes in itself a moral conquest, more striking, more durable, and far more solid than the physical conquest which renders it possible. It exercises an influence over the minds of the people in many ways comparable to that of a new religion. . . . Our law is, in fact, the sum and substance of what we have to teach them. It is, so to speak, the gospel of the English, and it is a compulsory gospel which admits of no dissent and of no disobedience.[14]

It was perfectly consistent with his approach to refer to law thus as a religion, because Stephen conceived of both law and religion as systems of organized coercions. And while he spoke of supplanting a physical conquest with a moral one, he referred simply to replacement of arbitrary force with orderly force. Such a view of law was as remote from Bentham and Mill as was Stephen's view of religion from that of Grant's. Bentham had stressed the role of the great Legislator who created laws for a people by greater perception which enabled him to see further and understand more than others. But he had assumed that such laws would be readily understood and joyously accepted by the people at large, for the laws simply facilitated their own interests and predilection for pleasure over pain. With Stephen, law was transformed into a system of coercion,

----

[12] J. F. Stephen, *Liberty, Equality, Fraternity*, London, 1873, p. 17.

[13] *Ibid.*, p. 18.

[14] Stephen, "Legislation under Lord Mayo," in W. W. Hunter, *Mayo*, II, 168-69.

whose sanction was fear rather than the rational calculation of how best to avoid pain, and the Legislator of Bentham had been transformed into the man—or nation—with power to inspire fear and compel obedience. Crucial to such a change was a radical revision of the Benthamite view of human nature. To Bentham, all men had seemed both rational and equal; to Stephen, drastic inequalities in human abilities, and the total irrelevance of rational calculation for the majority of mankind seemed equally axiomatic.

In formulating such views, Stephen reflected the widespread change in attitudes of the substantial middle classes in business and the professions toward political democracy, which had taken place between the suffrage reforms of 1832 and those of 1867. In 1832 the middle classes had been fighting for their own enfranchisement, and in doing so had often appealed to the standard of democracy and innate human rights. After the monopoly of the franchise was opened to the middle classes in 1832, however, they rapidly lost their enthusiasm for seeing the monopoly extended further. By 1867 the same classes that had rallied to the standard of democracy when it had seemed equivalent with their own interests now rejected it vociferously. As the specter of universal suffrage loomed on the horizon, the cry went up that anarchy was imminent and individual liberty in danger. Some thinkers such as Mill and de Tocqueville were worried by the dangers they saw, but reluctant to do more than express reservations about what they assumed was inevitable. Others such as Carlyle defied and rejected the democratic trend unequivocally. "Count of Heads to be the Divine Court of Appeal" fumed Carlyle. Englishmen " 'free' more and more to follow each his own nose, by way of guide-post in this intricate world." "Manhood Suffrage—Horsehood, Doghood, ditto, not yet treated of. . . ."[15]

It was not surprising that India should begin to look increasingly attractive to people dismayed by what they considered

[15] Thomas Carlyle, *Shooting Niagara: And After?*, London: Chapman & Hall, 1867, pp. 1-4.

the vulgarization of English life, and the chaos they felt would result from the expansion of the English electorate. The ambition of the majority of Englishmen who came to India in the second half of the century was not to undercut the aristocratic basis of English society but to acquire aristocratic status for themselves. They were naturally opposed to any political developments that would dilute the meaning of the very privileges they were striving to annex for themselves. India now gained a further merit in the eyes of the ambitious middle class: to the opportunity of living a life on the aristocratic pattern was added the attraction of an escape from democratic vulgarity at home. As Fitzjames Stephen put it, India was "the one sphere in which an Englishman who is neither born in the purple nor minded to flatter mobs, can hope just at present to serve his country to any serious purpose."[16]

Stephen himself served in India for only three years, as Law Member of the Viceroy's Council, but he followed Indian events with intense interest even after returning to England, and engaged in a voluminous correspondence with Lord Lytton while the latter was viceroy. And while Stephen's views were in some respects extreme they represented a complete and logical exposition of attitudes which were not at all uncommon, though they found fewer public advocates than did more liberal views.

Stephen had come to India in 1869, two years after the passing of the Reform Bill, with the anguish resulting from this victory of democracy still fresh. India transformed him. He found there a viable and efficient autocracy, unfettered by Parliaments and democratic suffrage, and the discovery affected the rest of his life. It convinced him that democracy was not only bad, but even more important, was entirely avoidable. He devoted, in consequence, a considerable portion of the remainder of his life to mounting a systematic attack on the viewpoints of John Stuart Mill and Alexis de Tocqueville, in the full confidence, which India had given him, that his own principles were perfectly practicable.

[16] Stephen to Lytton, 20 December 1876, Stephen Papers.

What Stephen found in India was a full-fledged bureaucratic state in no direct way answerable to the people it governed. India's rulers were not elected; nor was their constant preoccupation an attempt to flatter and gratify the people they were expected to govern. A bureaucratic state, insofar as it is a hierarchical organization of career specialists, is inevitably reluctant to modify its decisions in accordance with popular pressures external to itself; though, insofar as it is a power unit, it must in order to survive acknowledge the bases of its power. No bureaucracy can thus ever be entirely its own master, and the instances in which the British Indian bureaucracy yielded to the pressures of private Englishmen in India suggest the reluctant acknowledgement the Indian Government was forced to make of the source of its mandate to rule. Despite this qualification, British-Indian government did come close to approximating the role in which it cast itself: a government of experts which could afford to ignore all considerations external to its own procedures of deliberation. It rewarded its own kind with the highest offices, encouraging the aspiration of subordinate bureaucrats to impress their superiors in the hierarchy rather than the people whose lives they controlled. The services encouraged their members to be active in the regulation and management of everything concerning their assigned area. Officials were expected to display mastery, rather than elicit cooperation, to make themselves indispensable, rather than nourish the grassroots of democracy. Such inherent tendencies of any state bureaucracy would inevitably have made India's civil servants unsympathetic to participatory democracy even if strong antidemocratic sentiments had not been widespread, for quite different reasons stemming from the aristocratic aspirations of Englishmen, the cult of conduct, and the fascination with the use of force. It was thus not surprising that Stephen found much to praise in India.

Stephen's political philosophy was already partially formed when he arrived in India, but India was crucial for its development. As he wrote in the introduction to his book, *Liberty, Equality, Fraternity*, his "Indian experiences strongly confirmed the reflections . . . which had been taking shape gradually in my mind for many years. The commonplaces and the vein of sentiment at which [the book] is levelled appeared peculiarly false and poor as I read the European newspapers of 1870-1871 at the headquarters of the Government of India."[17] In a letter to Lytton, Stephen referred to the book as "little more than the turning of an Indian lantern on European . . . problems."[18] His discussion of liberty, for instance, contained an elaborate Indian metaphor:

> The Brahmins, it is said, being impressed with the importance of cattle to agriculture, taught people to regard the bull as a holy beast. He must never be thwarted, even if he put his nose into a shop and ate the shopkeeper's grain. He must never be killed, even in mercy to himself. If he slips over a cliff and breaks his bones and the vultures are picking out his eyes and boring holes between his ribs, he must be left to die. In several Indian towns the British Government has sent half the holy bulls to Mahommedan butchers, and the other half to commissariat wagons. Many matters go better in consequence of this arrangement, and agriculture in particular goes no worse. Liberty is Mr. Mill's Brahminee bull.[19]

Stephen praised the way in which Indian government was conducted, arguing that because power was exercised by a small group of enlightened men, Indian affairs could be handled with speed and intelligence.

> I do not believe that one act of Parliament in fifty is considered with anything approaching to the mastery of the subject with which Indian Acts are considered and discussed. . . . [Speed of enactment] was possible because in India there are neither political parties nor popular constituencies to be considered, and hardly any reputation is to be got by making

[17] J. F. Stephen, *Liberty, Equality, Fraternity,* unpaged introduction.
[18] Stephen to Lytton, 2 May 1876, Stephen Papers.
[19] J. F. Stephen, *Liberty, Equality, Fraternity,* pp. 132-33.

speeches. Moreover, everyone is a man under authority, having others under him. . . .[20]

.   .   .   .

The comparative fixity of tenure of the higher Indian officials, who usually hold their posts for a term of five years, and the practice which prevails of carrying on the legislative business continuously, and not in separate sessions, at the end of which every Bill not passed is lost, all give a degree of vigour and system to Indian Legislation unlike anything known in England, and which I hope and believe compensate to a considerable extent for its unavoidable defects and shortcomings.[21]

The emphasis is unmistakeable. A person accustomed "only to England" could scarcely be expected to imagine what a genuinely efficient form of government was capable of accomplishing. Stephen considered British Indian government superior to the indigenous English form and perfectly well suited to adoption, with some modifications, in England itself. Many things might with profit be run by specialists, he commented, not only India but many parts of English life.[22] "As for the manner in which the Viceroy and his Council do their share of the work, I will say only that there are things which it is much easier for seven men to do than for 700, and that the direction of the government of an Empire is one of them."[23] Stephen argued that it was impossible to "build much of a superstructure with a general plan on such a basis as a House of Commons selected by large masses of voters."[24] Stephen considered the association of "large masses of voters" with the important business of government both unfortunate, and unnecessary. While at his Olympian seat at Simla, acting with thorough relish as a "Benthamic

[20] Leslie Stephen, *Life of Fitzjames Stephen*, p. 270.

[21] J. F. Stephen, "Legislation under Lord Mayo," in Hunter, *Mayo*, p. 148.

[22] J. F. Stephen, *Liberty, Equality, Fraternity*, p. 250.

[23] J. F. Stephen, *Letter to the Times*, 4 January 1878.

[24] Stephen to Lytton, 29 December 1879, Stephen Papers.

Lycurgus," Stephen had penned a "Minute on the Administration of Justice," in which he had argued,

> I do not think that it would be at all in accordance with the general principles on which our policy proceeds to consider the feelings of Natives on a subject on which we are clearly right, as a final reason for adopting this or that system.[25]

Though it never materialized, Stephen planned to follow his attack on Mill with a companion volume in refutation of de Tocqueville's *Democracy in America*. He informed Lytton that he possessed

> a notebook in which is a heading "The English in India" under which heading notes of chapters . . . are slowly accumulating. My ambition would be to make it, if vanity may be forgiven, a sort of counterblast to de Tocqueville's *Democracy in America*.[26]

What his argument would have been can be traced in his references to American democracy:

> How far they actually are equal now, and how long they will continue to be equal when the population becomes dense, is quite another question. It is also a question whether the enormous development of equality in America, the rapid production of an immense multitude of commonplace, self-satisfied, and essentially slight people is an exploit which the whole world need fall down and worship.[27]

To counter de Tocqueville's assumption that such democracy was indeed the wave of the future, Stephen pointed to the flourishing aristocracy based on national conquest which existed in India, and argued on this basis that acquiescence to the supposed inevitability of democracy was not an act of realism, but of cowardice. If aristocracy had managed to preserve its privileges in

[25] J. F. Stephen, "Minute" (title page destroyed), p. 42.
[26] Stephen to Lytton, 16 October 1878, Stephen Papers.
[27] J. F. Stephen, *Liberty, Equality, Fraternity*, p. 254.

India, there seemed no reason why aristocracy should not be equally successful in dealing with the lower orders elsewhere.

The analogy between the "natives" of India and the lower classes of England—and Ireland—was a favorite one among the British upper classes, from the latter decades of the nineteenth century well on into the twentieth—and explained, incidentally, much of the sympathy that grew up between the Indian nationalist movement, the independence movement in Ireland, and the labor movement in England. It was felt, quite rightly, that theirs was in some degree a common cause, if only because they were treated in a similar manner by the British upper classes. Philip Mason has noted Lord Curzon's surprise at the whiteness of the skin of certain English enlisted men he discovered bathing;[28] he had seemingly, by an unconscious analogy, assumed that because they were members of the English lower classes, they must have dark skins. The prejudices of race and class were mingled, and made mutually reenforcing. The distasteful qualities of the English lower classes were attributed to Indians, and vice versa. Many a disgruntled member of the English upper classes shared Stephen's longing to be able to "deal" with English and Irish impertinence in the way it might still be dealt with in India, a feeling accounting perhaps for the strange outburst of English sympathy for General Dyer who ordered the Massacre of Jallianwallah Bagh at Amritsar in 1919, which, though causing the death of several hundred people, was justified by Dyer and Dyer's supporters as an effective method of forestalling further violence.

In Stephen's view, England's Empire was an achievement of past national greatness whose relinquishment would be an act of national cowardice reflecting a failure of the will to rule. He could envision the ultimate possibility of such a failure resulting from the growing democratization of English politics, but he hoped that even if England herself went to democratic perdition

---

[28] Cf. his *Prospero's Magic*, for an extended discussion of the relation between race and class attitudes in this period. The reference to Curzon is on p. 1.

she would at least keep her liberalism at home and not insist on exporting it to India.

My soul has been, and is always being, more or less vexed by the folly people talk and write about India. In today's *Times* are a letter from a rather foolish fellow called Monier-Williams, Sanscrit professor at Oxford, and an article thereon, which show how rubbishy little commonplaces, caught up by what they call in India a TG (Travelling Gent) in a few weeks tour get worked up into what is here described as public opinion. However this indifference of the British nation to India is as great a blessing in one way as the indifference of most people to . . . nominal religion is in another. A real, active, imaginative belief in heaven or hell would turn the world into a priest-ridden convent and a similar belief in the commonplaces of the *Times* about India would turn India into a mad scene of confusion and anarchy. Happily people don't really believe much either in heaven or hell or liberalism as applied to India.[29]

Strong resentment among the English community in India was focused on what Stephen called the "TG's," visitors from England whose unfavorable impressions were attributed to the superficiality of their observations. Kipling created a character to exemplify the type, his "Pagett, M.P.," to whom he devoted both a poem and a short story in which he sought to discredit the "sneers of the travelled idiots who duly misgovern the land."[30]

The accusation of superficiality against critics from England was to a degree persuasive, and to a degree beside the point. Decisions about India did rest ultimately with the British Parliament, which could not indiscriminately support its servants simply because of their specialized knowledge; the government of a subject people was "too important to be left" to the civil serv-

[29] Stephen to Lytton, 17 April 1876, Stephen Papers.
[30] Kipling, "Pagett, M. P.," in *Departmental Ditties*, New York, 1913, pp. 61-64.

ants. It was furthermore necessary for liberal criticism to be voiced by visitors, because it no longer had a foothold within the administration itself. "Free and temperate criticism of the measures of Government by officials was not permitted in 1872,"[31] in the opinion of John Beames, I.C.S., who was penalized for indulging in criticism. The Indian Civil Service was effectively organized to discourage lively disagreement in the ranks. It has been suggested[32] that the training of the Company's civil servants at Haileybury before 1859 may have encouraged a spirit of independence in the service by inducing civil servants to look for approval to their former classmates at Haileybury rather than to their bureaucratic superiors; and that those who entered the service by competition in the second half of the century, who began their careers as isolated individuals rather than as a self-conscious group, may have found it more difficult to follow an independent line and have been more inclined than their predecessors to pattern their thoughts and actions in ways likely to appeal to their superiors. The end of the era of wars and pacification, moreover, meant that the route to distinction lay in administrative promotion, not on the remote frontiers where idiosyncrasies might be safely indulged. Nor was the criticism which Beames and others desired to offer intended to push the government closer to a liberal position. With few exceptions, the officials who offered criticism were less, rather than more, liberal than the government they criticized. John Stuart Mill had been eager to shield what he assumed was a liberal official class from what he assumed would be illiberal Parliamentary meddling; the later nineteenth century saw just the reverse of Mill's expectation emerge, with a conservative official class, dedicated to preserving the status quo as a way of insuring their own privileges and position, indignant at the intervention of liberal Parliamentarians. The almost total absence of liberal criticism among the administrative specialists made it possible to label as superficial the outsiders who persisted in it. And yet, the dis-

[31] Beames, *Memoirs*, p. 203.
[32] By Professor Bernard S. Cohn, in informal discussion.

tasteful "TG's" were only repeating what the Company's specialists had themselves said when the specialists were still liberal.

Stephen, in summing up his political views, noted that he and Lytton considered themselves "much finer fellows than the rank and file of society at large and think that they ought to defer to our views. In a word we are not unlike what the English in India would be if they had no England to back them up and no European troops."[33] In England the autocratic Stephen felt like a general without an army; but, as he noted, in India the autocrat still had his army. And yet, as Stephen also noted, the position of the autocrat in India was guaranteed ultimately by the support of the British nation. Stephen was forced to base his hopes for the continuance of that guarantee on the shaky foundation of national indifference to Indian affairs, and would scarcely have been surprised, though hardly pleased, by England's refusal in the twentieth century to continue to underwrite a rule for others she had refused for herself.

[33] Stephen to Lytton, 14 April 1880, Stephen Papers.

CHAPTER VII

Nation and Empire

National pride may be a valuable possession, but
when it becomes a consciousness of racial superiority, it ceases to be an Imperial virtue.

—RAMSAY MAC DONALD[1]

ONE of the many lessons of the Mutiny was that India could no
longer remain the preserve of a few British families; India belonged to the entire British nation, and thinking about India
was deeply involved with many other things. India had come
into the mainstream of English politics and was heavily implicated in the major undertakings of the British nation all over
the world. If England required troops in China, or coolies in
South Africa, India might be called upon to supply them. India
was viewed in terms of what were presumed to be India's own
needs, but also as the century advanced, India was increasingly
viewed in the broader context of imperial requirements. India
had become an essential link in the widening circle of colonies
and possessions which composed the British Empire.

In the middle years of the nineteenth century it was assumed
that England's colonies of white settlers, following the American example, would ultimately break free of England's control
and become independent nations. It was hardly a matter whose
merits deserved discussion; independence for the colonies
seemed so unavoidable that it was scarcely worth the trouble to
lament. The prospects for self-government in a possession such
as India, inhabited by people of a different cultural tradition and
ruled by England by right of conquest, were less unanimously
subscribed to, but there were people such as Mill and Macaulay
who looked forward to the time when India, as well as the white
colonies, would manage her own affairs as a sovereign state. In

[1] Quoted in George Bennett, ed., *The Concept of Empire, Burke to
Attlee, 1774-1947*, London: Adam and Charles Black, 1962, pp. 353-54.

the first half of the century England had been prepared to contemplate abandoning control over colonies and possessions
alike.

These were years, however, in which England's Empire was
distant, and in which overseas possessions were not actively
sought by her European competitors. Under such circumstances,
it was possible to look forward to a time when British commercial interests would be securely guaranteed in a world of self-
governing nations linked pacifically by free trade. The advocates
of Indian independence in the first half of the nineteenth century had never imagined that Indian independence would harm
England; they presumed that political independence would simply be a new phase in the formal relationship between the two
countries which would not affect the most important aspect of
their relationship, that involving trade. Charles Grant, belit-
tling in 1792 the prospect that India would ever be independent,
had added that, if India ever were to become independent "our
commerce might still be necessary to it, and possibly even continue to increase." For, Grant suggested, the "dangers" that India might some day be able to govern herself were "the dangers
of prosperity"[2] implying only a greater ability on India's part to
absorb British manufactures. Such had also been the theme of
Munro, and Macaulay, and John Stuart Mill, who imagined that
trade between independent nations could not be harmful in any
way to British economic interests. Such was the optimistic assumption of the era of liberal nationalism and free trade. Anom-
alous and easily terminable forms of rule seemed the only ones
suitable for colonies and possessions distant from Europe, un-
challenged by foreign foes and difficult to consider governing on
a permanent basis.

With the quickening of communications by telegraph and
steamship and the opening of the Suez Canal, however, the
colonies seemed increasingly less remote. With the ebbing of
faith in the nation–state as the necessary form of government

[2] Grant, "Observations," p. 110.

for all peoples, the ultimate independence of the colonies began to seem less unavoidable. And with the resurgence of the competition for empire among European nations, free trade seemed less feasible, and the advantages of India as a reserve of military strength as well as a trading partner became more apparent. It seemed unlikely that England's economic interests would remain intact if she withdrew from India, for there were now competitors—French and German imperialists—ready to step in when England withdrew. And of course the military resources of India, which seemed more important in later years than in the heyday of pacific nationalism, could only remain available so long as political control was maintained. There was also an awareness throughout Europe of the growing power of Russia and the United States, countries much larger than the traditional nation-state. The result was the emergence of European imperialisms which attempted to weld into permanent political units territories scattered in various parts of the world. The English brand of imperialism was initially conceived as a crusade to save the white colonies for England by welding them into a new political community which would enable England to hold her own against any of the vast new trans-national states emerging in the latter years of the century. And yet, the potential cornerstone of any British empire could never be any or even all of the young white colonies, but India. To be important the British empire would have to include India.

The idea of a permanent *Raj*, which initially had referred simply to the continuation of a British presence in India, and whose advantages had been viewed simply as insuring order and progress for India and continued profit and employment for individual Englishmen, now become subsumed into a more ambitious notion. England could and should remain permanently in India, it was argued, and the question was no longer merely of isolated interest. British India became an essential building-block for much larger schemes. The white colonies and England would be linked together by ties of race and mutual interest. India would be tied to England because India needed England to rule her; and the combination of India, the colonies, and England would produce a gigantic political organism which not even Russia or America could hope to surpass. In the words of Lord Milner,

> Physical limitations alone forbid that [the British isles] by themselves should retain the same relative importance among the vast empires of the modern world which they held in the days of smaller states—before the growth of Russia and the United States, before united Germany made those giant strides in prosperity and commerce which have been the direct result of her military and naval strength. These islands by themselves cannot always remain a Power of the very first rank. But Greater Britain may remain such a Power, humanly speaking, for ever, and by so remaining, will ensure the safety and the prosperity of all the states composing it, which, again, humanly speaking, nothing else can equally ensure.[3]

This concept was first popularized in two books—Charles Dilke's *Greater Britain* and J. R. Seeley's *The Expansion of England*—each of which sought to prove that "what we call our Empire is . . . not properly, if we exclude India from consideration, an Empire at all . . . it is a vast English nation."[4] Dilke and Seeley excluded India from what they considered the natural boundaries of England's domain because they were still liberal nationalists as well as imperialists. They subscribed to the doctrine that political government ideally should reflect the existence of a community joined together by natural bonds. They believed in national self-determination and self-government, and that no nation had the right to deprive another of its right to determine its own destiny. In all these respects, they shared the liberal creed. They differed only in the suggestion that a natural community existed where no one had previously perceived it— a community consisting of England and her white colonies—in their awareness of the relevance of larger political units for the

---

[3] Quoted in Bennett, *Concept of Empire*, p. 352.
[4] Seeley, *Expansion of England*, p. 75.

future and in their skepticism about the universality of a sense of national identity.

India was consequently not included in the nation–empire, but relegated to a special category. The conflicting claims of national self-determination and England's desire to be a transnational state were reconciled by the argument that India was not a nation. For if India were not a nation then England could not be accused of depriving her of her rights as a nation to self-government. In the early years of the nineteenth century, Englishmen had commonly spoken of an "Indian nation," or of several Indian nations, if regions such as Bengal were considered separate nations. India's nationhood was not something requiring specific proof; it was assumed that all mankind was divided into nations. "The rising generation will become the whole nation in the course of a few years," C. E. Trevelyan had written in 1838 in his essay *On the Education of the People of India.*[5] "The time has arrived for taking up the subject of national education."[6] Liberals assumed, without feeling it was necessary to argue the point, that India was inherently national; conservative opponents of reform shared the assumption. At the time of the Mutiny Disraeli in the Parliament and Ellenborough at the Board of Control both spoke of the Mutiny as a "national" protest against the meddling efforts of reformers.[7] And yet within a couple of decades, the concept of Indian nationality, once uncritically accepted by men of all political affiliations, had almost entirely disappeared. The Indian nation had been transformed in the English mind first into a subcontinent and thence into an empire. India, English commentators now informed their readers, was only a "geographical expression." Seeley wrote, "The fundamental fact then is that India had no jealousy of the foreigner because India had no sense whatever of national unity, because there *was* no India and therefore, properly speaking, no foreigner." "What is India? What does the name India really

[5] *Op. cit.*, p. 134.   [6] *Ibid.*, p. 164.
[7] Metcalf, *Aftermath of Revolt*, pp. 73, 144.

signify?" Sir John Strachey asked the undergraduates at Cambridge.

> The answer that I have sometimes given sounds paradoxical, but it is true. There is no such country, and this is the first and most essential fact about India that can be learned.

.   .   .   .

> India is a name which we give to a great region including a multitude of different countries ... there is not, and never was an India, or even a country of India, possessing, according to European ideas, any sort of unity, physical, political, social, or religious; no Indian nation, no "people of India," of which we hear so much.[8]

Paralleling the denial of India's nationality was the transformation of British nationalism into one of the secular religions that grew to importance in the wake of the decline of Christian faith which, in the words of Melvin Richter, "set out to demonstrate that already existing forms of social organization presupposed social solidarity and moral duties of a sort hitherto not recognized."[9] While the new religious nationalism was not necessarily destructive of a commitment to human brotherhood and equality, the emphasis on local affiliations as a source of moral obligations prepared the way for an idea of service to the nation involving participation in the nation's struggle with its foes. Such a concept of competitive nationalism was wholly compatible with imperial control of subject peoples, for it was assumed that service to the nation involved proving its strength at the expense of others and, further, that real nations were rare. Fitzjames Stephen advocated both the merits and restricted sphere of relevance of nationalism in a letter to Lord Lytton:

> Nations are for the present at least and are likely to be for as long a time as we can look forward to with any distinct-

[8] John Strachey, *India, its Administration and Progress*, 4th edn., London, 1911, pp. 1-5.
[9] Richter, *op.cit.*, pp. 33-34.

ness, infinitely the most important of human institutions or organizations. Tribes, families, hordes, small town and village communities like those which the very latest school of historical speculators busy themselves with so much, belong to the infancy of the world, and have only a historical speculative interest. You cannot get much that is worth having out of a village community, or a clan of Rajpoots, or out of the tribes of Central Asia. On the other hand associations or societies which go beyond the limits of nations, are on various points of equally little value. The Humanity of our positivist friends is only a ghost which rather pedantic unsuccessful professors see in their dreams. . . . A nation is therefore on the whole the greatest, the wisest, the best thing authentically known to us to exist, and the service of a nation is the noblest of human employments, the one which affords the fullest scope for all a man's powers of mind and body and the most durable and widest object for his affections. In short, to my mind the nation is the unit in and for which we all of us live move and have our being. Now nations are admirable amongst other reasons for this, that they are not in the least degree abstractions. They are real associations and there are not above a dozen of them if there are so many, and they are coherent, developed, organized in infinitely various degrees. France and England are *pucka* nations, but I think no others are so in an equally distinct emphatic manner, except perhaps the United States. . . .[10]

England was a nation, one of several nations, but a nation in a world where the principle of nationality was by and large absent. England reserved the virtues of nationality to herself and offered to India the alternative attractions of government by the imperial British nation.

One can trace England's developing sense of her imperial

[10] Stephen to Lytton, August 30, 1877, Stephen Papers. "Pucka" is an Indian word which literally means *ripe*, but by extension has become a term of generalized approbation, denoting genuineness, completeness, high quality, etc.

destiny in the changing treatment by English writers of the imperialism of ancient Rome. The study of Comparative Empire had always been a favorite pursuit of the classically educated servants of British India. For centuries classical analogies had come naturally to the lips of Englishmen discussing any subject; the subject of empire was no different and in fact lent itself more easily to classical analogy than did many other things.

It was common in the early years of the nineteenth century to select illustrations designed to point British policy in a liberal direction, and to liken, for instance, India's present position to that of England under Roman rule. This was a standard theme in the writings of Grant, James Mill, and Macaulay. C. E. Trevelyan even compared the position of Rome itself to that of India.

It is a curious fact that an intellectual revolution similar to that which is now in progress in India actually took place among the Romans. At an early period, the Etruscan was, as Livy tells us, the language which the young Romans studied. No patrician was considered as liberally educated who had not learned in the sacred books of the augurs of Clusium and Volaterrae, how to quarter the heavens, what was meant by the appearance of a vulture on the left hand, and what rites were to be performed on a spot which had been smitten by thunder. This sort of knowledge—very analogous to the knowledge which is contained in Sanscrit books—was considered as the most valuable learning, until an increased acquaintance with the Greek language produced a complete change. Profound speculations on morals, legislation, and government; lively pictures of human life and manners; pure and energetic models of political eloquence, drove out the jargon of a doting superstition. If we knew more minutely the history of that change, we should probably find that it was vehemently resisted by very distinguished Etruscan scholars....[11]

Trevelyan drew upon the experience of Rome to bolster his

[11] *Education of People of India*, p. 38.

arguments in favor of liberal policies; but the classically educated were not always liberal, and it was equally possible to re-
sort to Roman precedents in defense of despotic rule. In the
years following the Mutiny, Rome became for India's administrators a source of substantiation for autocratic policies, a school
of practical experience in imperial governance from which useful techniques and ideas might be drawn. When Lt. Col. Davidson, for example, proposed that in view of the untrustworthiness of Indian sepoys, British India should be garrisoned in substantial measure by "Hottentots, Caffres, Negroes, etc.," he defended the reasonableness of this policy by pointing to Rome.
"So far as the differences of circumstances admit," he suggested,
"we might do well to imitate the Roman policy, which jealously
excluded the employment in the conquered provinces of troops
native to the place, and substituted for them men having no local sympathies of country and kindred."[12]

Kipling wrote a number of illiberal stories about an imaginary
Roman Britain which bore a much stronger resemblance to British India than it did to Roman Britain. The central figure of
several of the stories is Parnesius, a devotee of Mithras and "A
Centurion of the Thirteenth." Parnesius is a Briton whose family has served loyally in the Roman Army for generations. He
describes how he first joined his Legion:

> "Like many of your youngsters, I was not too fond of any-
> thing Roman. The Roman-born officers and magistrates
> looked down on us British-born as though we were barbari-
> ans. I told my father so. 'I know they do,' he said; 'but remem-
> ber, after all, we are the people of the Old Stock, and our duty
> is to the Empire.' "[13]

Kipling implies a parallel between Parnesius's situation and

[12] Lt. Col. Davidson, Resident, Hyderabad, "Papers Connected with the
Reorganization of the Army in India Supplementary to the Report of the
Army Commission," *Parliamentary Papers* (H. C.), 1859, p. 229.

[13] Kipling, "A Centurion of the Thirteenth," in *Puck of Pook's Hill*,
Garden City: Doubleday, Page, n.d., p. 123.

that of the martial races of India; his description of the trans-
mural Picts, moreover, is highly suggestive of Bengali nationalists. "We are the Little Folk—we!" Kipling choruses in "A Pict
Song."

> Rome never looks where she treads
> Always her heavy hooves fall,
> On our stomachs, our hearts or our heads;
> And Rome never heeds when we bawl,
> Her sentries pass on—that is all,
> And we gather behind them in hordes,
> And plot to reconquer the Wall,
> With only our tongues for our swords.
>
> .   .   .   .
>
> We are the worm in the wood!
> We are the rot at the root!
> We are the germ in the blood!
> We are the thorn in the foot![14]

There is no question that Kipling in writing his Roman tales
intended them to be parables of the Indian Empire. And the
point of all of his parables was that Indians would be wise to
suffer their fate with better grace.

Kipling's Rome is a vigorous and viable Empire, admirable in
every respect. Kipling seems even to have taken his personal religion from Rome, to have preferred the Mithraism of his hero
Parnesius to the Christianity of his own day. Kipling's biographer, Edward Shanks, writes that Kipling "does not seem to
have looked with any confidence to Christianity for the conso-
lation and assurance that he needed. There are signs that he was
attracted by another religion . . . Mithraism."[15] Shanks traced the
appeal of Mithraism to the "fact that Mithraism was essentially
a military religion and was widespread through the armies of
the Empire."[16] Also it had

---

[14] *Ibid.*, p. 181.
[15] Edward Shanks, *Rudyard Kipling*, London: Macmillan, 1940, p. 259.
[16] *Ibid.*, p. 260.

something of the character of a semi-secret society, with initiations, and degrees of advancement and ceremonies which were guarded from all but the initiates of the proper degree. This appealed to something very deep in Kipling's nature. It engendered, he felt, an intimacy of strength and cooperation which satisfied a craving in him.[17]

Shanks points out the similarity between what Kipling envisioned in Mithraism and the public school cultic rites of the boys in *Stalky & Co.*, who ultimately grow up to be soldiers of the British Empire. Kipling's Mithraism is also reminiscent of the conception Cecil Rhodes had of the society whose establishment he endowed and in the creation of which he was advised by Kipling. The vision Kipling hinted at was of a unified British imperial army spread over the world and joined by a common bond of devotion to "Mithras, also a soldier," paralleling the association of Anglo–Saxon administrators sponsored by Rhodes.

C. E. Trevelyan had seen in Roman history promise for the development of emerging nations. Kipling, satisfied with empire

[17] Kipling wrote a poem entitled "A Song to Mithras," as follows:
Mithras, God of the Morning, our trumpets waken the Wall!
'Rome is above the Nations, but Thou art over all!'
Now as the names are answered, and the guards are marched away,
Mithras, also a soldier, give us strength for the day!

Mithras, God of the Noontide, the heather swims in the heat,
Our helmets scorch our foreheads; our sandals burn our feet.
Now in the ungirt hour; now ere we blink and drowse,
Mithras, also a soldier, keep us true to our vows!

Mithras, God of the Sunset, low on the western main,
Thou descending immortal, immortal to rise again!
Now when the watch is ended, now when the wine is drawn,
Mithras also a soldier, keep us pure till the dawn!

Mithras, God of the Midnight, here where the great bull dies,
Look on thy children in darkness. Oh take our sacrifice!
Many roads Thou hast fashioned; all of them lead to the Light,
Mithras, also a soldier, teach us to die aright!

in *Puck of Pook's Hill*, p. 157.

as a normal state of affairs, was interested in the practical working of the Roman empire and eager for the British empire to be
a more perfect copy thereof. But Kipling, for all of his popularity, was nonetheless essentially a rebel, a pagan critic of his
age. It was more common in the closing years of the nineteenth
century to compare the Roman empire unfavorably with that
which Britain had created, and to refer to the Roman analogy
most often for the purpose of self-congratulation on the degree
to which Britain had improved on the ancient example. The
British empire was conceived to be at once Christian, reformist,
and democratic, and on each count presumed to be a substantial
advance upon the Roman example. Rome had opposed its
might against Christianity, British rule had been imbued from
its inception with Christian intentions. W. H. Russell recorded
in his *Indian Mutiny Diary* attending

> divine service in the Mess-tent today . . . an eloquent . . . ser-
> mon from the Rev. Mr. McKay, wherein that excellent divine
> sought to prove that England would not share the fate com-
> mon to all the great empires of the world hitherto, because she
> was Christian, whereas they had been heathen. . . .[18]

The Roman empire had only rarely, and then for rather dubious reasons, interfered with the customs of subject peoples,
noted Lord Cromer in his discussion of *Ancient and Modern
Imperialism*:

> Traces of the existence of a humanitarian policy are, indeed,
> to be found in the records of Roman Imperialism. The cruel-
> ties of Druidical worship, which were left untouched by
> Julius Caesar, were suppressed by Claudius, although in this
> instance the humanitarian action was possibly dictated by the
> political consideration that nationalism drew its main element
> of strength from religion. . . .[19]

[18] Russell, *Diary in India*, I, 356.
[19] Lord Cromer, *Ancient and Modern Imperialism*, New York, 1910,
p. 49.

The Roman empire had been an arbitrary autocracy; the British empire was ruled, not by a despot with military legions at his command, but by an entire nation, and that nation one which possessed liberal institutions of government insuring the just nature of the rule it would provide to subject peoples.

> From this thraldom to the past, to the ideal of Rome, Imperial Britain, first amongst modern empires, completely breaks. For it is a new empire which Imperial Britain presents to our scrutiny, a new empire moulded by a new ideal. . . . [The Imperialism] of the ancient world, little modified by medieval experiments limits itself to concrete, to external justice, imparted to subject peoples from above, from some beneficent monarch or tyrant; the later, the Imperialism of the modern world, the Imperialism of Britain, has for its end the larger freedom, the higher justice whose root is in the soul not of the ruler but of the race.[20]

Comparisons of this sort between Roman and British imperialism involved a dubious and also dangerous presumption: that a nation could be Christian without wishing that its subjects be Christian; that a nation could have the best interests of its subjects at heart without wishing them to be free; and that a nation could itself enjoy self-governing institutions without feeling an obligation to extend them to its subjects. England in these years attempted to act simultaneously the role of a democratic nation and an imperial autocrat, a feat possible only by conceiving of its basic principles as exclusive attributes of the British race.

British imperialism, precisely because it was national, was inescapably discriminatory in nature. The Roman empire had not been characterized by rigorous social exclusiveness. As Lord Cromer pointed out, "Trajan, Marcus Aurelius, and Seneca were Spaniards. Septimus Severus belonged to a Gallic family,

[20] J. A. Cramb, *The Origins and Destiny of Imperial Britain*, London, 1915, p. 18.

and was born in Africa."[21] An empire based on law was capable
of extension to a multitude of peoples. Roman citizenship was
not defined in racial terms, and because of this, Rome was able
to enlist the genuine allegiance of peoples of varying origin. As
C. E. Trevelyan noted,

> The provincials of Italy, Spain, Africa, and Gaul . . . re-
> mained to the last faithful subjects of the empire; and the
> union was at last dissolved, not by internal revolt, but by the
> shock of external violence, which involved conquerors and
> conquered in one common overthrow. The Indians will, I
> hope, soon stand in the same position toward us. . . . It will be
> a shame to us if, with our greatly superior advantages, we also
> do not make our premature departure be dreaded as a
> calamity.[22]

But England's greatly superior advantages had not only won
her an empire, they had produced a national pride in that very
superiority which, far from inspiring loyalty and enthusiasm
among the provincials, was capable of inspiring only resigna-
tion or reaction. England's empire was never one in which the
provincials could feel they had an important stake. In the days
of St. Paul, Roman citizenship had been a legal status whose
possession entitled any provincial, whatever his nationality, to
certain privileges. Citizenship in the British empire, regardless
of promises contained in proclamations by the Queen, was
firmly based on national exclusiveness, on "the straightforward
assertion of . . . the superiority of the conquering race."[23]
The national character of British imperialism affected it from
beginning to end and influenced to a greater or less extent every
Englishman who went to India from the earliest times. Even
when sexual liaisons were common between Englishmen and
Indian women, the relationships were casual and children of
mixed parentage were poorly provided for. Charles Grant spoke

[21] Cromer, *Imperialism*, pp. 36-38.
[22] C. E. Trevelyan, *Education of People of India*, pp. 196-97.
[23] J. F. Stephen, *Letter to the Times*, 1 March 1883.

for every school of thought, both before and after his time, when in 1792, after praising the efforts of Alexander the Great to make his European and Asiatic subjects "one people," he added: "It would never suit us, nor our subjects, to act universally as Alexander proposed. We ought not to wish, that the distinctions between the two races should be lost."[24] Grant hoped to see British and Indians—though racially distinct—"one people" in rights, religion, and manners, not realizing that laws, religion, and manners associated with an exclusive conquering group could never form the basis of the stable dominion with which even the conquered could identify—as had once been provided by a Roman law open to all without distinction of nationality. What most distinguished British from Roman imperialism was not the fact that Britain was Christian, reformist, or democratic; it was that British imperialism was based on nationality rather than law.

In the eighteenth century, when English merchant adventurers, pillaging and scavenging on the dying Moghul Empire, contended that they should be judged according to Oriental custom, they were judged in England by very different standards. The assumption in England even at this time was that Englishmen in India were not simply independent predators but were essentially Englishmen in India, whose conduct was a proper concern of other Englishmen. The English nabobs did not dispute the contention; in fact, they created the political issue of their conduct themselves by their insistence on recognition in England for their achievements in India. They were not interested in sinking into the obscurity of an Oriental despot's harem; they wanted to be English lords and treated as heroes of the English nation. They wanted their conduct to be judged by Eastern standards, but their success admired by English standards. In this sense, Clive and Hastings were just as alien to India as the civil official of a century later who sent his children to schools in England and sighed for his retirement home at Tunbridge Wells.

[24] Grant, "Observations," p. 114.

The English in India never became anything other than Englishmen, never were content with any form of honorable recognition other than that which their own country could provide; and England was never content simply to watch her merchant company sink or swim as fortune dictated. The great French adventurer Dupleix was dishonored, imprisoned, and beheaded by the French monarch as a reward for his services in India. England both censured and honored Clive and Hastings; in doing so, she implicitly recognized that they could not be made scapegoats because the nation was involved with their activities. The handful of East India Company servants who conquered India felt themselves, and were felt to be in England, ultimately representatives of the nation. This identification with England served to inspire lone adventurers to perform feats of daring and to sustain them with material aid when their daring led them into perilous straits.

England's national cohesiveness had won her an empire, but not the right to deny nationality to others. The attempt to transform England's conquered territories into permanent appendages was shipwrecked on the same rock which had provided England with her empire in the first place. National identity, national pride, national exclusiveness, could fire England to great exploits, but was not a basis on which a permanent multinational empire could be built up. Theories might be devised denying Indian nationality as a logical impossibility, but theories could not dispose of Indian nationalism once it did in fact exist.

CHAPTER VIII

The Attempted Orientalization of British Rule

> That [the British government] was a despotism was
> not to its discredit in Indian eyes. The Oriental
> understands no other form of government. . . . To
> the Oriental, if he could understand it, a democracy
> would appear a mere irreligious anarchy, and an
> aristocracy a confederate band of robbers.
>
> —AL CARTHILL[1]

> "Your sentiments are those of a god," she said
> quietly. . . .
> Trying to recover his temper, he said, "India likes
> gods."
> "And Englishmen like posing as gods."[2]

ONE of the results of the determination to make British control
of India just and enduring was a seemingly paradoxical resurgence of Orientalism. Reformers from Charles Grant to Fitzjames Stephen had all presumed that England's rightful claim
to dominance in India was founded on the efficacy of English
character and law. Grant considered that the Indian tradition
was productive only of political rebelliousness and instability;
Stephen felt that the determination of British policy should
never take into account native views, or be bound by accepted
forms. In the latter years of the century a very different point
of view emerged which sought to demonstrate the validity of
the traditional Indian way of doing things. Instead of studying
how to reconcile Indians to Western concepts—whether it
should be by education or force—some Englishmen now talked
of what was required by "an Oriental country like India." Almost all Englishmen partook of this perspective to an extent; it

[1] Al Carthill (pseud.), *The Lost Dominion*, Edinburgh: William Blackwood and Sons, 1924, p. 44.
[2] Forster, *Passage to India*, p. 50.

was developed in its most complete form, however, by men in subordinate positions in the hierarchy who advanced their proposals as part of an attack on what they considered to be unimaginative bureaucratic government. Much more "Orientalization" was thus proposed than actually implemented, but its effect on some areas of British policy was substantial.

The ultimate superiority of English culture and character was not brought into question by this approach; Englishmen were content to remain the same people with the same values. What changed was the perception of the relevance and relationship of English character and values to Indian society. It was not proposed that England abandon her principles but rather that she dramatize and embellish them to appeal to her Oriental audience. The Orientalizer agreed with Grant and disagreed with Stephen in feeling that Indian opinion was important; but disagreed with the conviction of both Grant and Stephen that India could be changed. Grant had felt that so long as India remained Hindu, she could feel no affection for her English rulers; the Orientalizer contended that British rule could and should be made appealing to the Hindu mind, which it now seemed hopeless to attempt to change.

Insofar as Indian values were held irrelevant to the practice of British government, no special advantage seemed to be attached to an appreciation of things Indian. Many Englishmen cultivated scholarly hobbies, and became specialists in Indian subjects, but the inability to sympathize with the Indian point of view, far from being disabling, had seemed to many an actual qualification, a necessary reflection of the superiority of British character. It was precisely because Englishmen were "immeasurably exalted above the natives by their European cultivation and character of intellect," in this view, that difficulties arose in attempts to understand "all these strange Asiatics, who live and move and have their being in an atmosphere of tradition in which Anglo–Saxon Christians cannot draw a single breath of life."[8] The attitude of the reformers had been typified by Lord

[8] Martineau, *Suggestions*, pp. 12-17.

Cornwallis, who had removed himself from personal contact with Indians in order to regulate their fate more justly; by Macaulay, who felt that familiarity with Indian languages whose range ran only from absurdity to obscenity, far from being a necessary preliminary to deliberation regarding their fate, could only result in contamination; and by James Mill, who ignored the relevance of existing social customs to the determination of new legal arrangements. Lack of understanding of Indian people, Indian languages, and Indian customs seemed to such people a proof of moral superiority; and lack of sympathy a necessary precondition to the dissemination among Indians of superior British ways. The Orientalizer's attitude, in contrast, presumed both that Indians could not be changed, and further, that the superiority of British character presented no obstacles to a full understanding of Indians. Englishmen remained ordinarily as isolated as ever from Indian society, captives equally of their official positions and the confining nature of British Indian society, but many prided themselves nonetheless on a knowledge of the complexities of Indian character. The Orientalizer's ideal was the man "in whom . . . a thorough knowledge of Asiatics and a thoroughly English spirit were united."[4] Ross Mangles, a prominent director of the East Indian Company, contended in 1853 that "there were hundreds of European servants of the Company who knew far more of India and of its inhabitants than any of the Natives themselves."[5] In 1908, when Morley proposed that an Indian be included in the Viceroy's Executive Council, he argued that it would be desirable to have someone on the council who "knew the country." This argument was answered by the Marquess of Lansdowne, a former viceroy, who exclaimed, "What country? There are a great many countries in India. If the noble Viscount could discover a native gentleman who knew the whole of the Indian Empire, and could speak authoritatively on behalf of all the different races and creeds con-

[4] Sir Herbert Edwardes' description of Sir George Clerk, in Edwardes and Merivale, *Henry Lawrence*, p. 323.

[5] Metcalf, *Aftermath of Revolt*, p. 262.

cerned, I should say by all means, give him a place on the Viceroy's Council. . . ."⁶ The implication of Lansdowne's remark that no Indian could be expected to "know India" was that Englishmen knew it much better.

A popular stereotype in British fiction, which has continued to thrive down to the present day, is the Englishman elaborately stained with walnut juice who can pass with complete freedom and anonymity along the byways of Indian society. This genre, of which Kipling's *Kim* is the classic, and of which John Masters is the best known modern practitioner, appealed to the British presumption that Indian society held no secrets for them. Despite the popularity of the legend, there was little substance to the idea that Britishers could easily pass as natives if they chose. Only a rare Englishman would not have been betrayed by his physique, carriage, accent, and manner, even if he were fluent in the language.

Englishmen constructed a myth of their own omniscience, and a further myth which presumed to describe the "real India." Conceived as a guide for adapting British government to Indian needs, it served to convince many Englishmen that they were serving Indian interests and successfully winning Indian appreciation. This "real India" consisted of the ancient India of the countryside; and of retainers and dependents of British power, of princes, peasants, and minority groups. Indians who lived in cities, engaged in business and the professions, who were not dependent on British favor, without an interest in preserving for themselves a privileged position guaranteed by British might, were designated "unrepresentative." After travelling for several months throughout India in 1883, consciously seeking out the acquaintance of the urban middle classes of Indians, Wilfred Blunt was told by Sir James Fergusson, Governor of Bombay, that the natives were satisfied with British rule. Blunt's reaction was to wonder, "Who then are the people Sir James gets his

⁶ Syed Razi Wasti, *Lord Minto and the Indian Nationalist Movement, 1905-1910*, London: Oxford University Press, p. 152, from Hansard, House of Lords, 4s, Vol. 198, Cols. 1995-1996.

ideas from? Who are the satisfied natives? I have not met a single one since I came to India."[7] Fergusson, like most Englishmen, felt that British rule "spoke for the voiceless masses" and could afford to ignore the articulated grievances of educated Indians. "There are some people who clamour for boons which it is impossible to give," noted Lord Curzon, "but the administrator looks rather to the silent and inarticulate masses."[8] The emergence of middle class Indians, to whose appearance Macaulay had looked forward with such pleasure, was now greeted by many with condescending disregard, such as that of Curzon, and with comments of the type, "Isn't it funny to see them eating with knives and forks?" Englishmen sought to impose on Indians their own conception of what Indians were supposed to be like, so that now "A European magistrate reprimands a native pleader for appearing in court with his shoes on"[9]—for acting, in other words, the way Englishmen were supposed to act rather than the way Orientals were supposed to act. An India of the imagination was created which contained no elements of either social change or political menace. Orientalization was the result of this effort to conceive of Indian society as devoid of elements hostile to the perpetuation of British rule, for it was on the basis of this presumptive India that Orientalizers sought to build a permanent rule.

Orientalization had serious consequences for British policy in regard to Indian society. Insofar as it concerned the internal conduct of British government, however, it involved not the essence of British government but rather the way in which it appeared to Indians. It was not ordinarily advocated that Englishmen should become Oriental in their personal lives, or that all legal process should be thrown to the winds. The concern was rather that the traditional sentiments of Indians toward their government be consciously appealed to in the hope that British justice might inspire the same enthusiasm as had the ceremonials of the

---

[7] Blunt, *India Under Ripon*, p. 223.

[8] Bennett, *Concept of Empire*, pp. 346-48.

[9] Dilke, *Greater Britain*, p. 469.

old regime. By the same token, it was occasionally proposed that Indians be encouraged in their belief that Englishmen had knowledge of the supernatural because they could illuminate Calcutta with "lamps without wicks," and practice telegraphy, "and other such necromancy"[10] inspiring Indians with awe and reverence. This notion, with which Kipling toyed with considerable pleasure, implied that Englishmen might be able to combine the hereditary position and authority of King Arthur with the know-how of Twain's Connecticut Yankee. In place of the earlier contention that Indians would be impressed and improved by a direct exposure to British principles, Kipling and others now urged that they should be retained, but shrouded in a "veil of illusion" which would make them appear in the light best suited to impress convention-bound Indians.

In pursuing this end, Orientalizers sought out those aspects of the Indian political, religious, and social traditions felt to be compatible with British rule and endeavored to give them as much encouragement as possible through measures of public policy. In regard to political ideas, for instance, new enthusiasm emerged for the Oriental tradition of despotic rule. Brigadier-General Jacob felt that "to the Anglo–Saxon race self-government is essential. But force the Oriental to take his share in government, and you will soon have no government at all. It is obvious that two races of men with principles of action and feelings different, can never be successfully managed by adopting one system, and forcing it alike on both."[11]

Theodore Morison, who served as the principal of the Mohammedan Anglo–Oriental College at Aligarh, as a member of the Viceroy's Legislative Council and finally as a member of the Secretary of State for India's Council in England, felt that many of the techniques of Oriental despotism could be used profitably by the British government of India. He noted that in a despotism the sovereign could solidify all factions behind it by acting willfully, by discriminating use of favoritism, and urged this course upon the viceroy. Fitzjames Stephen had written,

[10] Martineau, *Suggestions*, p. 46.   [11] Pelly, *John Jacob*, p. 1.

I believe that the real foundation of our power will be found to be an inflexible adherence to broad principles of justice common to all persons in all countries and all ages, and enforced with unflinching firmness in favor, or against, everyone who claims their benefit or who presumes to violate them, no matter who he may be. To govern impartially upon these broad principles is to govern justly, and I believe that not only justice itself, but the honest attempt to be just, is understood and acknowledged in every part of the world alike.[12]

Stephen's watchword was impartiality; but it was precisely *partiality* whose necessity Morison urged. Impartiality, Morison felt, had, far from gaining the enthusiastic respect of Indians, dangerously alienated their wavering affections:

Monarchy [he wrote] has from its very essence this advantage over democracy, that whereas the demagogue wins to power by expatiating to the sovereign people upon the multitude of their grievances which the existing government has failed to redress, even the most opposite factions at court will vie with each other in protesting their satisfaction with the existing constitution. . . . It is only in obedience to one great master that all can unite without heart-burning.[13]

It is difficult to believe that an heir of the traditions of England, containing the histories of King John, Charles I, James II, and George III could urge such a principle of government. But Morison's description of monarchy was not designed to evoke images from England's past, but rather those of traditional India.

If any tourist . . . wishes to enter into the political ideas of the people of India . . . when the glare of day has softened to a golden haze and the dusty droves of cattle are returning to their stalls, let him accompany the Rajah on his evening ride.

[12] J. F. Stephen, quoted in Leslie Stephen, *Life of Fitzjames Stephen*, pp. 263-64.

[13] Theodore Morison, *Imperial Rule in India*, Westminster: Archibald Constable, 1899, pp. 44-45.

From the gateway of the fort, the Rajah's elephant, in long housings of velvet and cloth of gold, comes shuffling down the steep declivity; on his back, in a silver howdah, sits the Rajah, laden with barbaric pearl and gold; behind him clatter his kinsmen and retainers on brightly caparisoned horses; these horses are, for the most part, pink-nosed, squealing brutes, but they are controlled by a standing martingale and a spiky bit, and make a brave show. As the cavalcade winds down the narrow streets the men pick up their swords and hurry forward; the women and children rush to the doors of their houses, and all the people gaze upon their prince with an expression of almost ecstatic delight; as the elephant passes, each man puts one hand to the ground and shouts "Maharaj Ram Ram." The most indolent tourist cannot fail to notice the joy upon all the people's faces; and when the cavalcade winds home and he realises the intensity of delight which the mere sight of their prince has caused the subjects, he will begin to understand the suitability of monarchy to certain phases of social evolution.[14]

English reformers from Macaulay to Fitzjames Stephen had possessed a hearty contempt for native principles of government, as well as for the persons and conduct of the native princes. Native rule had had defenders in the first half of the century, people reluctant to witness the destruction of all foci of traditional loyalty, but even they usually advocated the maintenance of the native states more as a matter of policy than from a conviction that native principles of government were positively beneficial, or superior to direct British government. Mountstuart Elphinstone, for instance, a warm advocate of the maintenance of princely government, urged the retention of the princes on somewhat cynical grounds. He felt that "Every Indian government (perhaps every Asiatic one) expires after a very short existence,"[15] and thus that the Company need not bother to dispense with governments who would so rapidly ex-

[14] *Ibid.*, pp. 48-49.   [15] Thompson, *Princes*, p. 277.

terminate themselves. In the meantime, while independent princes still managed to maintain themselves,

> Their territories afford a refuge to all those whose habits of war, intrigue, or depredation make them incapable of remaining quiet in ours; and the contrast of their government has a favourable effect on our subjects. . . . If the existence of independent powers gives occasional employment to our armies, it is far from being a disadvantage.[16]

Even Colonel Tod, for all his enthusiasm for Rajput history and his dedication to maintaining Rajput independence, defended the Rajput princes because of their vices almost as much as their virtues. In his *Annals and Antiquities of Rajasthan,* published between 1829 and 1832, he argued that the chivalric code of the princes of Rajasthan made them incapable of cooperation with one another; they were always fighting amongst themselves over some question of honor. The only thing that might unite them in a common cause was supersession by the British. Tod thus argued that the maintenance of the privileges of the princes would not be harmful to British sovereignty, while their supersession might have dangerous results. Despite his nostalgic admiration for the noble Rajput ready to stake everything on a question of honor, Colonel Tod did not suggest that the princely states represented political systems which the government of British India would be wise to emulate. But the reconstruction of at least the externals of Indian government on the pattern of the native states was precisely what Morison was eager for.

> Even the dullest imagination would be kindled at the sight of the royal standard floating over the majestic gateway of Akbar's fort in Agra; of the British horse guards in their polished cuirasses, lining the gloomy court of guard; and of the royal cavalcade, emerging from beneath the venerable archway.[17]

Morison argued that the Indian in his present state of develop-

[16] *Ibid.,* p. 271.   [17] Morison, *Imperial Rule,* p. 146.

ment needed colorful pageantry much more than he needed representative government. And though Morison was eager that more be done in this line, the Indian government in the second half of the century was undoubtedly much more preoccupied than previously with the creation of spectacles; the Viceregal durbar became a regular event.

Some Englishmen advocated that British India should also adopt the procedures of government followed in the princely states, not simply their trappings. Lt. Col. Davidson, in 1859, for instance, defended the employment of foreign mercenaries in preference to Indian troops by noting that,

> The native governments have long since given us a practical lesson as to their opinion of the loyalty and fidelity of the sepoy soldiery of India. It will be found that their most trusted troops were always foreign mercenaries. The Nizam has at this present moment in his employ 18,000 Arabs and about 5,000 Rohillas (Affghans) and many more of the latter tribes are in his territory seeking employment. Not a petty rajah in Guzerat but has, or endeavors to have, his Arab or foreign guard, however small it may be numerically for the protection of his person and treasury; alleging they find the foreign mercenaries faithful while their own immediate subjects cannot be trusted.[18]

Law enforcement as practiced in the princely states also drew substantial praise, which increased with the emergence of the Indian nationalist movement. Many Englishmen pointed to the way in which the princes dealt with political troublemakers in their own states and deplored the chaos which English administrators seemed incapable of checking in British India where legal process played into the hands of agitators. British India seemed to these men to be characterized by a growing systematization of government, rigidifying into a mindless formalism,

[18] *Parliamentary Papers*, 1859, "Papers Connected with the Reorganization of the Army in India Supplementary to the Report of the Army Commission," p. 229.

spiritless and incomprehensible to Indians. The objection was not only to bureaucratic petrification, however, but to the very concept underlying the bureaucracy: that system and regularity were in any sense desirable. Just as Indians were thought to require the stimulation of pageantry and the drama of a personal sovereign, so also were they presumed to need government personified at every level. Only if authority were clearly summed up and embodied in the official of government with whom Indians had to deal directly, and the authority to decide a point of dispute placed clearly in the official's power rather than entangled in the mystical interpretation of incomprehensible printed regulations, they argued, could government at any level command respect.

Bartle Frere, in a letter to Lt. Col. Durand of November 6, 1858, warned against what he called "pseudo-centralization":

> Our attempts at centralization during the last 25 years . . . have been all by departments instead of by persons. I know of no successful instance of the kind in history, and it appears to me to be the true, almost the only source, of general decay of vital power ominously coincident with dropsical increase in the extent of the body. . . . To our native subjects nothing is more bewildering than this infinite subdivision of authority.[19]

In his written reply, dated two days later, to the questions submitted to him by the Commissioners on Army Organization, Frere elaborated his reasons for objecting to the dilution of authority in discussing the merits of Army Regulations. He wrote,

> Asiatic soldiers . . . come all of races habituated to despotic government. . . . The grant of rights which they can enforce against their sovereign and employer simply puzzles them, and a code like the articles of war and army regulations, by giving rise to vague notions of some ill-understood rights, which some unknown authority is apparently suspected of wishing to subvert, creates a vague feeling of suspicion and

[19] *Ibid.*, pp. 61-62.

discontent. . . . An Englishman asks "What are my rights and duties?" The Asiatic guesses what they will be by the answer to his question, which is always, "Who is my master?" and amid all the intricacies and divided responsibilities of our present system, this is a question to which he can rarely get a clear and decided answer. In some respects his adjutant or commanding officer, the brigadier or adjutant-general, the commander-in-chief or governor in council are all, more or less, his masters; but he can never clearly understand the exact relation of each authority to the other, still less can he find the one master whose will to him is law, for he still perceives behind the government itself some power which prevents the government from being absolutely despotic.[20]

Such a state of affairs would not have existed for long if S. S. Thorburn had had his way. Thorburn, best known for his work for cooperative credit among the peasantry,[21] also had plans for the revitalization of the entire government structure, which he embodied in a novel published in 1897 entitled *His Majesty's Greatest Subject*. His grievance against the government was that it honored the wrong men for the wrong reasons:

> To oscillate between an office stool in Calcutta and Simla, occasionally see villages from a first-class compartment in a mail or special train, and frequently accord interviews to polished native gentlemen, one and all veneered imitations of Englishmen, is not the way to learn India . . . yet this had usually been all the previous experience of India undergone by the men selected to fill . . . high offices . . . the Viceregal Council, or the Governorship of a Province. . . . It was a system excellently suited for a commercial nation with a preponderance of sharp practitioners [i.e., the Hindu merchant] but utterly unsuited for the good governance of ignorant peasants. . . .[22]

[20] *Ibid.*, p. 58.
[21] Praised by Woodruff in *The Men Who Ruled India*, II, 159-62.
[22] S. S. Thorburn, *His Majesty's Greatest Subject*, New York: Appleton, 1897, p. 101. Fitzjames Stephen wrote to John Stuart Mill that "though it

Thorburn's remedy for this situation was unfolded in a narrative of two brothers, one of whom, because he is several minutes older, becomes a Lord, while his younger duplicate is forced to seek his fortune in the backwoods of India. The younger brother Jack learns to speak Indian languages like a native and ultimately ends up posing as the aged counselor of the Princess of Sunderabad while in fact serving as her lover. The older brother, having become a nondescript and timorous Lord, is appointed Viceroy of India. During a visit to Sunderabad the Viceroy dies while in private conference with the Princess and her aged advisor, who instantly assumes his brother's position, determining to live a lie for the sake of the preservation of the Empire. Though he would now have been the rightful Lord in any case he would not in the normal course of events have succeeded as well to his brother's appointive position, the Viceroyalty. The crisis which the Empire faces and his own superior perception of how to deal with it, however, justify in his eyes his assumption of the Noble Lie that he is in fact the very Viceroy appointed by the Crown.

Through this less than inspired literary device, Thorburn has provided India with the Oriental despot which he feels the situation requires. The crisis the Viceroy is called on to face is both internal and external. On the domestic front, the new Viceroy acts with dispatch. "Now and again we caught a preacher of sedition, *flagrante delicto*, and hanged him quietly without fuss; otherwise life rolled on as usual."[23] "One morning India awoke to find that three hundred leading busybodies had disappeared."[24] Externally, the long-anticipated war with Russia had finally materialized. Russia and France had combined and the decisive war was finally to be fought. The Viceroy cuts the telegraph cable to London, attributing the failure in communica-

---

may seem absurd to talk of seeing a country merely by hurtling through it in a railway, I really have seen a good deal of India. . . ." Stephen to Mill, dated Simla, 3 August 1871, Stephen Papers.

[23] Thorburn, *His Majesty's Greatest Subject*, p. 72.

[24] *Ibid.*, p. 98.

tion with England to the perversity of the French. Thus cut off
from his Secretary of State for months at a time, the Viceroy is
free to pursue his policies without challenge or contradiction.
Vast congresses of Hindus and Muslims are convened at Bena-
ras and Delhi and their loyalty secured through patronage of
learning. The Viceroy's final triumph comes with the decisive
defeat of the Russians at Kabul. "If my friend, Sir Power Oli-
phant [the Commander-in-Chief] was now celebrated as Siva,
the war god, I was adored as Indra, the storm-compeller, and
controller of the universe."[25] Though worshipped as a Hindu
deity, the Viceroy nonetheless remains faithful to his Muslim
princess whom he marries in a triumphant consolidation of the
interests of the princely states and the Empire as well as of the
"two masterful races of India,"[26] the "two peoples of the Book,"
Christians and Muslims. "It brought home to all wealthy and
educated Hindu malcontents, throughout the length and
breadth of the peninsula, their own impotence in the face of
such a combination."[27]

Here is the program of the Orientalizers in the full flower of
wish-fulfillment. The external problem is a simple one: a war
between empires into which Germany has not protruded. The
internal crisis is a simple one: unrepresentative and self-seeking
Hindu malcontents whom indecision has permitted to flourish
require only a show of strength, a vigorous expression of favoritism, to wilt. The administrative problem is a simple one: cut
the cable to England, undercut the bureaucrats of Simla and
institute ruthless, direct measures by an Orientalized despot who
thinks instinctively as an Akbar would, who speaks like a native, is worshipped by one religious faction and marries a Princess of the other.

Thorburn's wholesale condemnation of the conduct of British
government, his advocacy of arbitrary personal rule at all levels
of government, his contempt for due process and the bureaucrats who thrived by adhering to it, were common attitudes in
the later years of the century among that class of administrators

[25] *Ibid.*, p. 299.   [26] *Ibid.*, p. 274.   [27] *Ibid.*

who had not prospered in an era of bureaucratic promotion, who served out their careers in subordinate positions in the provinces and who resented both the growing extent of supervision of their local concerns by those higher in the bureaucracy, and their own supersession for promotion. Combining a dislike for those who had advanced where they had failed with a dislike for the system which seemed to undervalue their own qualities, many disgruntled district officers, making common cause with private Englishmen who also felt neglected, predicted ruin would result from following the current procedures of government. The proposal to Orientalize the whole governmental structure was normally a form of attack on current practice mounted by people with grievances, personal as well as ideological, and had no major effect on official policy; the attack, in fact, characteristically took the form of private complaints, or was expressed in fiction or books published anonymously indicating the uneasiness which was felt about publicly attacking official superiors on whom one was dependent for promotion or favors. The preferred procedure of officialdom was to maintain bureaucratic forms, and employ Oriental political notions only to provide a facade of dramatic brilliance for the customary framework of impartial bureaucracy.

Just as most Englishmen began to stress the useful aspects of Indian principles of government, so also did they find Indian religions compatible with British purposes and consequently worthy of praise. Muslims were "People of the Books," believers in a religion nurtured in the same environment from which Christianity had sprung—and usefully antagonistic to Hindus. And surely Hinduism's very power of survival seemed to argue —Bentham notwithstanding—that it possessed considerable merit. Those who spoke in defense of Indian religions were not likely to have repudiated their own Christian beliefs. There were few men in official positions inclined to follow the path taken by Annie Besant in championing the superiority of Indian religions over Christianity. The argument characteristically was that Hinduism—or Sikhism or Islam—was good for Indians and useful for British ends. W. W. Hunter, for instance, expounded the social role of Hinduism in a fashion which anticipated the modern findings of anthropologists:[28]

> Recent careful observers . . . think that Hinduism has yet much work to do. They point out that its old task of absorbing the races of India into a religious and social federation is still unfinished. The low castes are yearly creeping upwards to higher standards of ceremonial observance, the outcastes are coming within the pale, the hill and forest peoples are entertaining Brahmin priests and copying Hindu rites. Whether the rise of the low castes in the ceremonial scale is a gain to them in this life seems doubtful, but it is not a question which they will ask us to decide. To the aboriginal races, with their witch-finders and murrain-spreaders, and perpetual fear of sorcerers and devils, the advantage is more evident. A Brahman has only to set up his leaf hut in their glens and to mark a stone or trunk of a tree with a daub of red paint, and the poor malignant spirits of the forest flee before the powerful Hindu gods. . . . I have no sympathy with those who would minimise the results of Christian missionary enterprise in India. But the Indian census,[29] in spite of obscurities of classification, proves that Hinduism is a religion which has not yet exhausted its mandate. For the hundreds which it loses to Christianity, or to Islam, or to the new theistic sects, thousands of the lower races crowd into its fold.[30]

Hunter presented a picture of a felicitous coincidence of interests between Hinduism and British policy. An episode of the 1850s has been noted above[31] in which the Indian desire for the construction of roads to a place of pilgrimage was scornfully overruled by British authorities in the name of trade; Hunter

[28] Cf., e.g., M. N. Srinivas, "A Note on Sanscritization and Westernization," in his *Caste in Modern India*, Bombay, 1962, pp. 42-43.

[29] Of which Hunter was director.

[30] Hunter, *India of the Queen*, pp. 35-36.

[31] Chap. VI.

contended that building railroads to pilgrimage sites was desirable for all concerned. The British made a profit, the Hindus got to their destination more rapidly, and (so Hunter trusted) by riding on Western rails inevitably lost something of their fanaticism:

> The railways, which have rendered the political unity of India under the Queen possible, tend also to the consolidation of the national faiths. The path of pilgrimage has been made smooth. . . . For the leading Hindu shrines convenient branch railways have been constructed, which give fair promise of 6 per cent dividends and shares at 25 above par. The more secluded temples still have their old fashioned worshippers. But the chances of a god doing a large and increasing business are greatly improved by a railway station. Juggernaut himself, after defying the calumnies of a century, now finds his popularity imperilled for want of railway communication. . . . But pilgrimage by return ticket, with children at half-fares, while it promotes joyous gatherings of the people in honour of the gods, is death to fanaticism.[82]

Hunter thus echoed the pious optimism of Lord Auckland that the pagan rituals of Hinduism might in time become "as innocent as Harvest-home," not to mention of profit to British investors. Indian religious sentiments were, moreover, as useful for political as for economic ends. Theodore Morison pointed out that all Indian religions taught obedience as a religious duty; why should Indians not be encouraged to believe that obedience to the British was similarly a religious duty? Queen Victoria, so Morison noted, was already viewed in some quarters as something of a divinity. He quoted an extract from the vernacular press which read,

> We are singing the praises of Mother Victoria . . . Queen Victoria protects as the Divine Mother. She is more than a human being. She is a goddess. . . .[83]

[82] Hunter, *India of the Queen*, p. 36.
[83] Morison, *Imperial Rule in India*, p. 52. Of such eulogies, John Beames

The fact could be pointed to that John Clevland's tomb was dec-
orated with flowers by Indians for years following his death and
that he was worshipped as a local divinity in the province he
had pacified. Or that an order of "Nikal Sehni Fakirs" dedicated
to the memory of the awesome Nicholson lasted for some years
after his death.[34] As Thorburn's novel had suggested, Indians
could find room in the Hindu pantheon for terrible as well as
benevolent divinities.

On a less intoxicating level, the uses of the Sikh religion for
British military purposes were noted. Just as railroads seemed to
serve equally British and Hindu ends, so did service in the army
by Sikhs seem a happy coincidence of interest. Edmund Candler
observed that

> It has often been said that the Indian Army has kept
> Sikhism alive. Without . . . the door open to military service
> the ineradicable instincts of the Hindu reassert themselves.
> . . . War is a necessary stimulus for Sikhism.[35]

If Sikhism needed the army, so obviously could the British exploit for their own purposes the martial traditions of the Sikh
community.

The British were discovering new virtues as well in the traditional organization of the society over which they ruled, as
ideas presented themselves of ways in which that society could
be turned to British account. The India of nineteenth century
British conceptions was a static rural society in most places controlled by an hereditary aristocracy. Utilitarian reformers had
sought to "get this society moving" by breaking down obstacles
to the working of a laissez-faire economy; an effort was now
made to stabilize Indian society, to keep it from moving, by
eliminating the sources of instability which Utilitarian reforms

---

commented: "Your Bengali Babu can reel out this sort of stuff by the
fathom from morn till dewy eve and then begin again." Beames, *Memoirs*,
p. 236.

[34] Cf. Woodruff, *Men Who Ruled India*, i, 148, 341.

[35] Candler, *The Sepoy*, London: J. Murray, 1919, p. 29.

had introduced. Cooperative credit, control of money-lenders, and restriction of land sales were among the reform movements that attracted the attention of men such as Thorburn and much that was useful and humane was accomplished. Somewhat less admirable, however, was the parallel effort to save the landed aristocracy from themselves.

British officialdom felt the need for a powerful class of natives loyal to British rule because of the stake they would have in its perpetuation. They consequently supported princes and landlords and justified their support by asserting that they were the natural leaders of Indian society. If they were natural leaders, and Indian popular loyalty was transferred uncritically from one generation to the next, as the myth protested was the case, it was presumably necessary for the British government to put up with this hereditary class whatever its merits might be. The British, whose energetic policy of destroying traditional positions whose occupants seemed no longer to justify their trust had helped bring down the Mutiny upon them, now actually set about resurrecting rulers of princely states and classes of landlords. No dereliction, incompetence, enfeeblement, or immorality would henceforth persuade the British to take the step which was taken in Oudh in 1856 when the debasement of the Oudh Court led to its extinction at the hands of Lord Dalhousie. Those who were designated natural leaders might have risen to power within living memory; but now their influence was declared to be sanctioned by the immemorial traditions of Indian society.

India, however, had never been characterized by serene social balance. Much more normal had been a struggle for power, in which no prince or landlord could maintain himself indefinitely merely on the credit of a distinguished ancestry. The introduction by the reformers of the concept of the legal alienability of land had not introduced change into a stable society; it had only supplanted one process of struggle and evolution by another. Indian society had never been incapable of change, nor had the British thought it was, until the initiation of efforts to make their own presence in India permanent. British officials opposed the disruption of traditional society which they felt Western legal and commercial institutions had caused; but the kind of traditional society they attempted to re-create had never existed before and existed now only by the conscious efforts of British policy. The British effort to make themselves permanent rulers of India led them to an attempt to arrest by artificial means the normal process of evolution that had always characterized India, and whose form alone had been affected by the early phases of British rule.

The "traditional" social structure which England attempted to guarantee was in a number of important respects actually an innovation on the Indian scene. As Sir Alfred Lyall observed,

> In Asia hereditary succession actually means the succession to each vacancy of the ablest and most popular of the ruling dynasty or tribal family, the incompetent being rapidly eliminated as failures after short and sharp experiment. When no able man turns up for a dynastic vacancy, the dynasty collapses. . . . A strict law of hereditary succession to petty Asiatic despotisms is not a very promising political innovation; it renders the chief independent of personal qualifications, and makes him reckless of offending anyone except only the British Government . . . the paramount power having arrested the operation of the natural law by which the fittest ruler prevails.[36]

Lyall's conclusion was that "The protected autocrat . . . has not yet turned out such a success that the English nation can feel proud of having brought him out upon the political stage."[37]

British officials were not blind to the difficulties such a policy had produced. They sought, however, to salvage the aristocrats at all costs, attempting to transform them into good natural leaders. The result was a solemn game of cat-and-mouse in which the British government hoped that the "natural" leaders of society would be just, and reprimanded them when they were

[36] Sir Alfred Lyall, *Asiatic Studies*, London, 1901, I, 233-34.
[37] *Ibid.*, p. 262.

not; hoped they would be good managers, and bailed them out by appointing British assistants when they fell into debt. British Residents and Prime Ministers helped princes govern their states, and British tutors oversaw the education of their sons. Wilfred Blunt described

> how young princes were brought up by the British Government when it happened to become their guardian. They are taught to ride and play lawn tennis, and the Resident writes that they are enlightened and loyal princes. Then they are placed on the throne, but find it dull, and go to Calcutta where they spend their money. Then they come back and grind their subjects with taxation, and the Resident writes that they are barbarous and unfit to govern. Lastly, the Government intervenes and administers the country for them.[88]

As Blunt's description suggests, the government's assumption about the correct form of education was the same as that current in England at the time. The public school emphasis on games as a training in character was confidently adapted to the training of Indian princes. A number of complete public schools designed for the sons of the aristocracy were also established. One such, the Colvin Taluqdars College at Lucknow, had as its motto, "Noblesse Oblige."

British officials felt compelled to assist the traditional aristocracy to do their duty by society, because they were convinced that society needed them. They went to extraordinary and embarrassing lengths to save the aristocracy from themselves—and from their society—on the assumption that they ought to be saved. In truth, however, it was the British who needed the nobility, not the peasantry. The British and the princes needed one another; India's need for either was highly doubtful and based on an assumption that India's needs and capacities would not change. The government's dependence on the political support of a class which could be kept alive only by artificial means marked the extent of the reversal in policy that had taken place;

[88] Blunt, *India Under Ripon*, p. 164.

once a radically revolutionary force in its impact on Indian society, British rule now devoted its vast resources to an attempt to prop up an enfeebled ruling class.

A further aspect of Indian society which seemed capable of exploitation for British purposes was its division into myriad castes and communities. Indian society was notoriously complex and compartmentalized, consisting of hosts of disparate communities living in greater or less isolation from one another. The British, until the middle years of the century, had been indisposed to take these divisions and distinctions seriously. The British were reluctant to make the distinctions their subjects made about themselves. Such distinctions seemed an inconvenience to the British and a reflection of the prejudice and oppressive traditionalism which were to be swept away by British reforms. The revitalized, egalitarian society envisioned as the result of the reforms seemed to make it incumbent on the British to refuse to countenance in their own administration the discrimination practiced by Indian groups toward one another. The new approach was to suggest that the British might with advantage exploit this divisiveness by playing Indian communities off against one another and by assuming that the complex divisions of Indian society made cooperation between them impossible. The British now conceived of themselves as a necessary buffer providing India with an invaluable service by their ability as an alien military power to keep Indian communities from falling upon one another. "England receives nothing from India except in return for English services rendered," observed Sir John Strachey. "In place of constant anarchy, bloodshed, and rapine, we have given to her peace, order, and justice; and if our Government were to cease, all the miseries from which she has been saved would inevitably and instantly return."[39] Lord Roberts, Indian commander-in-chief from 1885 to 1892, reported that intelligent Indians were not unaware or unappreciative of this service. He recounted

[39] Strachey, *India: Its Administration and Progress*, pp. 212-13.

a remark made to me by the late Sir Madhava Rao, ex-Minister of the Baroda State. Sir Madhava was one of the most astute Hindu gentlemen in India, and when discussing with him the excitement produced by the "Ilbert Bill," he said: "Why do you English raise these unnecessary questions? It is your doing, not ours. We have heard the cry, 'India for the Indians,' which some of your philanthropists have raised in England; but you have only to go to the Zoological Gardens and open the doors of the cages, and you will very soon see what would be the result of putting that theory into practise. There would be a terrific fight amongst the animals, which would end in the tiger walking proudly over the dead bodies of the rest." "Whom," I inquired, "do you consider to be the tiger?" "The Mahomedan from the North," was his reply.[40]

Such a view assumed that the natural condition of India was chaos, and that the various elements of Indian society were incapable of pacific cooperation with one another. The intricate procedures earlier Indian rulers had devised for eliciting cooperation among communities by honoring their separate distinctness were ignored; mutual animosities were considered ingrained, cooperation impossible, and the exploitation of communal animosity not oppressive but only a reflection of India's own desires and requirements. An important part of the "changeless East" of British conceptions were the enduring hatreds of Indian communities for one another, which made them all thankful that the British did not pitilessly leave them to their fate by withdrawing the force which stood between India and chaos.

The impressions of Indian character of the earlier part of the century, reflecting the wholesale condemnation of the reformers, had made little effort to distinguish between the relative merits of separate Indian communities. Bengali Hindu and Kashmiri Muslim were both described in terms of a relatively uniform Indian character. So long as the crucial determinant of character

[40] Roberts, *Forty-one Years in India*, II, 388.

was thought to be religion or social institutions, distinctions on the basis of community or region were out of the question. With the growth, however, of climatic and racial speculation, linked to the waning of hope for the rapid transformation of traditional Indian society, grew a new interest in making distinctions between the innumerable Indian communities. As part of the new British undertaking to preserve Indian society from chaos and mutual annihilation, an effort was made to pinpoint and utilize for British purposes the specialized abilities of India's numerous communities, as well as to regulate and neutralize their destructive propensities.

The clearest illustration of the implementation of this policy was in the reorganization of the Indian Army which followed the Mutiny. Englishmen in pre-Mutiny days had not been eager to recognize distinctions among their Indian recruits. What attention the British did pay to caste was usually a result of persistent Indian pressure. The army of the Marathas was organized on the basis of caste regiments, but the British in recruiting Marathas to oppose the successors of Shivaji initially neglected caste origin in forming companies. It was only as a result of the protests of high-caste soldiers against the indignity of being thrown together indiscriminately with such low-caste men as the Parwaris that the British reorganized the Bombay army on the basis of one company, one caste.[41]

Throughout the half-century preceding the Mutiny, a constant effort was made to eliminate the vestiges of caste which remained in the army. In 1807 the Paragraph in the "Code of Regulations relative to the Recruiting of the Army" which specified that

> Mussulmans and Hindus only are eligible to be enlisted for the cavalry or horse artillery; nor shall recruits of the inferior castes, viz., Pullah, Pariah, and Chuckler, be listed for the golundaze of infantry but under the most urgent necessity, when

[41] Sir Patrick Cadell, *History of the Bombay Army*, 1938, p. 15.

a special report shall be made to headquarters of the events, and of the circumstances which may have led to it. . . .[42]

was removed because of the feeling on the part of the commander-in-chief that this was unfairly discriminatory and that the lower castes should not be thus explicitly excluded from eligibility. On December 31, 1834 it was announced that

> The Governor-General of India in Council is pleased to direct that all objections to men belonging to the respectable classes, on account of caste or religion, shall cease to operate in respect to their admission into the ranks of the Bengal army.[43]

The British demonstrated a concern with counterpoise by maintaining the territorial isolation of the three Presidency Armies, and concentrating their recruitment among groups traditionally hostile to their immediate foes,[44] but they systematically sought to remove internal divisions within the Armies to make them more uniform and serviceable forces. This process culminated in 1856 with the adoption of the General Service Enlistment Act, under which the grouping in the armed services according to caste would have been formally abolished altogether, and all future recruits would be required to agree to march wherever ordered. The Act was only the logical conclusion of a series of efforts to make the army a rational and modern force. The reply came the following year in the great

[42] *Parliamentary Papers* (H.C.), "Returns (East India)," "Orders issued regarding the Castes of Hindoos from which the Native army is to be Recruited," 5 Feb. 1858, pp. 2-3.

[43] General Orders by His Excellency the Right Honourable Governor-General of India in Council; Fort William, 1834, No. 252 of 1834. *Ibid.*, p. 13.

[44] In the wars against the Hindu Marathas preference was given to Muslims. The situation was reversed in the wars against the Muslim prince Hyder Ali and his son Tipu Sultan which occupied the company in the south throughout the latter part of the eighteenth century. In Bengal the army was from the beginning overwhelmingly Hindu just as the company's rivals in that region remained predominantly Muslim.

Mutiny which similarly culminated a series of protests from the army against British disregard for Indian feelings. In these pre-Mutiny days, castes had to fight to preserve their integrity. After the Mutiny, it would be the British who would do everything they could to preserve caste and racial distinctness—a paradoxical success for the ideals of the mutinous sepoys.

The Mutiny of 1857 left intact only a fraction of the Bengal Army. Of eighty-four regular regiments existing in 1856, only seventeen survived even as administrative units by 1859. A new army had to be created, and there were obvious arguments in favor of altering the basis on which it was founded. The dominant feeling during and immediately after the Mutiny was the desire to reduce the entire army to an equality of contempt, to impose forcibly the uniform system to which high-caste Indians objected, "experience having taught that it was better to mingle the castes and disregard the prejudices so greatly pampered before."[45] The official "Report of the Commissioners appointed to inquire into the Organization of the Indian Army" recommended in 1859 "That the Native Army should be composed of different nationalities and castes, and as a general rule, mixed promiscuously through each regiment."[46] Such a procedure, it was felt, would minimize the danger of conspiracy. "The more the different classes and races are mixed so that no one tribe shall unduly predominate," observed Sir Patrick Grant, "the less chance there will be of combination against authority."[47]

The appeal of such a policy came not alone from the mood of righteous vindictiveness with which the Mutiny was suppressed, but in addition from a number of quite rational considerations. The Mutiny had taken place only in the Bengal Army, while

[45] T. H. Kavanaugh, *How I Won the Victoria Cross*, London: Ward and Lock, 1860, p. 172.

[46] *Parliamentary Papers*, (H.C.), 1859, "Report of the Army Commission" p. xiv.

[47] *Parliamentary Papers*, (H.C.), 1859 "Appendix to Minutes of Evidence taken before the Commissioners appointed to inquire into the Organization of the Indian Army" Memorandum dated July 16, 1858, pp. 126-27.

the armies of Madras and Bombay remained loyal. The armies of Bombay and Madras had long been egalitarian and indiscriminate in composition, while in the Bengal Army the large numbers of high-caste Brahmins had been effective in protecting their own caste privileges. The Mutiny seemed to argue forcibly against the policy of "pampering" the Brahmins and in favor of the egalitarian policy practiced in Madras and Bombay where the Presidency Armies had remained loyal throughout the temptations of the Mutiny. Bitter experience seemed to second the policy of rational efficiency and uniform treatment.

As more settled times succeeded the turmoil of the Mutiny, however, the merit of a policy of equal treatment was brought into question. It was pointed out that it was in large measure a defensive policy, designed to forestall seditious collusion by scattering all natural communities as widely as possible. The advantages were put forward of an alternative procedure which would concentrate recruitment in certain communities which would thereby be encouraged to be loyal to British rule. It was suggested, for instance, that "aboriginal races, like the Sonthals, Bheels, etc., and segregated tribes, such as the Bundeelas and Gonds"[48] should be enlisted, not for philanthropic purposes alone, but further because they would be useful as "counterpoises."

In a series of lengthy memoranda submitted jointly to the Commissioners on Army Reorganization in 1858, John Lawrence Neville Chamberlain, and Herbert Edwardes had outlined military proposals which, though disregarded at the time, within a few years became the basis of army organization. They criticized the "promiscuous mixing" of native troops as an ineffective method of discouraging disaffection on a permanent basis and recommended instead the isolation of communities from one another.

Regiments of native infantry should be provincial in their

[48] *Ibid.*, Memorandum by John Lawrence, Neville Chamberlain and Herbert Edwardes, July 1, 1858.

composition and ordinary sphere of service; as we cannot do
without a large native army in India, our main object is to
make that army safe; and next to the grand counterpoise of a
sufficient European force, comes the counterpoise of natives
against natives. At first sight it might be thought that the best
way to secure this, would be to mix up all the available military races of India in each and every regiment and to make
them all "general service corps." But excellent as this theory
seems, it does not bear the test of practice. It is found that different races mixed together do not long preserve their distinctiveness; their corners, and angles, and feelings, and prejudice get rubbed off; till at last they assimilate, and the object
of their association to a considerable extent is lost. To preserve
that distinctiveness which is so valuable, and which while it
lasts makes the Mahomedan of one country despise, fear, or
dislike the Mahomedan of another, corps should in future be
provincial and adhere to the geographical limits within which
differences and rivalries are strongly marked. . . . By [this]
system . . . two great evils are avoided; firstly, that community
of feeling throughout the native army, and that mischievous
political activity and intrigue, which results from association
with other races and travel in other Indian provinces; and sec-
ondly, that thorough discontent and alienation from the service which has undoubtedly sprung up since extended conquest
has carried our Hindostanee soldiers so far from their homes.[49]

Lawrence, Chamberlain, and Edwardes objected to General
Service Corps because they feared that they might actually ac-
complish what an earlier generation had hoped they would: the
elimination of communal prejudices. Though thus acknowledging the role played by conditioning, they also laid the foundations of what was ultimately to provide the "scientific" justification for a policy here frankly advocated on the grounds of ex-
pediency, by giving their sanction to the theory that certain Indian communities were more warlike than others though they

[49] *Ibid.*, Memorandum of July 1, 1858.

did so in assessing, not the superior loyalty of the warlike races, but rather their greater menace. They wrote:

> On the subject of proportioning natives to Europeans, it should be remembered of how many races the population of India is made up; that some are much more warlike and robust than others; and that the European check ought to vary with the native power. Thus, in the Punjab and Upper India less than one European to two Sikhs or Pathans or Goorkhas would not be safe; whereas with the Hindostanees it might be one to three; and with the southern races one to four.[50]

Their proposal thus contained all the elements of the developed theory of later recruitment policy, but not as yet combined into a single statement. They advocated the patronage of communities, such as the Bhils and Sonthals, whose previous degradation would make them loyal to their patrons; they advocated the isolation of natural communities in order to maintain their distinctive characteristics, and to stimulate their enthusiasm for the service by making it local and communal in composition; and, they adhered to the belief that certain communities made inherently better soldiers. It required only the additional conviction that the martial communities could be trusted as fully as the lowly Bhils to arrive at a theory which seemed to eliminate the repressive and calculating element in the British policy of favoritism.

The dispute concerning the theory of the martial races was partially one between an earlier liberal and a later conservative generation; it was also partially a dispute between Bengal and the other Presidencies where an egalitarian policy had long proved workable. The attempt to introduce the Bombay and Madras system into Bengal had contributed to the outbreak of the Mutiny there; following the Mutiny the more conservative Bengal policy was slowly spread to the other Presidencies.

General Jacob's defense of the Bombay system led him to re-

---

[50] *Ibid.*, Memorandum of June 26, 1858.

ject categorically all talk of the relative merits of different castes or tribes. In Jacob's opinion,

> The attending to, acknowledging at all, in any way, any distinctions of races, tribe, caste, etc., as giving any rights or implying any merits, appears to me to be a very great error.
>
> Men should be enlisted with reference to individual qualifications only. Any race, tribe, or caste, the individuals of which possessed high personal qualifications, would necessarily predominate over the other, but not by reason of race, tribe or caste, but simply on account of their personal and individual qualifications. This cannot, I think, be too much insisted on, or too frequently kept in view.[51]

Jacob debunked the merits of the so-called martial races. The Afghans, whom Macaulay so admired, Jacob called "quarrelsome, unruly, and murderous . . . and . . . given to the most detestable vices."[52]

> But these Affghans, etc., are also utterly faithless . . . their absolute faithlessness and treachery appear incredible to those who do not know them, and form a startling contrast to the frank, open manner, the free, manly *bearing*, the burly forms and fair faces, of these Affghan men; which, until taught by experience we naturally associate with the possession of European virtues. . . . I have seen these great, strong, tall fairfaced warriors throw themselves from *their horses, and weep like children* in fatigue, difficulty and danger, amidst the derision of the Hindostanees . . . [they are] immeasurably inferior to the men of India in all military qualities, and, in fact, in everything but personal appearance.[53]

Jacob not only opposed all recruitment policies based on community; he also had the strongest objections to the claims of the particular communities which were favored.

Indian racial characteristics were, however, pronounced by

[51] *Ibid.*, p. 78.   [52] Pelly, *John Jacob*, p. 372.
[53] *Ibid.*, p. 372.

theorists of the martial races to be immutable, or at any rate incapable of alteration in a desirable direction. Numerous "Caste Handbooks" were produced, designed to guide recruitment officers by delineating the martial qualities of the various castes. Recruiting, in the words of Lord Roberts, "was made the business of carefully selected officers who understood Native character, and whose duty it was to become acquainted with the various tribes inhabiting the districts from which the recruits for their own regiments were drawn."[54] Lord Roberts, while commander-in-chief, personally initiated the replacement of recruits from the more politically advanced Bombay and Madras Presidencies with the "martial races" of the north. He justified the elimination of communities which had long provided soldiers to the army by contending that "long years of peace . . . had evidently had upon them, as they always seem to have on Asiatics, a softening and deteriorating effect; and I was forced to the conclusion that the ancient military spirit had died in them."[55]

Instead of attempting to shake the hold of caste from the mind of the recruit, British officers consciously attempted to keep their army orthodox. While before the Mutiny individual officers had sought to convert their men to Christianity, now Hindu, Muslim, and Sikh priests were put on the military payroll.[56] The standing regulations of the 11th Sikh Regiment stated that

> Men will observe the customs of their faith. A Sikh found smoking tobacco, or with his beard, moustache, or the hair of his head cut, or who dyes or pulls out the hair of his head or face—and a Musalman found drinking alcoholic liquor or disobeying in part or whole . . . the rules laid down for observ-

[54] Roberts, *Forty-one Years in India*, II, 442.

[55] *Ibid.*, II, 383.

[56] Hindu and Muslim priests received Rupees 8 monthly; Sikh priests, Rupees 10. These figures are from Sir O'Moore Creagh, *Indian Studies*, London, 1920, p. 267.

ance of *Ramzan* will render themselves liable to punishment for disobedience of regimental Standing Orders.[57]

The British characteristically believed they had mastered the subtleties of Indian society and learned how to turn them to British advantage. It was also believed that British rule was itself Oriental, as ideally suited to Indian conditions as Hinduism itself. Fascinated by what was traditional in India society, many Englishmen had become incapable of dealing with the fact of change. Fascinated by Indian tradition, they hoped to make British rule a part of that tradition.

Rudyard Kipling's "The Tomb of his Ancestors" tells the story of an old British-Indian family, the Chinns, whose Indian service had spanned four generations and who had become a legend in the remote areas where they invariably served. The story relates how the young John Chinn, a police sergeant, is welcomed upon his return to the Bhil territory with all the instinctive warmth of family retainers welcoming the eldest son. His old servant remembers him as a boy. The villagers quickly spread the word that "a Chinn" has returned. As the story develops, Chinn is required to kill a tiger which it is assumed the spirit of his grandfather rides through the countryside. Killing the tiger ultimately reconciles the Bhils to accept vaccination. Chinn thus by the end of the story has vindicated his lineage, assured his position as protector of the Bhils, and provided by this route for the extension of their material welfare. Chinn has a special birthmark which all the Chinns have carried; the special seal of Heaven which confirms their consecration to Indian service, the stamp of their legitimate heredity. The Bhils await his return, they remember him as a child, they tell him tales of his ancestors, they respond instinctively to his claim to determine their fate—even if it means submitting to vaccination. John Chinn may be only an officer in the British police, but to call him such would be the reckoning of an unimaginative bu-

[57] Chaudhuri, "The Martial Races of India," *Modern Review*, Calcutta, February 1931, p. 219.

reaucrat. He is not simply a British official, but the hereditary ruler of an aboriginal tribe. Chinn was not only expected to kill his grandfather's tiger; he was expected in due course to produce a male heir.

At one point in Kipling's story, John Chinn's servant mentions to him that, in his opinion, "Foreigners are bad people."[58] The furthest thing from his mind, Kipling suggests, was that the Chinns might be foreigners in central India.

[58] Kipling, "The Tomb of his Ancestors," *The Day's Work*, Garden City: Doubleday, Page, n.d.), p. 101.

CHAPTER IX

The Response to the Nationalist Challenge

Where then is the rational ground for apprehending,
that such a race will ever become turbulent for English liberty? A spirit of English liberty is not to be
caught from a written description of it, by distant
and feeble Asiatics especially.

—CHARLES GRANT, 1792[1]

Why did they teach us to read about liberty and
justice and self-government, if after all we are to
have none of these things?

—RAJAH NIL KRISHNA, 1884[2]

IN THE COURSE of the nineteenth century, British notions of the
way in which India was kept in subjection shifted from an emphasis on moral force and the influence of the example of British
character, to the less ambitious idea that India was held simply
by military power. British aspirations for India had shifted similarly from a hope for total and immediate reform, to a belief
in the possibility of slow and indefinite reform, to a view finally
that England's mission in India was to "keep order." The persistent stress on this latter theme, which continued dominant
from the end of the nineteenth century until independence, the
constantly reiterated emphasis on the fact that England had
given India peace and security, was a tacit admission that she
had abandoned her interest in giving India anything more than
this.

In personal values India's rulers had changed from being
proudly and self-consciously middle class individualists, fighting
for their rights as a class in opposition to the English aristocracy,
to being members of a middle class seeking to retain its privileges from lower class attack, concerned with preserving the

[1] Grant, "Observations," p. 106.
[2] Blunt, *India Under Ripon*, p. 130.

status quo and eager to live like privileged aristocrats. Their image of what constituted a viable society had shifted from one emphasizing freedom and competition, to one stressing classes and duties, the stable relationship of lord and peasant in a static society. It was now assumed that India would never change, as Englishmen projected their own desires onto the elusive—and changing—reality of Indian society. British Indian memoirs of the late nineteenth and early twentieth centuries are imbued with a sense of timelessness. Native India was seen personified in the princes, whom British policy had endowed with a strong vested interest in changelessness. The nationalist movement, to an astonishing extent, drew no response from the British imagination in India. It is almost impossible to find references to nationalist politics in contemporary memoirs. Nationalism was simply ignored, wished out of existence, or dismissed with the presumption that nationalists did not represent the "real" India. Nationalism of the urban, professional middle classes reflected only the peevishness of a rootless minority which "represented only the anomaly of their own position." Though themselves members of an English middle class which had had to struggle for recognition, India's rulers now turned on the emerging Indian middle classes a biting aristocratic scorn. In a curious reversal of roles, the Indian middle class preempted the position the British middle class had abandoned for aristocratic pretensions. Indians went into business and the professions; they developed an urban life and organizational skill while Englishmen consorted with princes and peasants. Indians assumed the championship of social reform, self-government, and nationalism at a time when the English had begun to question their value. While Indians read Mill and talked of rights and constitutions, the English were obsessed with princely ceremony.

In the India of British conceptions, cities, business, and politics were of minor importance. To demonstrate their conviction, the British moved the capital of the Empire from the premier city of politics and business, Calcutta, to Delhi, the noncommercial, nonpolitical center of ancient Imperial splendor. The classes which engaged in business and politics were considered both impotent and contemptible; impotent because of their insignificance, contemptible because their talk of rights and parliaments was not sincere, but simply another exemplification of Indian cunning and deceitfulness. Nationalist rhetoric was only a further demonstration of that intellectual "suppleness and . . . tact" which moved "the children of sterner climates to admiration not unmingled with contempt."[3] The English suspicion of intellectual glibness even among their own countrymen was intensified with regard to Indians, whose espousal of liberal concepts was held to be devoid of any real conviction. Englishmen refused to believe that an Indian could be a genuine nationalist, just as they refused to believe that India could ever be a genuine nation.

It might be difficult to convince the world that he, to whom caste was all in all, was really a democrat, that a polygamist and a worshipper of the phallus had much in common with Western civilization, that a believer in a lofty, if nebulous philosophy was really an admirer of the shallow nominalism of the West. But much might be done in a good cause. Just as without in the least compromising his Brahminhood, he had invested Akbar with the sacred thread, and in return accepted the spiritual guidance of the Most Great God, just as he had in the drinking parties of Jehangir capped the merry monarch's improper Persian verses, so he might learn to talk the jargon of democracy and utilitarianisn.[4]

The Imperialist refused to believe that a veneer of Western dress or Western verbiage had altered the basically immutable Indian character; the nationalist movement was conceived as only another exemplification of that character.

Some few Anglicized Bengalee baboos have caught up and travestied the English commonplaces which have, in my

---

[3] Macaulay, "Warren Hastings," in *Essays and Poems*, p. 567.
[4] Carthill, *Lost Dominion*, p. 55.

opinion, most injudiciously been made a part of their education . . . [wrote Fitzjames Stephen] but the great mass of the population and in particular the best part of it, the warlike and vigorous races of Northern India, have never shown the smallest sympathy with such views.[5]

The nationalist movement also demonstrated the basic incompatibility of the various groups of which Indian society was composed, just as it exemplified the true character of those groups. The "better sections" of Indian society, the rulers of the princely states and the vigorous races of the north, were staunchly loyal, as befitted their honest and manly character; the disloyalty of the nationalist baboo seemed equally to reveal his true nature, that of a deceitful flatterer. The agitator, half-devil, half-child, was perversely intent on causing trouble, but only in the fashion of an adolescent who is unaware of the implications of his revolt and who would be incapable of coping with the consequences of its success. The agitator would in reality be hopelessly at sea without the protective father against whom he rebelled—and would never have rebelled at all had he not been convinced it was the best way to impress his father. Defiance of the British, coupled with a secret admiration and desire to win their respect, appeared to follow the classic pattern of adolescent revolt.

One of my friends . . . spent much of his time denouncing me . . . as a satanic and cold blooded murderer . . . [related one British official whose reminiscences are reported by Woodruff]. In the front row of the audience [of the agitator's meeting] would be a police sub-inspector, interrupting now and then to ask for a repetition of a difficult passage. Then, the meeting over, the Sub-Inspector would come round to my bungalow with his version of the proceedings. But my perusal of his report would be interrupted by the arrival of the orator himself. . . .

[5] J. F. Stephen, "Foundations of the Government of India," in *Nineteenth Century*, LXXX, October 1883, 563.

"I'm sure you'll be interested," he would begin "in these rather beautiful old Assamese paintings. Illustrations to the Mahabharata. . . ." And the small hours would find us still talking hard. . . ."[6]

Clearly, such adolescent rebellion against the protective father could never lead to a healthy maturity. If the adolescent were ever to lose his father whom he attacked so virulently, his very success would spell his downfall. Unshielded, he would quickly fall prey to the rule of force. The implication was that the agitator probably knew this himself; and that the last thing he really wanted was to have his demand for independence granted.

The slogans the agitator employed were drawn from the familiar canon of English liberalism for reasons which the Imperialist understood only too well. Such slogans were not employed because they represented ideas valued by the agitator or because they were capable of impressing the Indian peasant; they were employed because they were calculated to impress English public opinion. The Imperialist who had turned to India as a refuge from the increasing democratization of English politics, now saw his command of India itself trapped in the vise of Oriental cunning and English gullibility. The two principal objects of his contempt, Indian nationalism and English democracy, were joined together in a common argument, one serving as an explanation of the other. Indian nationalism took the form it did because of the existence of English democracy; more than that, English democracy was directly responsible for the emergence of Indian nationalism in the first place. Nationalism on the part of Indians was a form of adolescent revolt; but there would not have been even that degree of disaffection had it not been for the injection of English politics into the Indian scene.

In short, but for the restless, dissatisfied officious interference of English theorists, there is no reason why the present

[6] Woodruff, *Men Who Ruled India,* ii, 250.

state of things in India should not continue indefinitely [wrote Fitzjames Stephen]. If the British Government in India is ever seriously disturbed and ruined it will be by reason of an agitation set up at the instigation of Englishmen against institutions with which the natives, if left to themselves, are perfectly satisfied.[7]

Valentine Chirol suggested in his book, *Indian Unrest,* that unrest was largely the result of the interference of a number of misguided Europeans. "It was in the polemical tracts of European writers," says Chirol "that the first protagonists of Hindu reaction against Christian influence found their readiest weapons of attack. . . . Certainly no Hindu has done so much to organize and consolidate the movement as Mrs. Annie Besant. . . . Is it surprising that Hindus should turn their backs upon our civilization when a European of highly-trained intellectual power and with an extraordinary gift of eloquence comes and tells them that it is they who possess and have from all time possessed the key to supreme wisdom. . . ?"[8] Not even Chirol's arch-villain, Tilak, a man who, as a Chitpavan Brahmin, possessed "Western daring and Eastern craft"[9] is allowed to escape the imputation that he is a victim of poison poured into his ear by Europeans. Why did Tilak hit upon the notion of establishing a cult of the Hindu hero, Shivaji? "Only a few years before an Englishman who had visited Shivaji's tomb had written to a local newspaper calling attention to [its] ruinous condition. . . . Some say it was this letter which first inspired Tilak."[10] Chirol thus led his readers to believe that if there had been no English intervention, if there had been no A. O. Hume, no Charles Bradlaugh, and especially no Annie Besant, there might never have been a nationalist movement, or, in Chirol's phrase, unrest. In John Masters' novel of the Indian Mutiny, *Nightrunners of Bengal,* a leading Indian conspirator, the Silver

[7] J. F. Stephen, "Foundations of the Government of India," p. 563.
[8] *Indian Unrest,* London: Macmillan, 1910, pp. 28-29.
[9] *Ibid.,* p. 38.   [10] *Ibid.,* p. 45.

Guru, a leprous ascetic who glows in the moonlight, turns out to be in reality an Irishman in disguise who has become embittered by England's treatment of himself and his country. The Indian Mutiny thus dissolves into a sort of extension and creation of the Irish fight for independence.

Indian unrest came to seem a mere reflection of England's domestic arguments, and English indignation against rebels like the atheist Bradlaugh, as well as English awareness of their isolated eccentricity, were appealed to in asking the English public to assess Indian nationalism. In some respects, this attitude was reminiscent of the suspicion of reforming missionaries at the beginning of the century. In each case the inclination was to discredit the efforts of reformers by attempting to call on aristocratic prejudices concerning them. Instead of attempting to debate the relevance of their proposals to the Indian scene, their critics attempted to discredit them by charging that it was not the Indian situation which elicited their energies but their English (or Irish) background which determined their concerns.

The regrettable fact, however, was that the English public did listen to the Indian nationalists and their English supporters, and the government of India found itself increasingly hamstrung by a self-conscious, conscience-stricken government at home, the result being a disastrously equivocal policy toward the nationalist movement. The government proceeded by "spanking the baby at one end while feeding it at the other,"[11] and moreover confused which baby should be spanked and which fed, in, for instance, rewarding the loyalty of the martial races in the First World War by granting concessions to disloyal nationalists. It was precisely this "habit of the English Government to 'come down' on the side of its late enemies"[12] which led to despair that "some caprice of Providence had made [the British Electorate] masters of the destinies of the human race."[13]

There was a clear notion of what would happen if further concessions were made to nationalists, "those infernal Baboos

[11] Carthill, *Lost Dominion*, p. 257.
[12] *Ibid.*, p. 243.   [13] *Ibid.*, p. 61.

who are no more fit to govern Sikhs and Afghans than to govern Englishmen," as Stephen had called them in a letter to Lord Lytton.[14] The result of putting administration in such hands was illustrated by Kipling in a story entitled "The Head of the District."

Kipling's story of a frontier district begins with the death of the British Deputy Commissioner, a man of the old school who had ruled his district in the ruthless and yet personal way with which frontiersmen were familiar, and had succeeded in winning "over to the paths of a moderate righteousness"[15] those savage and manly people. The decision concerning the successor to "Orde Sahib" was made by a Viceroy whom the press and public opinion in India labelled "a fool, a dreamer of dreams, a doctrinaire, and, worst of all, a trifler with the lives of men."[16] The Viceroy had won these titles in the estimation of the British community by his sympathetic encouragement of the idea of Indian self-government. "The very simplicity of the notion was its charm . . . appointing a child of the country to the rule of that country."[17] Self-government for India, so Kipling implies, was a sort of childish nonsense which could only appeal to the innocent or ill-informed. And yet, the Viceroy managed to have his way, and a Bengali member of the Civil Service was posted to take charge of the district. On his arrival, the English-speaking, English-educated Bengali was a subject of intense interest to the people of the Northwest Frontier.

> Bengalis were as scarce as poodles among the simple Borderers, who cut each other's heads open with their long spades and worshipped impartially at Hindu and Mahomedan shrines. They crowded to see him, pointing at him, and diversely comparing him to a gravid milch-buffalo, or a broken-down horse, as their limited range of metaphor prompted.[18]

[14] Stephen to Lytton, 20 July 1876, Stephen Papers.
[15] Kipling, "The Head of the District," in *Life's Handicap*, London, 1952, p. 118.
[16] *Ibid.*, p. 125.   [17] *Ibid.*, p. 122.   [18] *Ibid.*, p. 133.

The arrival of a despised Bengali whom the vigorous borderers had always considered the prey of conquerors, the slave of all mankind, to assume a position as their ruler, seemed to confirm the warnings of such inveterate opponents of British rule as the Blind Mullah. "Because you listened to Orde Sahib and called him father and behaved as his children," warned the Blind Mullah, "thou shalt slip thy shoes at the tent-door of a Bengali, as thou shalt hand thy offering to a Bengali's black fist."[19]

As the story progresses, both borderers and Bengali official act predictably, according to type; the borderers revolt, and the Bengali retreats helplessly, and ultimately is transferred back to his native Bengal.

Kipling's story presents, in a very few pages, a summary of virtually the entire Imperialist case. There is first, a portrait of Oriental dominance in the person of Orde Sahib, ruling his violent children with a hand of iron, and yet providing from his deathbed for the remission of land revenue in a few stricken villages. Orde knows his people, he speaks their language; his successor speaks only English. Orde knows that his people respect only force, and is able to use it as vigorously as circumstances require; his successor is an intellectual, a literate, report-writing, suit-wearing man who would be useless in the Punjab even if he were not a Bengali. Orde is a true Oriental; the Bengali, a false Englishman.

The experiment with self-government which Kipling relates comes, not at Indian insistence, but as a result of misguided English liberalism; and the experiment only reveals the total incompatibility of Indian races. He's "a black Bengali dog . . ." the Punjabis exclaim of their new ruler. "He's a *kala admi*—a black man—unfit to run at the tail of a potter's donkey."[20] And the Punjabis carelessly sever the head of the Bengali gentleman —a relation of the new Deputy Commissioner—and casually

[19] *Ibid.*, p. 128.   [20] *Ibid.*, pp. 130-31.

deposit the bespectacled head at the Englishman's feet. The real Indians, the ones who count, so we are left to believe, are pre-pared to serve the English indefinitely, if the English will only justify their trust by ruling Orientals the way Orientals expect to be ruled.

CHAPTER X

The Fragility of Imperial Confidence

BRITISH IMPERIALISM in India reached its highest stage of self-consciousness and self-satisfaction at the turn of the century, just as the Empire itself was becoming no longer viable. The Empire was never more fragile than at this moment when it seemed most secure; the rationalizations of the necessity for continuing British rule were never more complete than at this moment when they no longer applied.

This illusion of permanence, in the form it assumed at the beginning of the twentieth century, had evolved into a full-blown theory encompassing every aspect of England's relationship to Indian society, justifying and confirming England's role in India with a confidence which would have amazed earlier generations of reformers and conservatives alike. And yet, this imperial confidence owed much to those earlier generations, for it represented a synthesis of reformist and conservative attitudes which had emerged during the course of the century. Evangelical and Utilitarian reformers, at the beginning of the century, had mounted a wholesale attack on Indian society; their intentions were benevolent and affirmative, but they succeeded in their destructive task of alienating Englishmen from Indian society, without inspiring later generations with their own enthusiasm for its reform. Their constructive program itself presented difficulties, in its determination to judge Indian society exclusively in European terms, and the prospects for Indian reform in terms of India's approximation to European standards. The Evangelical emphasis on conduct, and the Utilitarian on government as regulation, moreover, contributed the primary components of the British-Indian conception of government as properly the administration of society's affairs by just and conscientious experts. The early nineteenth century reformers intended only India's rapid development; their effect was to provide the ideological framework for India's permanent administration by Englishmen.

India's experience with other liberal movements had been similar. There was much talk early in the century by liberal nationalists of the virtues of nationality and self-government and of England's task in India as that of preparing India for independence. Such talk was quite sincere, but also hypothetical. It furthermore presumed a future world made up of democratic national communities linked by the friendly ties of commerce, in which India could be a valuable partner even though independent. The possibility of continuing free trade with an independent former possession seemed less conceivable in the hostile, competitive world of the late nineteenth century, and the necessity for and the desirability of self-government for all came concurrently into question. India's claim to be a nation was now denied by men still committed to the national ideal. An aggressive English nation found gratification in the control of other nations, and opportunities provided by their subjection to pursue its rivalries with other major powers.

The tenets of England's liberal faith were usually not repudiated but rather presumed to be applicable only to those who were ready for them. India's right to self-government might thus still be upheld, but made contingent on conditions which it was assumed would never be fulfilled. India's reform and transformation might still be championed by men who conceived of the process as of almost infinite duration. England's special creeds, her Christianity, her technology, her governmental institutions, seemed no longer capable of transforming the entire world rapidly into nations on the English pattern, because they were now viewed as uniquely identified with England's national character and history, just as India's presumed vices were pronounced enduring national characteristics rather than the result of past misfortune. The radical identification of Englishmen with men everywhere was replaced by a notion of inherent English superiority, and an unwillingness to envision other peoples quickly arriving at a similar level of advancement.

This narrowing of English liberalism was related, not only to the growing competitiveness of the international situation in Europe, but also to changes in the social and political position of the English middle classes. The middle classes abandoned their earlier concern with gaining privileges for themselves by championing the cause of all mankind, for a concern with maintaining privileges already won for themselves but not yet extended to all mankind. The same classes which led the fight for expansion of the suffrage in 1832 in the name of human equality and democratic suffrage opposed the reforms of 1867 with warnings against popular anarchy. Middle class aspirations to an aristocratic status, encouraged by the growing economic and political power of the business and professional classes, were not compatible with attempts to reduce the value of such aristocratic status. The middle classes opposed the growth of democracy in England, and hoped to forestall its emergence in India.

Even before 1832 the middle class had been somewhat divided on the question of whether it was better to advance themselves by reforming the aristocracy, or by buying into it. India had been for some at least an avenue to a fortune sufficient to buy one's way even into the unreformed aristocracy. India in the latter half of the century still provided a route to social advance, but in a modified form. India became, not a place where one could earn enough money to return to England and live as an aristocrat, but a place where one could live like an aristocrat on limited means. Middle class aspirations to social advance, transposed thus to Indian soil, contributed to the determination of Englishmen to remain in India, and to preserve in India the conditions which enabled them to live as they wished.

The mentality of Englishmen in India in this era was in some respects a variant of that which had been current in the pre-reform days of the eighteenth century. Englishmen in India at that time also had instinctively adopted the stance of British aristocrats, and endeavored to preserve intact traditional Indian society. English advocates of Indian nationalism in the nineteenth century were treated by India's middle class rulers with the same aristocratic indignation with which missionaries had been treated a century before. The current of "Orientalism" similarly echoed sentiments common in the Hastings era. Static, conservative views of both English and Indian society, which had been challenged by the reformers, now regained popularity among Englishmen no longer enthusiastic for change. This revival took place, however, in drastically changed circumstances which necessarily modified the nature of the new conservatism. The fear of missionaries in the eighteenth century had stemmed from concern that they might jeopardize England's tenuous position in India; the English proponents of Indian nationalism seemed mere meddlers in a strong, sovereign, and permanent British Empire. The earlier "Orientalism" had been an appreciation of a society not dependent on British favor, an appreciation implying a parallel humility about the unique merits of Western civilization. The new Orientalizers were uncompromising in their commitment to British superiority, and stressed the manipulable aspects of traditional Indian society which they assumed could be bent to British purposes. A strong and confident ruling class incorporated into a policy of control attitudes which a century before had characterized culturally adaptable men concerned to stabilize a precarious British position.

India seemed to offer the prospect of aristocratic security at a time when England itself was falling prey to democratic vulgarity. To those with aristocratic or autocratic ambitions, India actually seemed in advance of England, preferable to the state of affairs in England. Englishmen looked to India as a refuge from English anarchy; but it could only be a vulnerable refuge, because it was ultimately guaranteed by that British nation which was now taking so regrettable a course. With the abolition of the East India Company, Indian affairs became subject to the strong pressures of popular politics. British national opinion initially endorsed British control at the time of the Mutiny of 1857 and continued to endorse it until the end of the century. There were sufficient signs, however, even before the end of the century, that the English democracy might ultimately sympathize with her Indian subjects against India's British rulers, to cause Englishmen in India to decry their relentless pursuit by democracy, even into their Indian refuge.

By the end of the century, India's rulers knew their existence was potentially threatened by political liberalism at home, but felt equally that British rule in India had been shown to be viable. It would never be necessary for Britain to leave; if Britain did leave, it would not be because India no longer needed her, but because the English democracy wantonly disregarded its responsibilities. British rule seemed fully and intelligently adapted to meet all of India's legitimate needs. Englishmen conceived of their own character, and of Indian character, in a fashion which suggested that the relationship of protection and dependence was ideally suited to both.

This imperial ideology seemed substantiated by science and experience. In concluding his defense of his particular brand of energetic imperialism, General Jacob wrote, "The principles advocated by me appear to be natural laws: I cannot conceive that they *could* fail of success when fairly acted on. I have applied them myself for fifteen years."[1] And yet, neither science nor experience had fully anticipated the twentieth century. The imperial method of settling disputes proved of little avail against the armies of Germany. The imperial disregard for democratic opinion and reliance on force proved of little avail against Indian nationalists or the English Labour Party. Neither a show of force, nor a rain of contemptuous abuse was capable of exorcising the unintended enemy. The imperial experience, while adding to British national power, at least temporarily, also fitted many men with blinders which hampered their ability to cope with new kinds of experience. And even at its height of splendor and self-confidence, the imperial position was the product of a highly artificial coincidence of circumstances. No matter how natural and self-evident its premises might seem, they were in large part merely a succession of mutually reenforcing misconceptions.

[1] Pelly, *John Jacob*, p. 444.

The illusion of British permanence in India was a significant component in the consciousness of the British nation; for the Englishman in India it was everything. Rationalizations and theories might emanate from England, but it was in India that they took on a vivid reality, as they were combined with the most intense aspirations and fears of individuals. The position of the British in India as a small elite in a vast and little-understood, alien society heightened their need for assurance and justification, and for constant and unqualified reenforcement from other Englishmen. As has been true of other dominant communities who have felt their privileges to be challenged, the British in India reacted by holding all the more tenaciously to their pretensions and by drawing sharp lines of distinction between those who were known to be sympathetic and those who were not. Men whose lives had been given meaning by the imperial ideology and who were personally strengthened and enabled by it to act effectively in the context in which it developed often preferred to retain the ideology defiantly and to go down fighting, indulging in dire warnings about the future of a world which no longer honored what they valued. For others, the insistently demanded accommodation to the dominant ideology, even when it seemed incontrovertible, had involved a reluctant effort.[2] For such people, the loss of Empire meant the regaining

[2] Two noteworthy examples of such efforts are recorded in the installment of Leonard Woolf's autobiography, *Growing, An Autobiography of the Years 1904 to 1911*, London: The Hogarth Press, 1961, which deals with his years as a member of the Ceylon Civil Service, and in various writings of George Orwell. Orwell recalled from his years in the Burma Police

> a night I spent on the train with a man in the Educational Service, a stranger to myself . . . for hours, while the train jolted slowly through the pitchblack night, sitting up in our bunks with bottles of beer handy, we damned the British Empire—damned it from the inside, intelligently and intimately. It did us both good. But we had been speaking forbidden things, and in the haggard morning light when the train crawled into Mandalay, we parted as guiltily as any adulterous couple.

(Orwell, *The Road to Wigan Pier*, New York: Harcourt, Brace, 1958, p. 177.) Woolf and Orwell both made efforts to enjoy their imperial posi-

of self-respect and the possibility of the reestablishment of the relationship between India and Great Britain on a more satisfying, more permanent basis.

---

tions and to live within the confining intellectual and social limits they imposed; both failed, resigned, and became bitter critics of the system they had served.

Bibliography

MANUSCRIPT SOURCES

India Office Library, London: *Despatches to India and Bengal*, 1829-1858.

Home Miscellaneous, No. 832 (record of Despatches by J. S. Mill).

Cambridge University Library, Cambridge, U.K.: J. F. Stephen Papers.

Records of the Government of India, National Archives of India, New Delhi: Stephen–Lytton Correspondence [microfilm].

PRINTED OFFICIAL SOURCES

Correspondence between the Court of Directors of the East-India Company and Her Majesty's Government with Draft of the Proposed Petition to Parliament, London, 1858.

Hansard, *Parliamentary Debates*, 3rd Series.

Parliamentary Papers.

Proceedings of the Governor-General of India in Council for the Purpose of Making Laws and Regulations, 1855-1900.

Report of the Indian Statutory Commission. London, 1930.

Statutes of the United Kingdom of Great Britain and Ireland.

NEWSPAPERS AND PERIODICALS

Calcutta Review, Calcutta.

Edinburgh Review, London.

Nineteenth Century, London.

The Times, London.

OTHER WORKS

Allport, Gordon W. *The Nature of Prejudice.* Garden City, N.Y.: Anchor, 1958.

Annan, Noel. *Leslie Stephen.* London, 1951.

Arendt, Hannah. *The Origins of Totalitarianism.* Cleveland, Ohio, 1962.

Arnold, Matthew. *Culture and Anarchy.* Cambridge, U.K.: Cambridge University Press, 1950.

Arnold, William Delafield. *Oakfield, or Fellowship in the East.* Boston: Ticknor and Fields, 1855.

Aron, Raymond. *War and Industrial Society*. London: Oxford University Press, 1958.

Atkinson, George F. *Curry and Rice*. London, 1911.

Ballhatchet, Kenneth. *Social Policy and Social Change in Western India, 1817-1830*. London: Oxford University Press, 1957.

Barzun, Jacques. *Race, A Study in Superstition*. New York: Harper & Row, 1965.

Beames, John. *Memoirs of a Bengal Civilian*. London: Chatto and Windus, 1961.

Bearce, George D. *British Attitudes towards India, 1784-1858*. Oxford, 1961.

Bennett, George, ed. *The Concept of Empire, Burke to Attlee, 1774-1947*. London: Adam and Charles Black, 1962.

Beveridge, Lord. *India Called Them*. London, 1947.

Blunt, Wilfred Scawen. *India Under Ripon, A Private Diary*. London: T. Fisher Unwin, 1909.

Bodelsen, C. A. *Studies in Mid-Victorian Imperialism*. London: Heinemann, 1960.

Brontë, Charlotte. *Jane Eyre*. New York: Modern Library edn., 1933.

Brown, Hilton. *The Sahibs*. London, 1948.

Burke, Edmund. "Speeches on the Impeachment of Warren Hastings," *Works*, Vol. vii. London, 1877.

Cadell, Sir Patrick. *History of the Bombay Army*. 1938.

Candler, Edmund. *The Sepoy*. London, 1919.

Carlyle, Thomas. *Occasional Discourse on the Nigger Question*. London: Thomas Bosworth, 1853.

———. *Shooting Niagara: And After?* London: Chapman & Hall, 1867.

Carstairs, R. *The Little World of an Indian District Officer*. London: Macmillan, 1912.

Carthill, Al (pseud.). *The Lost Dominion*. Edinburgh: William Blackwood and Sons, 1924.

Cash, W. J. *The Mind of the South*. New York, 1941.

Chaudhuri, Nirad. "The Martial Races of India," *Modern Review*, Calcutta, Four-part series, 1930-31.

Chesney, General Sir George. *Indian Polity, A View of the System of Administration in India*. London, 1894.

Chirol, Valentine. *Indian Unrest*. London: Macmillan, 1910.

Churchill, Winston. *My Early Life, A Roving Commission.* New York: Scribner's, 1958.

Cobden, Richard. *How Wars are Got up in India.* London: William and Frederick G. Cash, 1853.

Cohn, Bernard S. "The British in Benares: a Nineteenth Century Colonial Society," *Comparative Studies in Society and History,* Vol. IV, No. 2, January 1962, pp. 169-99.

Cramb, J. A. *The Origins and Destiny of Imperial Britain.* London, 1915.

Creagh, Sir O'Moore. *Indian Studies.* London, 1920.

Cromer, Evelyn Baring Earl of, *Ancient and Modern Imperialism.* New York, 1910.

Curtin, Philip D. *The Image of Africa, British Ideas and Action, 1780-1850.* Madison, Wis.: University of Wisconsin Press, 1964.

Davies, A. Mervyn. *Clive of Plassey.* New York, 1939.

Desika Char, S. V. *Centralised Legislation.* Bombay: Asia, 1963.

Dicey, A. V. *Lectures on the Relation Between Law and Public Opinion in England During the Nineteenth Century.* New York: Macmillan, 1926.

Dilke, Charles. *Greater Britain.* New York, 1869.

Dodwell, H. H. *The Indian Empire.* Delhi, 1964.

———. *Sepoy Recruitment in the Old Madras Army,* Calcutta: Indian Historical Record Commission, 1922.

Dubois, J. A. Abbé. *Hindu Manners, Customs and Ceremonies.* Trans. Beauchamp. London: Oxford University Press, 1959.

Eden, Emily. *Up the Country.* London: Humphrey Milford, 1930.

Edwardes, Sir Herbert and Herman Merivale. *Life of Sir Henry Lawrence.* New York: Macmillan, 1873.

Edwardes, Michael. *The Necessary Hell.* London: Cassell, 1958.

Elkins, Stanley. *Slavery.* New York: Universal Library, 1963.

Embree, Ainslie. *Charles Grant and British Rule in India,* New York: Columbia University Press, 1962.

Emerson, Rupert. *From Empire to Nation.* Boston: Beacon, 1962.

Evans, Humphrey. *Thimayya of India: A Soldier's Life.* New York: Harcourt, Brace, 1960.

Fay, Mrs. Eliza. *Original Letters from India (1779-1815).* London: Hogarth, 1925.

Forrest, G. W. *Sepoy Generals,* 1901.

Forster, E. M. *Abinger Harvest.* London, 1953.

Forster, E. M. *The Hill of Devi.* London, 1953.

———. *A Passage to India.* New York: Harcourt, Brace, 1924.

Frykenberg, Robert E. "British Society in Guntur during the Early Nineteenth Century," *Comparative Studies in Society and History,* January 1962, pp. 200-208.

Fuller, Bampfylde. *The Empire of India.* 1913.

Furber, Holden. *John Company at Work.* Cambridge, Mass.: Harvard University Press, 1948.

Godard, J. G. *Racial Supremacy.* Edinburgh, 1905.

Gopal, S. *The Viceroyalty of Lord Ripon.* London, 1953.

Graham, Lt. Col. G. F. I. *The Life and Work of Syed Ahmed Khan.* Edinburgh, 1885.

Grant, Charles. "Observations on the State of Society among the Asiatic Subjects of Great Britain, particularly with respect to Morals; and on the Means of improving it." *Parliamentary Papers* (H. C.), "Report from the Select Committee on the Affairs of the East India Company," 16 August 1832, Appendix.

Green, Graham, ed. *The Old School.* London, 1934.

Gupta, Sulekh Chandra. *Agrarian Relations and Early British Rule in India.* Bombay: Asia, 1963.

Halevy, Elie. *England in 1815.* London, 1949.

———. *The Growth of Philosophic Radicalism.* Boston: Beacon, 1960.

Hardie, Keir. *India, Impressions and Suggestions.* London, 1909.

Hayes, Carlton, J. H. *A Generation of Materialism, 1871-1900.* New York: Harper & Row, 1963.

Heber, Reginald. *Narrative of a Journey through the Upper Provinces of India.* 3 vols. London: John Murray, 1829.

Hervey, H. *The European in India.* London, 1913.

Hobson, J. A. *Imperialism, A Study.* New York, 1902.

Hovell–Thurlow, Hon. T. J. *The Company and the Crown.* London, 1866.

Hunter, W. W. *The India of the Queen and Other Essays.* London, 1903.

———. *Indian Musalmans: Are They Bound in Conscience to Rebel Against the Queen?* London, 1872.

———. *Life of the Earl of Mayo.* 2 vols. London, 1876.

India: Geographical, Statistical, and Historical. Compiled from the London *Times* Correspondence, McCullock and Others. London: George Watts, 1858.

Isaacs, Harold R. *Images of Asia, American Views of China and India*. New York: Capricorn, 1962.

Iyer, Raghavan. "Utilitarianism and all That (The Political Theory of British Imperialism in India)." *South Asian Affairs* (Iyer, ed.), *St. Anthony's Papers Number Eight*. London, 1960, pp. 9-71.

Jacquemont, Victor. *Correspondance*. 2 vols. Paris: Garnier Frères, 1846.

Kavanaugh, T. H. *How I Won the Victoria Cross*. London: Ward and Lock, 1860.

Kaye, John William. *The Administration of the East India Company*. London: Richard Bentley, 1853.

Kincaid, Dennis. *British Social Life in India, 1608-1937*. London: G. Routledge & Sons, 1938.

Kipling, Rudyard. *Works*. 36 vols. New York: Charles Scribner's Sons, 1937.

Kisch, H. M. *A Young Victorian in India, Letters of H. M. Kisch*. London: Jonathan Cape, 1957.

Knorr, Klaus E. *British Colonial Theories 1570-1850*. Toronto, 1944.

Langer, William L. *The Diplomacy of Imperialism*. 2 vols. New York: Knopf, 1935.

Lenin, V. I. *Imperialism, the Highest Stage of Capitalism*. New York, 1933.

Lyall, Sir Alfred. *Asiatic Studies*. London, 1901.

Macaulay, Thomas B. "Lord Clive," *Essays and Poems*. Vol. ii, pp. 390-463. Boston, no date.

———. "Warren Hastings," *Essays and Poems*. Vol. ii, pp. 554-656. Boston, no date.

Mack, Edward C. *Public Schools and British Opinion, 1780-1860*. New York, 1939.

Maclagan, Michael. *"Clemency" Canning*. London: Macmillan, 1962.

MacMunn, Sir George. *The Martial Races of India*. London, no date.

MacMunn, Sir George and Lovett. *The Armies of India*. London, no date.

Magnus, Philip. *Kitchener, Portrait of an Imperialist*. London, 1961.

Maine, Sir Henry. *Village Communities in the East and West*. New York, 1880.

Mannoni, O. *Prospero and Caliban, The Psychology of Colonization*. Trans. Powesland. New York: Praeger, 1956.

Martineau, Harriet. *British Rule in India*. London: Smith, Elder, 1857.

Martineau, Harriet. *Suggestions towards the Future Government of India*. London: Smith, Elder, 1858.

Marx, Karl and F. Engels. *The First Indian War of Independence, 1857-1859*. Moscow, 1959.

Mason, Philip. *Call the Next Witness* (published under the name of Philip Woodruff). New York: Harcourt, Brace, 1946.

———. *The Men Who Ruled India* (published under the name of Philip Woodruff). 2 vols. New York: Schocken, 1964.

———. *Prospero's Magic; some thoughts on class and race*. London: Oxford University Press, 1962.

———. *The Wild Sweet Witch* (published under the name of Philip Woodruff). New York: Harcourt, Brace, 1947.

Masters, John. *The Deceivers*. London, 1952.

———. *Nightrunners of Bengal*. London: Michael Joseph, 1955.

Maugham, W. Somerset. "The Outstation," *Collected Short Stories*. Vol. IV, pp. 338-65. London, 1963.

Mayhew, Arthur. *Christianity and the Government of India*. London: Faber and Gwyer, 1929.

———. *The Education of India*. London: Faber and Gwyer, 1926.

Metcalf, Thomas R. *Aftermath of Revolt: India, 1857-1870*. Princeton: Princeton University Press, 1964.

Mill, James. *The History of British India*. 6 vols. London, 1820.

Mill, John Stuart. *Autobiography*. London: World's Classics edn., 1944.

———. *Memorandum of the Improvements in the Administration of India During the Last Thirty Years* (published anonymously by the East India Company). London, 1858 (India Office Library Tract No. 790).

———. *Utilitarianism, Liberty and Representative Government*. New York, 1951.

Miscegenation: The Theory of the Blending of the Races applied to the American White Man and Negro. Anon. New York, 1864.

Mitra, Dinabandhu. *Nil Durpan, or the Indigo Planting Mirror*. Trans. Dutt. Calcutta: Sri Debi Prasad Mukhopadhyaya, no date.

Montesquieu, Baron de. *The Spirit of the Laws*. Trans. Nugent. New York: Hafner, 1962.

Morison, Theodore. *Imperial Rule in India*. Westminster: Archibald Constable, 1899.

Morris, Morris David. "Toward a Reinterpretation of Nineteenth-

Century Indian Economic History," *Journal of Economic History*, December 1963, pp. 606-18.

Mosley, Leonard. *Curzon, The End of an Epoch*. London: Longmans, 1960.

Muir, R. *The Making of British India, 1756-1858*. Manchester, 1915.

Napier, Sir Charles. *Defects, Civil and Military, of the Indian Government*. London, 1853.

Orwell, George. *Burmese Days*. London, 1949.

———. *The Road to Wigan Pier*. New York: Harcourt, Brace, 1958.

———. "Rudyard Kipling," *Dickens, Dali and Others*. New York: Reynal and Hitchcock, 1946.

———. "Shooting an Elephant," *A Collection of Essays*. New York: Anchor, 1957.

Panikkar, K. M. *Asia and Western Dominance*. London: George Allen & Unwin, 1953.

———. *The Indian Princes in Council*. Oxford, 1936.

Pelly, Lewis, ed. *The Views and Opinions of Brigadier-General John Jacob C.B.* London: Smith, Elder, 1858.

Philips, C. H. *The East India Company, 1784-1834*. Manchester: Manchester University Press, 1940.

———, ed. *Historians of India, Pakistan and Ceylon*. London: Oxford University Press, 1961.

Philips, C. H., H. L. Singh and B. N. Pandey, eds. *The Evolution of India and Pakistan, 1858 to 1947* (Vol. IV of the Series, *Select Documents on the History of India and Pakistan*, Philips and Singh, eds.) London: Oxford University Press, 1962.

Plamenatz, John. *On Alien Rule and Self-Government*. London: Longmans, 1960.

Prasad, Rajendra. *India Divided*. Bombay, 1947.

Richter, Julius. *A History of Missions in India*. Trans. Moore. New York, 1908.

Richter, Melvin. *The Politics of Conscience, T. H. Green and His Age*. Cambridge, Mass.: Harvard University Press, 1964.

Rivett-Carnac, Col. S. *The Presidential Armies of India*. London, 1890.

Roberts, Lord. *Forty-one Years in India*. 1905 edn. 2 vols. London, 1897.

Robinson, Ronald, John Gallagher and Alice Denny, *Africa and the Victorians*. New York: St. Martins, 1961.

Russell, William H. *My Diary in India, in the Year 1858-1859.* 2 vols. London: Routledge, Warne and Routledge, 1860.

———. *My Indian Mutiny Diary.* ed. Edwardes. London: Cassell, 1957.

Schumpeter, Joseph A. *Imperialism and Social Classes.* New York, 1951.

Seeley, J. R. *The Expansion of England.* Boston, 1883.

Sen, S. N. *Eighteen Fifty-seven.* Calcutta: Government of India, Ministry of Information and Broadcasting, 1957.

Shanks, Edward. *Rudyard Kipling.* London: Macmillan, 1940.

Sharan, Parmatma. *The Imperial Legislative Council of India (From 1861 to 1920).* Delhi: S. Chand, 1961.

Simcox, A. H. A. *The Khandesh Bhil Corps.* Bombay, 1912.

Singh, Hira Lal. *Problems and Policies of the British in India, 1885-1898.* Bombay: Asia, 1963.

Singh, S. N. *The Secretary of State for India and his Council 1858-1919.* Delhi: Munshi Ram Manohar Lal, 1962.

Sleeman, Lt. Col. W. H. *Rambles and Recollections of an Indian Official.* London, 1844.

Spear, Percival. *The Nabobs.* London: Oxford University Press, 1963.

Srinivas, M. N. *Caste in Modern India.* Bombay, 1962.

Stanford, J. K. *Ladies in the Sun, the Memsahibs' India, 1790-1860.* London: Galley, 1962.

Stanton, William. *The Leopard's Spots: Scientific Attitudes toward Race in America, 1815-1859.* Chicago: University of Chicago Press, 1960.

Stephen, James Fitzjames. "Foundations of the Government of India," *Nineteenth Century,* Vol. LXXX, October 1883.

———. "Legislation under Lord Mayo," in W. W. Hunter, *Life of the Earl of Mayo.* Vol. II. London, 1876.

———. *Letters to the Times,* 4 January 1878, 1 March, 1883, *The Times,* London.

———. *Liberty, Equality, Fraternity.* New York: Holt & Williams, 1873.

———. *Memorandum on the Administration of Justice.* (Title page destroyed; written and published during Stephen's tenure in India, 1869-72; in the National Archives, New Delhi.)

Stephen, Leslie. *The Life of Sir James Fitzjames Stephen.* New York: Putnam's, 1895.

Stocking, George W. Jr. "Matthew Arnold, E. B. Tylor and the Uses of Invention," *American Anthropologist*. Vol. LXV, No. 4, August 1963.

Stokes, Eric. *The English Utilitarians and India*. Oxford, 1959.

Strachey, Sir John. *India, its Administration and Progress*. 4th edn. London, 1911.

Strachey, John. *The End of Empire*. New York: Random House, 1960.

Sundaram, Dr. Lanka. *India's Armies and their Costs*. Bombay, 1946.

Tagore, Rabindranath. *Nationalism*. New York: Macmillan, 1917.

Taylor, William R. *Cavalier and Yankee, The Old South and American National Character*. New York: George Braziller, 1961.

Thackeray, William Makepeace. *The Newcomes*. London, 1904.

———. *Vanity Fair*. New York, 1930.

Thompson, Edward. *The Life of Charles, Lord Metcalfe*. London: Faber & Faber, 1937.

———. *The Making of the Indian Princes*. London: Oxford University Press, 1943.

———. *The Other Side of the Medal*. London: Hogarth, 1925.

Thompson, Edward and G. T. Garratt. *Rise and Fulfillment of British Rule in India*. Allahabad: Central Book Depot, 1958.

Thorburn, S. S. *His Majesty's Greatest Subject*. New York: Appleton, 1897.

Thornton, A. P. *The Imperial Idea and its Enemies*. London: Macmillan, 1959.

Tod, James. *Annals and Antiquities of Rajasthan*. 2 vols. London, 1957.

Trevelyan, C. E. *On the Education of the People of India*. London, 1838.

Trevelyan, G. O. *Cawnpore*. London: Macmillan, 1910.

———. *The Competition Wallah*. London, 1866.

———. *The Life and Letters of Lord Macaulay*. 2 vols. New York: Harper & Bros., 1876.

Wasti, Syed Razi. *Lord Minto and the Indian Nationalist Movement, 1905-1910*. London: Oxford University Press, 1964.

Weber, Max. *The Protestant Ethic and the Spirit of Capitalism*, trans. Parans. New York: Charles Scribner's Sons, 1958.

West, Algernon. *Sir Charles Wood's Administration of Indian Affairs, From 1859 to 1866*. London, 1867.

Whish, C. W.? (pub. anon.) *Essays Fin de Siècle, by an Anglo-Indian Optimist*. Allahabad: Pioneer Press, 1895.

Wilkinson, Rupert. *Gentlemanly Power, British Leadership and the Public School Tradition*. London: Oxford University Press, 1964.

Wolpert, Stanley. *Tilak and Gokhale*. Berkeley: University of California Press, 1962.

Woolf, Leonard. *Growing, An Autobiography of the Years 1904 to 1911*. London: The Hogarth Press, 1961.

———. *Imperialism and Civilization*. New York: Harcourt, Brace. 1928.

Yeats-Brown, Francis. *The Lives of a Bengal Lancer*. New York: Viking, 1930.

Young, G. M. *Victorian England, Portrait of an Age*. London: Oxford University Press, 1953.

INDEX

Lightning Source UK Ltd.
Milton Keynes UK
UKOW04f1402260716

279251UK00001B/134/P